# THE GLOBAL REGION

*Production, State Policies
and Uneven Development*

DAVID SADLER
*University of Durham, UK*

## PERGAMON PRESS

OXFORD · NEW YORK · SEOUL · TOKYO

UK          Pergamon Press plc, Headington Hill Hall,
            Oxford OX3 0BW, England

USA         Pergamon Press Inc., 395 Saw Mill River Road,
            Elmsford, New York 10523, USA

KOREA       Pergamon Press Korea, KPO Box 315, Seoul 110–603,
            Korea

JAPAN       Pergamon Press Japan, Tsunashima Building Annex,
            3–20–12 Yushima, Bunkyo–ku, Tokyo 113, Japan

First edition 1992

**Library of Congress Cataloging in Publication Data**
Sadler, David.
The global region: production, state policies, and
uneven development / David Sadler. — 1st ed.
p.  cm. — (Policy, planning, and critical theory)
1. Great Britain—Industries.  2. Industry and state—
Great Britain.  3. Great Britain—Economic conditions—
1945– —Regional disparities.  I. Title.  II. Series.
HC256.6.S23 1991        338.941—dc20        91–33929

**British Library Cataloguing in Publication Data**
Sadler, David
The global region. — (Policy, planning & critical
theory)
I. Title     II. Series
338.09
ISBN 0–08–040485–5 Hardcover
ISBN 0–08–040484–7 Flexicover

*Printed in Great Britain by BPCC Wheatons Ltd, Exeter*

# THE GLOBAL REGION

*Production, State Policies*
*and Uneven Development*

# Policy, Planning and Critical Theory

*Series Editor:* **Paul Cloke**
Saint David's University College, Lampeter, UK

This major new series will focus on the relevance of critical social theory to important contemporary processes and practices in planning and policy-making. It aims to demonstrate the need to incorporate state and governmental activities within these new theoretical approaches, and will focus on current trends in governmental policy in Western states, with particular reference to the relationship between the centre and the locality, the provision of services, and the formulation of government policy.

**Forthcoming titles in this series include:**

Policy and Change in Thatcher's Britain
*Edited by* **Paul Cloke**

Beyond the Housing Crisis
**Mark Goodwin, James Barlow & Simon Duncan**

People, Place, Protest: Making Sense of Popular Protest in Modern Britain
**Michael J. Griffiths**

Policy and Planning for Internationalized Agriculture
**Richard Le Heron**

Gender, Planning and the Policy Process
**Jo Little**

Selling Places: The City as Cultural Capital, Past and Present
**C. Philo and G. Kearns**

Uneven Reproduction: Economy, Space and Society
**Andrew Pratt**

The Power of Apartheid: Territoriality and Government in South African Cities
**Jennifer Robinson**

# Contents

vi *Contents*

# List of Figures

# List of Tables

# List of Abbreviations

| | |
|---|---|
| AEU | Amalgamated Engineering Union |
| AGR | Advanced Gas-cooled Reactor |
| BC | British Coal |
| BSC | British Steel Corporation |
| CEGB | Central Electricity Generating Board |
| EC | European Community |
| ECSC | European Coal and Steel Community |
| ECU | European Currency Unit |
| EETPU | Electrical, Electronic, Telecommunications and Plumbing Union |
| EFTA | European Free Trade Association |
| FGD | Flue Gas Desulphurisation |
| GATT | General Agreement on Tariffs and Trade |
| GMBU | General, Municipal and Boilermakers' Union |
| IISI | International Iron and Steel Institute |
| IRB | Independent Review Body |
| ISTC | Iron and Steel Trades Confederation |
| NACODS | National Association of Colliery Overmen, Shotfirers and Deputies |
| NCB | National Coal Board |
| NIC | Newly Industrialising Country |
| NIDL | New International Division of Labour |
| NUM | National Union of Mineworkers |
| OMS | Output per Man Shift |
| OPEC | Organisation of Petroleum Exporting Countries |
| PWR | Pressurised Water Reactor |
| SMMT | Society of Motor Manufacturers and Traders |
| TGWU | Transport and General Workers Union |
| UDM | Union of Democratic Mineworkers |

# Preface

In the course of the 1970s and the 1980s, social scientific debate on and investigation into the relationships between systems of production and processes of uneven development grappled at first uncertainly, then with growing confidence, over a number of closely related concerns. One of these involved a recognition that the *organization* of production—the precise combination of productive machinery and labour, and the way in which this was managed and ordered—was integrally engaged in questions to do with the geographical *location* of production. *How* a good or service was produced or delivered was intimately related to—both affecting and affected by—*where* such processes took place, and this held true at a variety of spatial scales. A second focal point was the increasingly apparent interlinking of the global economy, as longstanding international investment flows seemingly gained ever-greater fluidity and the worldwide circulation of capital accelerated. This heightened degree of international connectivity was evidenced also in the emergence of new centres of accumulation, and the challenges which they posed to an established order. And a third (closely related) theoretical and practical agenda entailed consideration of the multitude of ways in which regional trajectories of socio-economic development were interwoven (via corporate and state policies) as part of a broader national and international fabric: simultaneously product of and condition for global change. An increasing number of decisions of immense day-to-day importance to particular regions and localities, so it seemed, were being taken in remote centres of international corporate power, as territorial and structural limits to the policies of national states became more and more evident. The world had (or so it appeared) become in some ways a much smaller place. Many of the constraints imposed by time and space had been overcome, if not by national states then at least by capitalist interests in their pursuit of profit.

Somewhat paradoxically, perhaps (at first sight) all of this meant that the significance of place was being (re)discovered in social science at just the same time as capital was apparently increasingly able to transcend space. Yet production still had a geography; not only in its physical location, but also more generally in the sense that key strategic decisions incorporated a heightened awareness of the competitive advantages and disadvantages to capital of particular places and regions from within the global web, and the diversity of ways in which they could be connected as part of truly international strategies. Such decisions rested on conscious evaluation of particular attributes to do with historical-geographic processes of development. Rather than conquer space, perhaps, capital had come instead to incorporate it and to seek new means of integrating global decisions with the particularity of national and local socio-economic circumstance. The class relation between capital and labour was being recast in ways which emphasized capital's subtlety in its incorporation of space and time, and heightened the problems posed for labour by its inability to transgress such dimensions. Much of this was also captured in the shifting character of, and balance to, state policies during these years. In this fashion, then, the integration of places and regions within broader national and international circuits via corporate and state policies posed some harsh challenges to people living and working *in* those places and regions.

Such developments—both their preconditions and their implications—underpin and inform the writing of this book. It is organized in two main sections. Part I begins with the global environment and examines how one national state, the UK, is integrated into that broader framework. It focuses upon three sectors—coal mining, iron and steel production and automobile assembly—not for their "representativeness" (for that would imply a wholly different conception of social scientific research than that which is adopted here) but for the different insights which they bring to bear on the key processes of change. It examines in detail the strategies of major actors, and the reasons for and impacts of particular state policies. The priorities of Part I, however, are not meant to imply that some kind of macro-scale and capital-led determination is at work. Instead, in Part II, the focus switches to one region—north east England—to investigate the ways in which this has been and is being both actively and passively repositioned within a shifting international environment. As the boundaries between global and local blur, regional development becomes not just a matter of international process (for arguably this has historically been the case, to some degree at least) as one of how the region can adopt to and adapt in an increasingly volatile international marketplace. What is significant here also is the interaction between the conditions created as part of a previously dominant form of investment and those associated with newly emergent forms. Here, too, the *geography* of production—and its relationship to questions of state policy—is important.

In a region such as north east England, once one of the heartlands of Britain's nineteenth-century industrial dominance, the effects of the combination of successive international and national changes were highly apparent in the 1980s. Massive disinvestment from the old economic base of coal and steel took place as one result of the UK state's chosen path of mediation of international market forces. This intertwined with the hesitant emergence of a new economy (also underpinned by the UK state), which was characterized by radically different versions of production organization and a marked reworking of the class relation between capital and labour. These were epitomized in Nissan's automobile assembly plant at Sunderland (which began production in 1986), Western Europe's first such Japanese "transplant" investment and the first automobile plant in north east England, and evident more generally in the forced acceptance of what were commonly labelled "flexible" employment practices. In the interaction between different global phases of development, and in the intricate involvement of the UK state, the region provided a further and pointed illustration of the associations between production and geography.

It would be wrong to argue, of course, that the three sectors examined here represented the sum total of recent global economic change; or that economic development in north east England was somehow reducible to just these three industries; or even that the impact of these transformations was spatially or socially even across the region. That is certainly not the intention (and it is in this sense that it would be wrong to describe the evidence presented here as in some way necessarily "representative" of an over-arching process or set of processes, other than the vagaries of capitalism as a system of production). However, the impact of global change in these industries in this region and the role of UK state policies have been significant in a number of ways. The story documented here describes a crucial period in the north east's economic history, and a sorry tale of UK state intervention in the national economy in general and the north east in particular. Yet just as importantly, the book is about the *interconnectedness* of the global economy just as much as it is about the overall significance of the precise cases analysed; the ways in which different processes came together and the detailed working out of different strategies in time and place. It also highlights—and the implications of this are far-reaching—the extremely narrow room for manoeuvre which all this gave to people living and working in the region. Conceptions of, and command over, space and time in the sphere of production, in other words, represent a challenge to and an opportunity for capital *and* labour, and—in even beginning to speculate about the future—it is vital to acknowledge this.

In writing this book I have drawn upon a variety of sources and incurred a range of debts. It draws in part upon the results of various collaborative research projects undertaken within north east England and more broadly during the 1980s. References in the text acknowledge the collective nature of many of these; but I would particularly like to record my gratitude to Huw Beynon and Ray Hudson for their help and advice, and also to Paul Cloke for encouraging me to develop my ideas in this form in the first place. I am very grateful also to the technical and secretarial staff at the Department of Geography, Durham University, for their ready and professional assistance. Finally, I would like to thank Jeanette for her patience and support (as well as for her perceptive comments about Fiat). The ultimate responsibility, though, is mine alone.

# Introduction
# The Interplay of Global, National and Regional Economic Change

## I.1 Changing times, changing concepts

From about the mid-1970s, the world's major capitalist economies plunged into a deep and traumatic recessionary slump, one which was all the more acute when contrasted with the prolonged phase of generally high economic growth rates that had characterized much of the postwar period. The immediate trigger of this transition was a fourfold increase in the price of oil, enforced by the OPEC states upon an imported-energy dependent advanced capitalist world; reinforced by a further near-doubling in oil prices in 1979/80 during the course of more political turbulence in the Middle East. But the signs of recessionary downturn were evident as far back as the mid-1960s, as the postwar boom led by the dynamism of the US economy stuttered to a halt in the face of increasingly saturated markets and a growing overproduction crisis, which was aggravated in several key sectors by the emergence of Japan as a major industrial power. The profitability of manufacturing industry had begun to decline from the late 1960s onwards. Other factors also combined to push the world closer to slump, including rising real wages and increased commodity costs. Collapse of the global financial regulatory system dependent on the strength of the US dollar, inaugurated by the Bretton Woods agreement in 1944 and terminated by abolition of the fixed currency exchange rate system in 1971, sealed the fate of the old order.

The results of this recessionary slump were readily apparent: falling corporate profits, massive job loss and rapidly rising unemployment, reaching levels only previously recorded in the

1

Great Depression of the late 1920s and 1930s. National economic growth rates in much of the developed world fell dramatically close to—in some cases even below—zero. In many of the newly industrializing countries (NICs) a collapse in demand for manufactured goods led to further problems for expensive debt-financed industrialization programmes, and a growing crisis of foreign indebtedness ensued. As the world struggled to come to terms with this new situation, the language of academic analysis—in particular of the regional impacts of slump in the developed world—came increasingly to resemble that of the devastated economic fabric. De-industrialization, regional crisis and global shifts were the order of the day (see, for instance, Bluestone and Harrison 1982; Carney *et al.* 1980; Dicken 1986; Martin and Rowthorn 1986; Massey and Meegan 1982; Thrift 1986).

This new phase of global development fuelled a growing interest on the part of social scientists in general, and urban and regional geographers in particular, in frameworks for explaining precisely what was happening to the world economy, and interpreting the spatial changes taking place. One strand of this awakened concern focused on the significance of the specifically capitalist nature of society, and the need to theorize in the abstract the uneven development of capitalist relations of production (see in particular, Harvey 1982). Another, closely related, focused on the interconnection between the social relations of production and the spatial composition of economic activity. The interdependence of the social and the spatial in the organization of capitalist production was particularly evident at the regional scale, and was developed by Massey to form the basis for her particularly influential conceptualization of "rounds of investment" in which different layers of social/spatial structures were laid down (see especially, Massey 1984).

Just as these new ways of understanding the world were gaining more widespread acceptance, so the object of this theorizing—the world economy—seemingly took another turn. From about the mid-1980s onwards a partial and uneven recovery from recession set in. This, allied to continued high rates of growth in some (but by no means all) NICs which had weathered the storm and maintained respectable rates of economic growth, appeared to herald the dawning of a new era. If not a comparable boom to that of the 1950s and 1960s, it was perhaps at least a sustainable upswing. Such observations were at first couched in hesitant terms, then increasingly argued with greater and more forceful stridency. Yet if the recovery was real enough, it was by no means clear what kind of geographical expression it was likely to take. For some, it was apparent that the new basis for dynamism rested not just on a wholly new system of production organization (variously labelled flexible specialization/production/accumulation, neo-Fordism or post-Fordism) but also on a different rationale of spatial organization, which contrasted to an emphasis on *decentralization* in the earlier era in that it depended upon *reconcentration* around new production complexes and new industrial districts (see, for instance, Scott 1988a). Such claims were by no means universally accepted; but the debate around the social and spatial characteristics of this new phase in the world economy came increasingly to focus around them.

These global developments, and new ways of interpreting them, form a starting point for this book, in which I hope to substantiate a number of claims. I want to argue that whilst valuable insights have been gained into the workings of the capitalist economy through the emphasis on flexible production and new industrial districts, a number of restrictive overgeneralizations have been made leading to an excessive concern with a few cases. Similarly, the (at times obsessive) championing of abstract theorization, and the casting of debate in terms of a dichotomy between abstract and concrete, theoretical and empirical, have led to an undue downplaying of the significance of regional analysis and the theoretical understanding which this can provide, albeit at a lower level of abstraction than an (equally necessary) investigation of the global capitalist relations of production. Further, I also want to argue that there are ways of integrating the international dimension of change—in this case production—with the national and regional, and that this is crucial to a satisfactory analysis of what is going on in contemporary capitalist society. For despite the insights which it brings, the focus on systems of production organization also crucially *downplays* the continuing significance of the national state dimension (and this *is* important despite—even in some cases because of—the increasingly internationalized character of economic activity) and *oversimplifies* the regional aspect to global uneven development. Hence, this volume presents an international sectoral analysis devoted to three industries (coalmining, iron and steel production and automobile assembly) in the context of one particular national state (the UK) and of one region (north east England) demonstrating the interconnections between global, national and local.

In this introductory chapter, these arguments are developed by outlining four aspects of the book. In section I.2 I investigate changing conceptualizations of the international division of labour in accounting for the increasingly global nature of capitalist activity. Then in section I.3 the focus shifts to different forms of production organization, introducing the literature on flexible production and new spatial forms. As indicated above, this tends to downplay the significance of national state policies and contexts, so these are introduced in section I.4. In section I.5, I consider the regional aspect of uneven development, illustrating the significance of the north east of England (which forms Part II of this volume) as a case study region. Finally, in section I.6, I briefly describe the importance of the three sectors which form Part I of the book, and outline the content of succeeding chapters.

## I.2 Global capital and the international division of labour

One of the remarkable features of the collapse of the old world economic order from the mid-1970s—apart from its severity—was its highly uneven impact across different sectors, national states and regions. The downturn was felt most acutely in those heartlands of industrial capitalism which had been based, since the nineteenth century, on the production of a few commodities such as coal, iron and steel, mechanical engineering and shipbuilding. In many of these localities—especially in Western Europe—such was the extent of capacity reduction that the whole social and economic base of the community was threatened, leading to concerted opposition which on occasion even spilled over into violence and civil unrest (see Hudson and Sadler 1986). Such problems provided a marked and poignant contrast with the situation in a few NICs, such as South Korea, Brazil and Mexico, where new industrial growth programmes—within the constraints set by external debt-financing—were based on precisely those industries, in particular iron and steel, which were in greatest decline in the advanced economies. In these and some other NICs, such as Taiwan, Singapore and Hong Kong, high rates of economic growth—albeit from a low base—contrasted starkly with the laggardly recovery from recession in Western Europe and North America (see Browett 1986).

In the case of iron and steel, there were some particular reasons for these differences, to do with the greater steel-intensity of early industrialization programmes in the NICs, and a tendency toward product-substitution for steel by other materials in the developed world. The comparison is nonetheless a revealing one, for it was difficult to escape the conclusion that the changing distribution of production was inextricably bound up, somehow, with the global crisis of capitalism. Yet precisely how to understand the relationship, particularly from the point of view of the UK economy, and what was responsible for the crisis, prompted a wide range of different answers.

It was apparent, however, that an increasingly significant vehicle of *integration* within the world economy (but not necessarily of equalization) was the multinational corporation, also often called the transnational corporation in recognition of its ability to transcend national frontiers. One particularly significant work in this context was that of Frobel *et al.* (1980), which set out to investigate the reasons for and implications of a shift in production via direct foreign investment by European and US-based multinationals in NICs, exemplified by the West German textile and clothing industry. Three factors were held to be responsible: increasingly sophisticated techniques of international communication; the technological capability to subdivide the production process so as to minimize skill requirements at certain stages; and existence of a vast, cheap labour reserve in the NICs. Together, it was argued, these provided a powerful incentive for the establishment of new production bases, frequently at the expense of employment in the older centres.

The thesis that in this way a new international division of labour (NIDL) was emerging was not without its critics. For instance, Gordon (1988) argued that it overstressed the power of multinational corporations, and that the globalization of production was not a symptom of health on the part of multinational capital, but an enforced response to the decaying world economic order. For Schoenberger (1989a), the NIDL model was far from the dominant trend, nor was it likely to be. She argued that it also took a very narrow view of technological change, and appeared to set workers in the core against those in the periphery. Whilst in the strict sense of a physical relocation of production from core to NIC economy, the evidence was largely confined to Frobel *et al.*'s (1980) study of textiles and clothing, and also to the electronics industry, the NIDL concept was nonetheless important. It pointed to the growing power and sophistication of multinational capital and its ability to take advantage of differing possibilities for profit by *decentralizing* production across the globe.

This decentralization of production was by no means a new phenomenon. In the 1920s and 1930s, the growth of American economic and political influence across the world was matched by a process of internationalization on the part of US-based companies, sometimes for markedly different reasons. Dimbleby and Reynolds (1988: pp. 96–115), for instance, gave two useful contrasting examples. In this period, Britain controlled over three-quarters of the world's supply of rubber via its colonial possessions, and exerted a commanding influence on the world price of this commodity, which was vital to the tyre industry. The US company Firestone invested heavily in alternative sources of supply from Liberia in West Africa, in the process ironically reproducing the same kind of economic dependence for which the American government had criticized the British Empire. In motor vehicles, by contrast, the US giants Ford and General Motors invested heavily in Western Europe, primarily to avoid stringent tariff barriers. These reached over 33 per cent in the UK; a key factor behind Ford's establishment of a wholly new production site at Dagenham, and General Motors' purchase of an established UK producer, Vauxhall.

In the 1950s and 1960s, the flow of American investment in manufacturing plant in Western Europe became a veritable flood, as US companies rapidly expanded their interests there and in other parts of the globe (and other Western European companies also increasingly invested across national frontiers). One example is the case of semiconductor production (see Scott 1987). In 1962, the first US-owned assembly plant in semiconductors was established by the Fairchild Corporation in Hong Kong. By 1985 there were 63 such US-owned semiconductor assembly plants in South East Asia, as the industry took full advantage of cheap labour reserves to relocate simple production tasks. American government legislation also helped by allowing re-export of the semi-completed devices back to the USA under beneficial tariff conditions. To this simple picture of offshore assembly could also be added a growing division of labour within South East Asia. There was a concentration of relatively high-skill testing operations in a higher waged core of Hong Kong, South Korea, Taiwan and Singapore, and an emphasis upon assembly in Indonesia, Malaysia, Philippines and Thailand. Nor was the process of US internationalization confined to Western Europe and South East Asia. In Mexico also, for instance, a large assembly complex developed under government encouragement via its Maquila programme (see Sklair 1989). The global sourcing of component production and assembly—whether to take advantage of lower labour costs, secure access to essential raw materials or gain entry to national markets protected by import barriers—had come to play a vital role in corporate planning. This was typified in the global operations of the major automobile manufacturers (see Beynon 1984a), but was the case for a wide range of sectors. It is difficult, then, to understate the growing significance of international production strategies in the postwar period.

Whilst American multinational capital dominated the flow of global direct foreign investment in the 1950s and 1960s, a new trend emerged in the 1970s and 1980s which epitomized the changing balance of power on the world stage, as the USA slipped from global hegemony and Japan became increasingly influential. This was the rise of the Japanese multinational corporation (see Dicken 1988; Douglass 1988). The growth of Japanese overseas investment was at first a relatively slow process; indeed in the initial stages of its phenomenal postwar boom Japanese industry instead depended upon drawing in massive rural labour reserves to a few growing metropolitan areas. From 1971 to 1980, as these supplies of cheap labour dried up, the first phase of Japanese foreign investment in manufacturing took shape, mostly targeted in East and South East Asia, especially South Korea and Taiwan. Growing hostility to this Japanese presence, coupled with increasingly evident trade barriers in Western Europe and North America, led to a sharp acceleration in the flow of outward investment in the first half of the 1980s, and a diversification of destination. But this upturn was dwarfed by the third wave of overseas investment set loose from around 1985 onwards in response to revaluation of the Japanese currency (one result of a massive Japanese trade surplus) and the increased competitive edge of overseas production in major markets as against exports from Japan.

The growth of the Japanese multinational corporation was deeply significant. As Douglass (1988: p. 425) put it, "by the mid-1980s Japan had not only become the principal vortex of global capital accumulation; it had also become the primary source of direct investment sustaining the world economy". It is nonetheless important to retain a sense of perspective in comparison, for instance, with the overall extent of American overseas investment, especially in Western Europe. In the UK, where Japanese investment was particularly concentrated, Japanese-owned manufacturing plant employed just over 10,000 in the mid-1980s, less than Ford's Dagenham plant and miniscule by comparison with the 450,000 working in US-owned factories (Dicken 1988: p. 634). Even after the upturn of the late 1980s, employment in Japanese-owned manufacturing plants in the UK stood only at around 30,000. However, whilst there was a mismatch in terms of absolute scale, there should be no doubt that Japanese investment—in Western Europe and North America—had taken on a dynamic character, being associated with new forms of production organization and new levels of efficiency. In the UK and elsewhere, a growing literature focused on the geographical location of Japanese companies and the apparent "Japanization" of British industry (see Morris 1988; Oliver and Wilkinson 1988). The characteristics of, and reasons for, this "Japanese model" are considered below (in section I.4), but for the moment it is sufficient to note that Japanese direct foreign investment, whilst still small in total *stock* in comparison to that of US-based multinational corporations, was nonetheless both growing rapidly and associated with the leading edge of production innovation and productivity improvement.

The growth of Japanese direct foreign investment in manufacturing was more than matched by developments in another increasingly significant component of the world economy, the international financial system. In this the interplay between Japanese and American hegemony was a complex one where the only clear losers were the chief debtors—the newly industrializing countries, as their international financial commitments choked off planned industrialization programmes. During the 1970s, NIC expansion was, in general, increasingly debt-financed as these countries sought and found foreign loans, often organized through international banks dedicated to recycling the OPEC surplus. During the late 1970s and early 1980s, slowdown in the world economy, coupled with volatile inflation and interest rates and (after 1981) falling oil prices, led to increasingly evident problems among many of the NICs in meeting their burdensome debt repayments. In 1982 and 1983, many countries, especially in Latin America, were obliged to forgo interest payments and arrange a rescheduling of their debt. Thrift and Leyshon (1988) described how in the wake of this near-disaster, the world's major banks and governments initiated a new international financial system characterized by deregulation, greater freedom of movement of global funds, and the rise of Japan alongside the decline of the USA. As they put it (p. 61), "in many ways the Japanese investor [was] now the key to the operation of the world's financial markets". Through the worldwide role of Japanese banks and finance houses, the Japanese economy had reinforced its growing global significance.

Thus, in different ways the world economic order which seemed to be emerging at the end of the 1980s out of the recessionary crisis of the mid-1970s to mid-1980s differed from that of the earlier postwar boom. Whilst multinational capital remained free to roam the globe in search of profit, to many the most "dynamic" source of direct foreign investment was no longer the USA, but rather Japan. The financial system underpinning the world economy had also changed as NIC debt which once threatened to wreck the whole structure was (at least temporarily) rescheduled, and a new international financial system had emerged in which Japanese companies, as well as American, controlled the ebb and flow of global finance capital. The global balance of economic power had undergone a subtle but potentially far-reaching transformation.

## I.3 Changing forms of production organization, new spatial outcomes?

Another strand of debate over this emergent "new" economy concerned its forms of production organization and spatial appearance. Much—though by no means all—of this was grounded in the "regulationist" perspective, which evolved during the 1970s (see especially, Aglietta 1979; also Lipietz 1986). It focuses on the idea that any given national social formation is characterized by a particular regime of accumulation, which is governed by a certain mode of regulation. The regime of accumulation signifies an approximate stabilization over time of the balance between production and consumption. This is secured by the mode of regulation, which is a body of rules and social processes that ensure the smooth running of accumulation. The significance of this approach lies in the way in which it identifies the central importance of a balance between production and consumption, and the role of nation-states in regulating that equation. In particular, Lipietz (1986) argued that after 1945 much of the developed world was characterized by a "Fordist" regime of accumulation, in which the long boom was secured by a social democratic consensus around the consumption norms of the welfare state, and a continued intensification of the labour process via the norms of Fordist-type production methods. He subsequently extended this analysis (Lipietz 1987) to consider the ways in which different nation-states were integrated into the world economy through a revised version of the new international division of labour. To the regulationist school, the crisis of world capitalism in the mid-1970s was a reflection of the breakdown of the Fordist regime of accumulation, as the balance between production and consumption disintegrated and the postwar consensus around the welfare state fell apart, leading to (and in part caused by) the growth of right-wing neo-conservative policies.

Such central ideas have to greater or lesser extent underpinned a range of interpretations of the evolving form of the world economic order as it appears to move out of recession[1]. In particular, there has been an emphasis upon the new forms of *production organization* which are held to be replacing the Fordist system that apparently broke down in the midst of crisis. From a number of different starting points, it has been argued that the old, Fordist system of production is being replaced by something new, variously described as post-Fordist, neo-Fordist, or flexible production/specialization/accumulation. For Piore and Sabel (1984), the change represented a response to the crisis of mass production: a shift in recognition of growing saturation in many markets and a heightened diversity of demand on the part of the consumer, requiring a much more differentiated product and, hence, flexible production process (though, see also Murray 1987). To others, more directly grounded in the regulationist school (for instance, Scott 1988a, 1988b; Scott and Cooke 1988; Storper and Christopherson 1987), the new system rested on a fragmentation of the labour process, as what previously seemed an inexorable trend towards larger, more vertically integrated units of production broke down under the weight of pressures towards vertical disintegration. In this model of economic development, there was also (so it was claimed) a tendency towards the spatial reconcentration of production as clusters of new small firms emerged in new industrial districts.

One example of the flexible specialization/regional agglomeration argument, which should help clarify what is meant by the reorganization of production, is that of the US motion picture industry (see Storper and Christopherson 1987). From the 1920s to the 1950s, motion picture production was characterized by a factory-like process under the control of large, vertically integrated firms. The seven major studios controlled their own cinema chains and, with market outlets thus assured, could standardize their product and routinize production, hiring permanently staffed production groups required to complete a film every five to seven days.

With the advent of competition from television, and US government legislation enforcing the sale of their cinema chains in 1948 on anti-trust grounds, a series of dramatic transformations was set in place. By the 1970s, motion picture production, while still dominated by a few major studios, was undertaken by independent production companies which subcontracted a lot of their work to smaller specialist firms. Because these companies, and their employees, required much face to face contact to secure business and jobs, it is argued that there has been a tendency towards spatial reconcentration in the motion picture industry around southern California. Hence the vertical disintegration which lies behind flexible specialisation creates powerful agglomeration tendencies at the regional level. Flexible speciali- sation itself leads to the recomposition of the industrial complex, through a new form of horizontal integration of production capacity. (Storper and Christopherson 1987: p. 115)

Whilst conceptually simple in outline, the idea that a whole new basis of production is emerging, characterized by a particular form of spatial organization, has generated a widespread debate. Broadly speaking, it is possible to identify three interrelated areas of contention: the extent to which available evidence supports the view that Fordist production is being replaced by something spe- cifically post-Fordist and/or flexible; the appropriateness of the characterization of the "new" regime's geographical expression; and the relationship between grand theorizations and explana- tions at lesser levels of abstraction.

In terms of the spread of sectors in which flexible specializa- tion/production is held to be occurring, there is quite a variety. Christopherson and Storper (1986: p. 305) observed trends to flexible specialization in "the textile industries of the Third Italy, the mini-steel mills in the USA, and the machine tool and electronic industries in Japan and the USA". Storper and Christopherson (1987: p. 104) argued that "the trend towards flexible specialization can be observed across a range of indus- tries, extending even to classical mass production industries like automobiles and steel". For Scott (1988a, 1988b), three groups of industries dominated the new production system: craft/design intensive, high technology and services. Finally for Storper and Scott (1989: p. 26): "many sectors once dominated by Fordist mass production methods, for instance cars and components, have now become, or are becoming, increasingly reorganized on the basis of flexible production methods". Whilst this collection is far from an exhaustive (still less a consistent) list of industrial activities, some bold claims have nonetheless been advanced for the generalizability of the model of flexible production. Scott (1988b: p. 175), for instance, argued that it has "begun to rival mass production as the dominant core of the advanced capitalist economies".

An alternative perspective holds that not only is this a large claim to make from available evidence, but also the evidence itself far from points to one inescapable conclusion. Meegan (1988) showed that Fordism—conceived in the narrow sense as a system of production characterized by moving assembly lines—was never that dominant anyway, at least in the UK. Hudson (1989a) likewise affirmed that in many regions, such as, for example, north east

England, Fordism only ever had a tenuous hold. To conceptualize in terms of a grand sweep from Fordist to post-Fordist methods of production was, therefore, too bold a generalization. As Sayer (1989: p. 666) put it, the notion of post-Fordism was "confused in its arguments, long on speculation and hype, and based on selected examples whose limited sectoral, spatial and temporal range is rarely acknowledged".

Even such reaction to the notion of post-Fordist production systems was relatively tempered in comparison with that to the particularly *flexible* character of the new regime. In the first place, it was argued that the term itself was far from precisely specified. Gertler (1988) identified a range of different uses of "flexible" in relation to production, ranging from machines to manufacturing systems and processes of accumulation (see also the reply by Schoenberger 1989b). Sayer (1989: p. 671) identified seven different kinds of flexibility, concluding that mass production was not necessarily *inflexible* in any case. Secondly, it was not clear how "flexibility" in one sense might relate to that in other senses of the term. For Scott (1988b: p. 177), "the counterpart of rising flexibility in the organisation of production [was] rising flexibility in labour markets". This elision between overall system flexibility and labour market flexibility was an important one, for it masked consideration of a whole range of different processes taking place. Analytically, it was crucial to distinguish flexibility in the sense of relationships between companies from flexibility in terms of the labour process, or the organization of production within any given company.

This mirrored closely an important debate taking place in the UK over the "flexible firm" and its "flexible workforce". Championed by the UK government, the "flexible firm" model rested on the supposition that production was increasingly organized by companies using a two-tier workforce. A core of full-time, relatively secure employees (from which employers sought greater *functional* flexibility in terms of reduced demarcation) was contrasted with a peripheral workforce consisting variously of part-time, short-term and casualized workers, along with the increased use of subcontracted labour. It was argued that such strategies enabled companies more easily to cope with fluctuations in demand since the peripheral workforce gave them greater *numerical* flexibility. As in the flexible production debate however, evidence for the adoption of such strategies was at best tenuous, at worst nonexistent. Even a study which set out specifically to find flexible firms (NEDO 1986a) could not produce any clear evidence indicating that this strategy was generally and consciously being adopted. As Pollert (1988a, 1988b) argued, the "flexible firm" concept was faulty in blurring production and labour requirements, and *description* with *prescription*. It carried heavy ideological connotations and was being selectively promoted by the private and public sector alike as an instrument to achieve greater control over labour.

If the supposed transition from Fordist to post-Fordist production, and the whole question of "flexibility", provoked alternative views, these in turn were nothing compared to responses to the geographic appearance of the "new" regime. Proponents of flexible production argued that this was characterized by the emergence of new centres of accumulation:

> the old hegemonic regime of Fordist accumulation has progressively been giving way to a new regime of flexible accumulation. With the steady ascendance of the latter regime, a number of new industrial spaces have also started to make their decisive historical appearance on the economic landscape. (Scott 1988b: p. 171)

Such spaces, he argued, were in areas well away from the old Fordist bases of accumulation, which were unattractive due to their high levels of unionization and relatively politicized working-class populations. Instead, the new industrial spaces were either enclaves within old manufacturing regions (such as Los Angeles and the zone along Route 128 in Boston's western suburbs) or on the geographical margins of capitalist industrialization (such as parts of Italy and cities like Cambridge and Grenoble). His major work (Scott 1988a) focused on three areas in particular: the Scientific City in southern Paris, Silicon Valley and the Third Italy.

This claim that a new form of spatial organization was growing to dominance drew a range of responses: not just that the evidence was very limited, but also that it was capable of quite different interpretations. One area in particular, the Third Italy, came to play a central role. This region, in the north-eastern and central provinces of Italy, was distinguished from the traditional heartland of the national economy in the north west, and the rural south of Italy (with its poles of state-sponsored branch-plant investment) by a high proportion of small firms. Brusco (1982) identified this as the salient feature of the "Emilian model", in which small companies were grouped in new industrial districts according to product, giving rise to "monocultural areas in which all firms have a very low degree of vertical integration and the production process is carried on through the collaboration of a number of firms" (p. 169). These groups of small firms formed a secondary component of the region's industrial structure, differentiated from the primary element of much larger companies, on which it largely depended for orders.

Whilst proponents of flexible production focused on the liberating qualities of the new regime, this example—often cited in support of such claims—was in fact far less clear-cut. For although Brusco (1982: p. 183) argued that the new industrial districts returned flexibility to the overall production system rather than exploit cheap labour, it was clear that a huge contrast existed between the two sectors in terms of wages, conditions of employment, job security and protection by government legislation. The region of Emilia-Romagna, so Brusco (1982: p. 183) argued, was "more authentically capitalist" than the rest of Italy, in that the market had a freer hand and the state played a lesser role. As Amin and Robins (1990: pp. 18–19) showed, the idea that such industrial districts were liberating for either labour or the companies concerned selectively downplayed other pressures in terms of their low technological base, limited marketing skills and (crucially) dependence upon larger companies (see also Amin 1989).

A further problem with the idea of new industrial spaces concerned not so much their problematic "liberating" qualities as the way in which the flexible production model envisaged such spaces being constructed. For an unfortunate by-product of the emphasis given to forms of organization was a tendency to abstract the spatial patterns from the social relations of production. In focusing on production organization, space became seen as a kind of end result, an inevitable consequence of changes in the social relations of production. For instance, Storper and Christopherson (1987: p. 108) observed that industrial complexes were the "*geographical means* by which producers realise the external economies of scale that are inherent in a complex social division of labour" (emphasis added). For Scott (1988b: p. 171), the transition from old to new regime similarly entailed particular determinate spatial consequences:

> the current situation is one of considerable complexity, for the old regime is far from having disappeared entirely, and the new one by no means universally regnant. Moreover, *the geographical outcomes proper to each regime* intersect with each other in a sometimes disorderly and confusing manner. (emphasis added)

Such problems were in part connected to the third set of criticisms of the flexible production approach: its tendency to overarching general theory, not just in terms of relations to available evidence but rather the explicit concern for abstract theorization. Scott (1988b: pp. 182–3) for instance bemoaned the fact that in the midst of sweeping changes in the organization of international capitalism, social scientists had apparently taken to focusing on the local and particular at the expense of the global and abstract. There was a desperate need, he argued, to re-open "macrotheoretical questions about the logic of capitalist society as a whole" because "only by clarifying these issues can we also effectively explain detailed *geographical outcomes* currently occurring on the ground" (p. 183, emphasis added). In this concern for abstract theory, Scott neatly if inadvertently reiterated the idea that space was produced as a by-product of broader social change.

Much of this debate has to be located within the context of apparent shifts within radical and Marxist geography from a focus on structures in the 1970s to one on smaller scale "locality studies" in the 1980s (see Cloke, Philo and Sadler 1991, chapter two). Whether or not such a shift had indeed taken place, the perception on the part of some that it had led to powerful cries for the development of more abstract theory. For instance, Harvey and Scott (1989) maintained that a drift from theoretical to empirical work had been a retreat in the face of neo-conservative policies, which had to be compensated for by the production of new holistic theories in order to come to terms with the new appearance of the capitalist system of production. Once again, however, there was far from a consensus on such views.

An alternative perspective was put forward by Hudson (1988) who argued as follows:

> there can be no general theory of the geography of production or spatial divisions of labour. Attempting to construct such a theory will inevitably involve a flawed attempt to over-generalise from an historically and geographically specific set of circumstances. Rather, new and old forms of organising production profitably over space have combined to produce changing spatial divisions of labour and have become intertwined in different ways in different times and places. (p. 485)

In this way, whilst recognizing the laws of motion of capital across the globe, he sought also to emphasize the indeterminacy of production reorganization. Such a stance was also evident in, for example, the work of Lovering (1990), who insisted that changes taking place in the world economy should be interpreted not as an inexorable process, but as a series of tentative corporate experiments with contingent local expressions. For Amin and Robins (1990), too, the grand theory of flexible production left no room for social struggle and agency in the making of structural change. Whilst reasserting the continuing power of the multinational corporation, they concluded:

> As far as the geography of change is concerned, it is necessary to grasp the coexistence and combination of localising and globalising, centripetal and centrifugal, forces. The current restructuring process is a matter of a whole repertoire of spatial strategies. (p. 28)

There were, then, a number of highly important issues raised in and through the debate on flexible production and new industrial spaces. Generally speaking, these were to do with the adequacy of evidence for post-Fordist forms of production organization, including the ideologically-laden idea of the flexible firm; the evidence for and conceptualization of spatial change; and the whole process of theorizing in such abstract fashion, along with the connections between this and other forms of analysis. The focus on the forms of appearance of capitalism through its changing systems of production organization brought many useful insights. The idea which emerged that a *variety* of spatial strategies was open to internationally mobile capital, ranging on a spectrum from decentralization to reconcentration, was especially important. It was partially mirrored too in a growing awareness that changes in work organization were by no means all headed in the same direction: flexibility coexisted with mass production and standardization (see, for instance, Wood 1989).

On the other hand, there were a number of difficulties with the account of flexible production running through the debates outlined above. In seeking general theory in terms of exchange relations between companies, it downplayed the relations of production between capital and labour. Its concentration upon production was often achieved at the expense of elision between Fordist production and Fordist regimes of accumulation, underemphasizing the significance of the consumption side of the equation. Partly because of these shortcomings, proponents of flexible production selectively downplayed the role of the national state in maintaining a particular regime, and indeed in managing the transition (if such was taking place) from one to another. Storper and Scott's (1989) attempt to consider the social regulation of flexible production complexes only revealed some of the difficulties in making connections between production and reproduction without regard for the national state dimension. Ironically, the flexible production literature could be criticized for side-lining the national state, even though the regulationist school—on which much of it was loosely based—leaned heavily on the importance of the state. As Lovering (1990: p. 165) put it:

> Any attempt to construct a general theory on the demise of Fordism which treats the *national state* and the international and cultural context *merely as parameters* would seem unpromising. In effect this is Scott's approach. (emphasis added)

Equally Sayer's (1989) rejection of post-Fordism was founded on an examination of the specifically Japanese pattern of social organization, where mass production was both alive and well, and solidly underpinned by the Japanese state. In the following section, therefore, we turn to this question of the national state.

## I.4 The national state dimension

Despite frequent references to its significance, the national state dimension has thus far played little explicit role in this chapter. The shortcoming is rectified here; for the national state is one of the principal building blocks of the world economic order, and national state policies can play a vital—at times even decisive—role regarding developments in the global economy. The post-1945 boom was ordered round a social consensus in which the national state played a key part in securing some of the preconditions for profitable production such as currency stability, free trade and growing consumer demand, in return for commitments to relatively full employment and welfare provision. The extent and precise format of this agreement took specific national expressions, but for several decades there was a consensus—at least in the advanced capitalist countries—on the necessity for some kind of state intervention, if not necessarily on its extent and scope. Then as the long postwar boom faltered to a close, the ideas underpinning this regulatory model fell from favour and a growing tide of neo-conservatism filtered through the political fabric, epitomized by the election of Margaret Thatcher as Prime Minister in the UK in 1979 and Ronald Reagan as President in the USA in 1980 (see Gamble 1988; Krieger 1986). This new reactionary orthodoxy held particularly strong views on the role of the state in regulating capitalist markets. In attempting to restore satisfactory conditions for capital to invest profitably, many of the earlier ideas on appropriate levels of (un)employment and the welfare state were swept aside. It is of far from academic importance, therefore, that capitalist activity takes on a specifically national expression and is regulated mainly at the national level.

As well as these broad similarities, it is important to stress that there are and have been vital differences in the constitution of capitalism within nation-states, both reflection of and condition for differing national regulatory state environments. Capitalism in the USA, for example, has taken on a markedly different nature to that in Western Europe or Japan, whilst within Western Europe there is a wide range of differences. The single most remarkable distinguishing feature of post-1945 US capitalism was the sheer size of the US economy. A massive national market gave ample scope for the economies of scale made possible by Fordist-type mass production methods to be realized. Expansion of consumer demand as the economy grew was ensured via carefully state-regulated consumption norms, including the provision of suburban housing with all the consumer durables that this presupposed, such as the motor car and domestic household appliances (see Florida and Feldman 1988). At the same time, the boom was sharply characterized by a particularly American labour-relations environment. Legislation, such as the Taft–Hartley amendment in 1947, made it relatively more difficult for trade unions to organize labour in the USA than in other countries, for they had to gain representation within firms on a plant-by-plant basis, and could only have a national agreement with a company when they had organized within all of its plants. In those sectors where there was national-level recognition, such as automobiles, national trade union leaders exerted a tight control over plant-level representation, bringing members into line if necessary as they sought and secured guaranteed regular wage increases. These were given in return for relative long-term stability on the factory floor, which greatly facilitated corporate strategic planning. Moreover, labour representation differed markedly across states. In over twenty, mostly in the south, right-to-work legislation was passed which further limited trade union influence (see Clark 1989).

The anti-union environment of the southern states in comparison to that of the old north eastern industrial heartland was significant in the changing geography of US manufacturing employment in the 1970s and 1980s, as new growth sectors (and new employment in old sectors) concentrated in the south. However, a further key factor—sometimes downplayed in accounts of the development of new "high-tech" complexes such as Silicon Valley—was the changing pattern of US defence expenditure. After a downturn following the close of the Vietnam War, this began to increase again in real terms after 1977, and the proportion committed to research and development—especially in electronics applications—continued a marked rise. Such changes played a vital role in the emerging geography of US manufacturing (see Markusen 1985a; O'huallachain 1987); one more indicator of the widespread influence of American state policies and expression of the peculiarly American pattern of capitalism.

In the UK it was possible to identify three distinct phases in the post-1945 period, each characterized by a particular conception of central government policy which largely cut across party political divides (see Hudson and Williams 1986). Until 1962 this consensus was grounded on pursuit of full employment as a main goal of economic policy, entailing nationalization of several key sectors such as coal-mining, and financial management of the economy. Then emphasis shifted to a pursuit of higher growth rates as successive governments sought to "modernize" the UK economy, adopting a tripartite corporatist approach which embraced government, trade unions and business in an attempt to make British manufacturing industry technologically and organizationally competitive. This was relegated as a priority in the face of mounting balance of payments difficulties. Manufacturing employment began to fall absolutely from 1966 onwards (although output continued to grow until 1973). By 1975 government policies had a new focus, the control of inflation. Public expenditure increases were cut back and control increasingly centralized—especially after the election of Margaret Thatcher's administration in 1979, which was committed to controlling the Public Sector Borrowing Requirement at practically any cost. A policy of high interest rates exacerbated the problems facing an already weak manufacturing base struggling to cope with international recession, and a massive collapse set in. National unemployment rates doubled from 6 per cent in 1979 to 12 per cent in 1981, as whole swathes of manufacturing industry were shut down. By 1984, the UK economy recorded its first ever deficit in manufactured goods (see House of Lords 1985) and this widened sharply in the rest of the decade. Equally, relaxation of capital controls further encouraged the flight of financial capital from the UK. British finance capital became integrated into a highly sensitive, internationalized circuit—one small cog in a wheel, rather than an engine of the system.

These changes took on particular regional forms, which can be related to the UK's changing international role (see especially, Massey 1986). Expansion in the old industrial regions such as north east England, south Wales and central Scotland based on coal, steel, shipbuilding and mechanical engineering hinged on the imperial dominance of British manufacturing. The decline of the British Empire was clearly reflected in collapse in these sectors and deindustrialization in those regions. In the 1960s, decentralization from the core regions of the economy—the West Midlands and the south east, and large urban agglomerations—coincided with growing investment by UK-based companies overseas. It led to a new layer of growth being added to peripheral regions such as the north east, as branch plant operations of multinational (either UK- or US-based) capital attracted by regional policy and plentiful labour reserves (including incorporation of women into the waged labour force) overlapped the declining heavy industrial complexes. This proved no more able to cope with heightened international competition and only worsened the unemployment crisis in these regions in the 1980s.

The extent of the decline in manufacturing in the 1980s, coupled with the spatial concentration of growth in a broad arc from the "M4 corridor" west of London to East Anglia, was captured in concern for a growing north-south divide within the country. Regional employment and unemployment differentials were matched by vast differences in socio-economic conditions (see Lewis and Townsend 1989; Martin 1988; Mohan 1989). It seemed that the national economy was in the midst of a major structural transformation whose outcome was far from clear. In the process, individual places and regions took on markedly different economic profiles and prospects.

These shifts were accompanied by a new emphasis in state policies, as the hand of the market was given freer rein under the aegis of an increasingly powerful central state. This produced several bitter ironies—for instance, a growing component of central government "regional" policy in the 1980s was the (to the individual, inadequate, but in aggregate, highly substantial) provision of social security assistance (see Walker and Huby 1989). But the clearest expression of the new policy emphasis was that with regard to the nationalized industries. Here, the objective was simple: to recreate the conditions for private capital to invest profitably by cutting back capacity drastically, with scant regard for the strategic role of the industries concerned in the UK's economic base. In this way nationalized industries, such as coal and steel, came to be a major proximate cause of economic collapse in the peripheral regions wherein they were concentrated (see Hudson 1986a). For the Conservative Government this policy fulfilled a double role, not just opening these sectors to international competition but also reinforcing another strand of the Thatcherite project. This was an assault on the power—whether perceived or real was immaterial—of trade unions, all the more so since these industries were amongst the strongest points of organized labour. New types of collective bargaining agreements based on the proclaimed success of the

Japanese model were espoused instead (see Bassett 1986, for examples) and the (relatively un-unionized) service sector was proclaimed as a mechanism of growth. This remained so in spite of powerful warnings of caution about the extent of employment creation to be expected from service sector expansion (see Rajan 1987). For regions such as the south east, service sector growth might mean well-paid jobs in activities such as financial services. These, though, were under-represented in the peripheral regions; there, service sector growth all too often meant low-paid part-time work in areas such as retailing and tourism (though this was of course also present in the south east), further reinforcing the new geography of inequality.

If the state played a major role in the deindustrialization of the UK economy, it played a different, but no less decisive, one in Japan. Contrary to the assumption—prevalent in the UK—that state intervention meant direct control of the production process, the Japanese state played a major guiding role in the country's phenomenal postwar economic growth. This extended well beyond the most obvious—but by no means insignificant—manifestation, international trade policies. The most influential body in this process was the Ministry of International Trade and Industry (MITI) advised by the Industrial Structure Council. This aimed to formulate visions of the future; prognoses of what lay ahead for Japanese manufacturing. Such "vision-making" was the Japanese version of indicative planning, building a consensus, ensuring continuity in industrial policy and producing vital information to assist companies in long-term strategic planning (see Fujita 1988). In the 1960s, the vision was that of high economic growth rates and export-led expansion. By the 1980s, a new concern had come to the fore, that of spatially redistributing growth within Japan. This was an especially important goal given the growing problems of congestion within the few large conurbations. Hence the Technopolis programme was unveiled, which sought to decentralize the economy through the establishment of dispersed high-technology industrial complexes (see also Glasmeier 1988).

The other distinguishing features of Japanese industrial success were the exceptionally *organized* nature of Japanese capitalism, resting on a tightly bound but vertically disintegrated structure; and a particular form of mass production which depended upon relatively weak trades unionism. In the early postwar years, the limited size of the Japanese economy precluded full adoption of the kind of large-scale mass production prevalent in the USA. Instead, a different form had to be evolved, which involved even tighter control over the labour force. In several sectors, especially motor vehicles, there were bitter industrial disputes in the early 1950s, especially at Nissan. By the 1960s, though, this system, which came to be known as Just-In-Time (JIT) was securely established, as a particular form of enterprise-based trade unionism became dominant.

JIT production is commonly contrasted with its Western counterpart, Just-In-Case (see Sayer 1986). In such distinctions the focus is on the tight stock control and regular deliveries of JIT against the high stock levels held against uncertain deliveries of components in JIC production. JIT is more than just a production system characterized by low stock levels though, even if this is one important aspect of it. For JIT rests upon a continuous learning about the production process, a never-ending search (incorporating, rather than excluding, labour) for improvements in overall production efficiency, including small detailed changes and, if necessary, major alterations in the overall layout of the factory. The production process is broken down into a series of identifiable, discrete stages so that:

> whereas the JIC system is a method of mass production based on a collection of large lot production processes separated by large buffers and feeding into a final assembly line, JIT is a system of mass production consisting of a highly integrated series of small lot production processes. (Sayer 1986: p. 56)

Crucially, though, it is still a system of mass production. Whilst it might bear some similarities with the model of flexible specialization outlined above, and might be expected (all other things being equal) to have similar geographical correlates, JIT is not *necessarily* geared to small-scale markets or to horizontal agglomeration.

This clarification of the Japanese production system is highly important, for its proclaimed superiority was one argument used forcefully by the UK government in support of the growing wave of Japanese manufacturing investment there during the 1980s. This was concentrated in a few sectors, principally electronics and motor vehicles, and a few regions, notably north east England and south Wales. The extent of the UK government's welcome was evident from the clean sweep which Britain made of the first round of full-scale Japanese car assembly plants in Western Europe during the late 1980s: Nissan at Sunderland, Toyota at Burnaston, and Honda at Swindon. For these companies, location within the European Community provided a convenient production base inside increasingly restrictive trade barriers; for the UK government they brought employment, new production techniques and, perhaps crucially, new patterns of industrial relations.

One of the earliest systematic studies of the impact of this Japanese investment in the UK was that of Dunning (1986). He concluded that the trend was to be encouraged, but that the Government should explore two areas of concern. These were the extent to which employment was created and components produced locally rather than in Japan; and the potential "Trojan horse" impact wherein the UK became an "offshore assembly house" (p. 194) for Japanese multinationals, with research and development activities remaining in Japan, leading to a growing technological gap. These fears were subsequently explored further by Morris (1988). Oliver and Wilkinson (1988) also argued that a process of "Japanization" was occurring across British industry, not only via Japanese investment but also through the imitation of Japanese practices by other companies.

Much confusion surrounded this proclaimed process of Japanization, due partly to modifications made to Japanese practices in the UK, and also to misinterpretations of the Japanese system in action in Japan. Subjected to critical evaluation, it became more difficult to equate the proclaimed impact with the reality of Japanese investment. In particular Graham (1988) argued that suggestions of the Japanization of the UK economy rested on a selective re-reading of the JIT system. As he put it,

> JIT techniques are described in Japanese literature as a means of reducing total cost, but in Western descriptions the potential savings in direct labour costs are highlighted .... For [Western] managers who have for many years seen improving labour productivity as their principal goal, any new management technique is assessed in terms of its potential as a means of achieving productivity increases, even if more significant overall increases could be achieved through adopting a more radical perspective and redefining management's objectives. (p. 72)

Since JIT as a concept, then, had been modified in the West, he asked why it was still regarded as "Japanese". The answer, he concluded, was simple: "The myth of JIT allows organisational changes to be implemented as an imperative, claiming that they must be introduced to defeat foreign competition" (p. 74). Equally, Briggs (1988) focused on the standard Western representation of the Japanese employment situation as an ideal, arguing that in truth the Japanese model rested on a number of far-from-idyllic labour practices. These included the proclaimed "job-for-life" held only by a minority of the workforce; the very real economic ties which bound such workers to their company;

low levels of job satisfaction; discontent with quality circles; and the unwritten norms governing the status of supposedly "equal" managers.

It would seem, therefore, that the welcome given to Japanese manufacturing investment in the UK rested on the impact of Japanese companies in terms of labour relations, not techno-logical or industrial/organizational change. Whether this was a satisfactory basis for renewal of the UK economy was hard to judge; even more so was its adequacy as a response to deep-set long-term problems. It clearly rested though on a selective re-interpretation of the Japanese model, and a partial adoption of some of its features. Such questions were particularly significant in areas such as north east England, where Japanese manufacturing investment was concentrated.

## 1.5 Theorizing regional change

The debate on flexible production and new industrial districts has been considered in relation to the significance of regional change and, more particularly, the process of theorization. The distinction between highly abstract theory concerned with the laws of motion of global capitalism and concrete case studies of the regional implications of this process has also been introduced, and criticized for conflating questions of abstraction with those of geographic scale. This section explores these issues a little further so as to provide a framework within which the account of changes in north east England can be understood both in its own terms and in relation to the rest of the book.

As Hudson (1988) has argued, there is clearly a place in social science for both analysis of the global workings of the capitalist system and for theoretically informed work on regional change, providing it is recognized that the extent to which the latter can produce generalizable conclusions is limited by the available evidence. In this sense, then, there is a difference of emphasis between the two kinds of theorization in terms of evidence and starting point, but little necessary dissimilarity in terms of ultimate objective—understanding the capitalist system of production—or in the significance attached to theory construction. This point has often been lost in the debate over regional and, in particular, locality research (see also Cox and Mair 1989). Much of the concern over the apparent "retreat from theory" which regional and local analysis supposedly represented could be understood in terms of an encounter between Marxist and postmodernist views of the world (see Cloke, Philo and Sadler 1991, chapter two). The postmodernist celebration of difference and disavowal of grand theory became closely associated, in the eyes of some at least, with work on the local impacts of change; and in defending the significance of macro-theory, some Marxist theorists (by and large wrongly) implicated regional analysis with the postmodernist project. More recently however, there has been growing concern for the re-integration of regional analysis within broader frameworks, expressed most clearly in calls for a "new", theoretically informed regional geography (see Gregory 1989; Smith 1989).

One way of understanding the relationship between regional change and broader processes is through the notion of "spatial divisions of labour" (see Massey 1984). Regional industrial structures, so it is argued, are associated with different layers of investment, which overlap and intersect to form a changing mosaic of economic opportunity. This geological analogy is subject to a number of analytical problems, including the primacy which it attaches to economic changes, and the relationship between these and social and political developments. The importance of cultural and political processes in regional development should not be underestimated, and the ways in which they take shape from and help to fashion the economy of a region are deeply significant. The notion of "spatial divisions of labour" is, however, conceptually simple and forms, if nothing else, a useful starting point for understanding and interpreting the argument presented in Part II of this book, which deals with north east England.

In many ways the north east of England is a classic old industrial region. Its heyday came in the Industrial Revolution, when there developed a social and physical infrastructure built on the traditions of paternal capitalism. The story of much of the region's industrial base for most of the twentieth century was that of three key sectors—coal, steel and shipbuilding—along with mechanical engineering in the conurbations along the Tyne, Wear and Tees, and newer arrivals such as heavy chemicals from the early twentieth century. These were subjected to seemingly ever greater pressures and stresses of international competition, mediated in a variety of ways by state intervention. The three leading sectors were all nationalized—coal in 1947, steel in 1967 and shipbuilding in 1977—and their respective workforces within the north east on the dates of being take into public ownership (149,000, 46,000 and 48,000) were but one indication of the extent of state influence within the region. To give some idea of both the scale of decline and the dominance of these sectors, their combined total of nearly 250,000 jobs (albeit from different dates) was practically identical to the number of jobs remaining in the entire manufacturing base of the north east at the end of the 1980s, whilst there were three times as many jobs by that date in the region's service industries. In this, and many more ways, the region could truly be labelled as state-managed (see Hudson 1986b, 1989b).

The focus in this volume is upon the transition within the economic base of north east England which took place during the 1980s, as near-terminal decline set in amongst the old staple industries of coal and steel. As these (in the main, still national-ized) sectors declined, other forms of activity began to make their appearance—epitomized in the opening of the region's first ever car assembly plant by Nissan at Sunderland. What Part II seeks to do, then, is not to present a detailed historical examination of the whole economic history of the north east of England, but rather to focus much more selectively upon the *interactions* between two rounds of investment within the region—the old base of the nineteenth century, and the new style of 1980s manufacturing—and to address some of the questions of *social change and state policy* which are raised in the process. In so doing it should be recognized that much of the intervening history, such as rise and fall in the branch plant economy from the 1950s to the 1970s, is downplayed. However, in so structuring the account, the impact of international changes (considered in Part I) in coal, steel and automobile production is written large across the region, and at the same time this re-shaping of the north east forms a crucial, constitutive element in the global process of restructuring. The focus is upon the *interpenetration* of international and regional industrial change (mediated by the particular character of UK state policies), and the social and political implications of all this for the region and its inhabitants.

## I.6 Coal, steel, motor vehicles, north east England: the organization of the book

Part I of this book, then, presents a global survey of three indus-trial activities: coal-mining (strictly speaking not a manufacturing sector as such), iron and steel production, and automobile assem-bly. These form a classic production sequence with the outputs of one being the inputs of another, although they are also each interlinked with other components of the global economy. Some of these other connections are introduced to demonstrate the complex nature of the manufacturing chain. Part I also focuses on one particular national context for these three industries, one

TABLE I.1

*Employment at British Coal, British Steel and in motor vehicles and parts*
*(SIC 35), 1979–89*

|  | (1000s) | | Change 1979–89 | |
|  | 1979 | 1989 | 1000s | %pa |
|---|---|---|---|---|
| British Coal | 297 | 105 | −192 | −6.5 |
| British Steel | 186 | 52 | −134 | −7.2 |
| Motor vehicles | 464 | 268 | −196 | −4.2 |
| Total | 947 | 425 | −522 | −5.5 |

Note: British Coal and British Steel columns refer to year ending 31 March; motor vehicles and parts to June. British Coal figures are for total employment, not colliery industrial manpower, to aid comparison with British Steel and motor vehicles columns which also include white-collar staff.

Sources: British Coal *Annual Reports*; British Steel *Annual Reports*; *Employment Gazette* (for motor vehicles and parts SIC 35).

where their decline has been particularly significant. The loss of 0.5 m jobs at British Coal and British Steel and in motor vehicles and parts production (see Table I.1) represented nearly one-quarter of the decline in employment in production industries in the UK during the 1980s. It meant also a phenomenal rate of job loss in these sectors of more than 5 per cent annually over the decade. The timing of these redundancies was significant too (see Figure I.1). Employment in motor vehicles and parts production slumped dramatically in the 1979–82 recession, taking with it other sectors such as iron and steel, especially after 1980. By contrast, employment at British Coal only really began to collapse after the defeat of the year-long miners' strike in 1985, but in the following four years it fell by more than half.

Chapter 1 focuses on the international coal industry, exploring the extent to which coal production and demand were affected by the oil crisis of the 1970s. This made coal a highly competitive fuel and led to widespread expansionary forecasts, along with major investment by oil-based multinational corporations in this alternative energy source. When demand failed to expand at anything like previously anticipated rates, the new capacity created an excess of supply over demand and prices fell heavily, leading to great pressures on established producers such as the UK coal industry. There, the impact of international market forces was mediated by the particular form of organization of coal production (mostly through the public sector British Coal Corporation, formerly the National Coal Board) and its

27

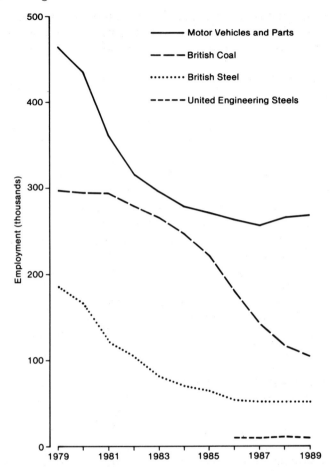

FIG I.1. Employment at British Coal, British Steel and United Engineering Steels and in motor vehicles and parts in the UK, 1979–89. (Sources: *Annual Reports* of British Coal, British Steel and United Engineering Steels; *Employment Gazette*. Company totals include white collar staff to ensure consistency with estimates for motor vehicles and parts employment.)

supply arrangements with the public sector electricity generating company, the Central Electricity Generating Board. During the 1980s government policy forced British Coal to respond to the global market situation via pit closures, an expansion of low-cost opencast output, improved capital utilization and flexible working practices. The tensions between adequate supply (including the issue of import capacity) and the price of UK production lay at the heart of British Coal's fortunes, especially during complex negotiations as the government prepared the electricity supply industry for privatization; this also affected patterns of demand. Finally, the chapter closes by considering the impacts of coal's changing fortunes within the UK energy supply sector on the electricity generating plant industry.

In Chapter 2 the emphasis switches to iron and steel, which has seen one of the most dramatic global shifts of production as capacity closed in Western Europe and North America and new works opened in many of the newly industrializing countries. In the former regions, iron and steel signified de-industrialization; in the latter, expansion. These contrasts are highly significant, partly representing diverging demand patterns (including product substitution in the advanced countries), but they also demonstrated a changing comparative advantage between nation-states in the global economy. The chapter considers the new patterns of steel production and trade which emerged after 1974, and efforts taken by the European Community to order decline in its steel industries. It then analyses the situation in the UK, where the major state-owned company (British Steel Corporation) followed a course similar to that of British Coal—capacity cutback and massive redundancy—before re-entering the private sector in 1988. New patterns of labour relations within BSC are evaluated before closing with the question of raw material supply to the industry.

Chapter 3 switches attention to motor vehicle assembly, a key manufacturing sector in the global economy and one which is heavily dominated by a few multinational corporations. The range of corporate strategies outlined above (in sections I.2 and I.3) on a spectrum from decentralization to reconcentration is a central focus, along with the growing trend towards (often temporary) tactical alliances. Japanese companies, such as Toyota and Nissan, have risen close to global ascendancy, rivalling even the American giants General Motors and Ford, and this chapter outlines the significance of Japanese expansion into production bases in North America and Western Europe. Within the latter, these plants are concentrated in the UK, so the chapter goes on to consider the new role of the country as a production base for the world motor vehicle industry, outlining consequences for existing manufacturers established there. Finally, changing patterns of component supply are analysed in the context of Japanese methods of production organization.

Part II then investigates how these trends have fashioned, and in turn partly taken their shape from, north east England. In Chapter 4 the decline of the old coal/steel based economy is described and contrasted with new forms of manufacturing, typified in the Nissan car plant at Sunderland. In coal and steel, state policies played a central role in organizing decline, despite (and in part because of) the expansionary prognoses of mid-1970s planning exercises. Instead of growth, public control was used as a mechanism to cut down these sectors with scant regard for the connections between them, or their links to the region. The implantation of companies like Nissan was similarly heavily underpinned (including substantial financial support via regional policy) by the UK state. The recruitment and labour relations policies of this "new" production complex marked it out as significantly different to the former basis of the old.

These issues are taken further in Chapter 5, which looks at one crucial precondition for such change in a heavily unionized labour stronghold such as the north east, the role of state policies in refashioning labour supply. This is considered via analysis of unsuccessful anti-closure campaigns, in steel at Consett in 1980, and in coal during the national 1984/85 miners' strike. The defeat of this opposition severely weakened labour within the region (and indeed the country) but most especially in these sectors, so that by the close of the decade they too displayed signs of changed labour practices and work intensification. Such changes were as nothing though compared to the conditions of employment which prevailed in many of the new companies introduced to coal and steel closure areas (again via state policy) in an attempt to develop new forms of manufacturing, which rested upon highly exploitative labour contracts and prevailing high levels of unemployment. The chapter closes with further consideration of the kind of new economy emerging in the north east; issues which are developed further in the concluding chapter.

## Note

1.  A useful review of some alternative approaches is contained in Harris (1988). He distinguished three types of explanation: long-wave, world-system and regulationist theories. Long-wave theories, associated particularly with the work of Kondratiev, focused on the bunching of innovations in products or production technologies every fifty years or so, to create the conditions for a new phase of capitalist expansion. Precisely why and how this bunching took place, and how technological change was generated, remained unasked and unanswered questions, and there was no clear relationship to the geography of change. World-system theories, in particular those of Wallerstein, were characterized by an emphasis upon a complete global economic system which was all-embracing; whilst regulationist theories, by contrast, saw each nation-state's internal structures as of primary significance. World-system and regulationist approaches, then, shared a concern for the integration of nation-states

in the world economy, but started from markedly different points of emphasis. Another perspective was that of Lash and Urry (1987), who argued that the growing consolidation of power in the hands of multinational corporations was leading to a *disorganization* of capitalist national states; although it was difficult to equate this notion with the growing sophistication of global financial management systems.

# Part I

# Global Restructuring:
# The Picture in Three Different
# Industries and Its Mediation by
# UK State Policies

# 1
# Coal on the Energy Market

## 1.1 Introduction

In 1984 and 1985 the UK miners' strike made headlines around the world. One of the longest, most intractable and bitterly fought industrial disputes of the century, it seemed both to capture a whole range of emotions and encapsulate the country's changing international role. Coal, the foundation on which an empire had been built in the previous century, became instead a symbol of national industrial decline. By the end of the 1980s the industry had been drastically cut back under competition from cheaper imports just as it had been in the 1950s and 1960s, in response then to the availability of low-cost imported energy in the form of oil (see Table 1.1). Whole coalfields, with their associated communities, faced a prospect of more or less complete extinction.

This chapter focuses not on the miners' strike and that turbulent year, but on the international and national economic and political conditions which created the possibility for such wholesale devastation of capacity and employment in the UK. It begins by considering (in section 1.2) the changing international environment after 1974, when fourfold oil price rises imposed by the major exporting countries suddenly made coal a relatively cheap and potentially highly lucrative energy source once again. In response, oil-based multinational corporations expanded their holdings in coal, at first in developed countries such as the USA, Australia and South Africa, later in partnership with developing countries such as Colombia. Much of the new capacity was worked by opencast methods, entailing the removal of first overburden, then coal, by huge dragline excavators. This produced relatively low-cost coal after a high investment in infrastructure; so that large volumes of cheap coal were thrown onto the world market in an attempt to recoup on the initial outlay. Crucially, however, demand failed to expand at anything like the rates predicted in the wake of 1973/74; global recession saw to that. So a chronic

TABLE 1.1

*UK primary energy consumption by source*

| % | 1950 | 1955 | 1960 | 1965 | 1970 | 1975 | 1980 | 1985 | 1988[1] |
|---|------|------|------|------|------|------|------|------|------|
| Coal | 90 | 85 | 74 | 62 | 46 | 37 | 37 | 32 | 33 |
| Oil | 10 | 14 | 25 | 35 | 45 | 42 | 37 | 35 | 34 |
| Gas | – | – | – | – | 5 | 17 | 21 | 25 | 24 |
| Nuclear | – | – | – | 2 | 3 | 3 | 4 | 7 | 7 |
| Hydro | – | 1 | 1 | 1 | 1 | 1 | 1 | 1 | 1 |
| Total | 228 | 254 | 269 | 303 | 337 | 325 | 329 | 327 | 340 |

(mt coal equivalent)

Source: Department of Energy *Digest of UK Energy Statistics* (various dates).
[1] 1988 figures also include 1 per cent net electricity imports.

temporary surplus of supply developed, and coal prices fell seemingly ever lower.

This situation underpinned the UK coal industry's decline, which is analysed in section 1.3. In the main market area, electricity generation, considerable pressure was exerted by the threat (whether actual or real was open to debate) of cheap imported coal, and of first nuclear, then later gas-fired generating capacity, as the electricity supply industry was prepared for privatization. The UK coal industry responded to the challenge by reducing capacity and cutting costs, but in the process any concerted national energy policy was ruled out of order, with the risk of leaving the UK as vulnerable to coal imports as it had been to oil imports in a previous era. The short-term market-generated and state-reinforced uncertainty also impacted upon other sectors dependent upon energy supply. Section 1.4 analyses one of these, power station equipment manufacture. Finally, section 1.5 considers further the longer term implications of coal's continuing decline in the UK and world market developments, and re-appraises the impact of UK state policies towards energy supply in general.

## 1.2 Coal and the international market

Coal is far from a uniform commodity. It is instead a highly differentiated one, with coals of varying origins distinguished on the basis of calorific value, chemical content (especially the amounts of sulphur and chlorine which are present), coking properties, amount of ash produced when burned, and even physical structure. There is a tremendous difference from the very high-grade anthracites at one end of the scale through to coking coals, steam coals and on to the brown coals or lignites at the other; and these are important distinctions in terms of end-use value. A steam-raising coal is generally unsuited for coking, and coking coals are wasted in steam raising. Coal should not be thought of as a uniform fuel capable of being used indiscriminately; it is a wide range of different fuels, each suitable for particular purposes (see also Foley 1987: pp. 55–7).

In the late nineteenth and early twentieth centuries, coal dominated global energy supply, and the major coal-producing nations were, not coincidentally, the major industrial powers. In 1913, the UK, France, Germany and the USA produced 90 per cent of the world's coal. Coal's dominance was a lasting one; as late as 1950, it supplied over 60 per cent of global energy demand. By 1960 this proportion was down to 51 per cent and, in 1967, oil overtook coal as the world's primary energy source. By 1970 coal's share of global energy supply was down to 35 per cent (see Chadwick *et al* 1987: pp. 1–2).

Much of the new oil production capacity was located in the Middle East and Latin America, so that the old coal-based European and American powers became heavy energy importers. Thus, in 1973, when a fourfold increase in the price of oil was initiated by the Organisation of Petroleum Exporting Countries (OPEC), both oil's seemingly inexorable rise to dominance, and the whole basis of the global economy, were severely shaken. Practically overnight, oil became a more expensive energy source than coal. As well as triggering longstanding trends pushing the world into recession, this threw considerable turmoil into the world coal industry. Spurred on by national governments concerned over the apparent domestic security implications of dependence upon imported energy supplies, the major (largely US-based) oil companies rapidly diversified into coal, oil's newly resurgent competitor.

In spite of coal's bulk and high transport cost in relation to value, the prospects appeared good for an increase in its international trading. After all it had, once again, become a prized commodity on the global energy market. So the oil majors—often referred to as the "Seven Sisters" (Exxon, Shell, BP, Gulf, Texaco, Standard Oil of California, Mobil; see UNCTC 1985: p. 144) purchased extensive coal reserves in the USA, Australia, South Africa and Latin America (see especially Rutledge and Wright 1985: pp. 310–4). This was principally steam coal—the direct competitor to oil—but new coking coal deposits were also opened up, largely on the strength of optimistic demand forecasts from the Japanese steel industry.

By the end of the 1970s, US oil companies owned 25 per cent of US coal reserves, major dock and handling facilities were being developed on the eastern seaboard of the USA and in Europe, especially in Rotterdam, and a string of optimistic forecasts seemingly confirmed the expectation that international trade in coal, and coal production generally, was set to boom. President Carter proposed to double US coal output by 1985 (Spooner and Calzonetti 1984: p. 3). The World Coal Study (WOCOL 1980) predicted that total world coal production would double from 2,200 m tonnes in 1977 to 4,400 m tonnes by the year 2000. It also envisaged the growth of major "coal chains", with supply networks from mine to port using purpose-built railways and oceangoing bulk carriers in one giant, integrated operation. Dramatic expansionary forecasts abounded, which were seemingly confirmed by a further massive rise in oil prices in 1979.

In the event, things took a radically different course. For a number of interrelated reasons, demand for coal totally failed to take off in the fashion so confidently expected in the late 1970s. Coal proved not to be so readily substitutable for oil in power station use as anticipated; major new investment which would have been required for conversion could not be merited by the price differential. The impact of energy conservation programmes which were initiated by many governments, in terms of reducing overall energy consumption, was underestimated. Suggestions of the impending exhaustion of oil and gas reserves within twenty

TABLE 1.2
*World's major coal producers, 1973 and 1987–89*

| (m tonnes) | 1973 | 1987 | 1988 | 1989 |
|---|---|---|---|---|
| China | 417 | 870 | 885 | 956 |
| USA | 530 | 761 | 591 | 608 |
| USSR | 461 | 516 | 523 | 498 |
| Poland | 156 | 193 | 193 | 178 |
| India | 78 | 177 | 180 | 186 |
| South Africa | 62 | 176 | nd | nd |
| Australia | 55 | 147 | 136 | 149 |
| UK | 132 | 104 | 104 | 100 |
| West Germany | 103 | 82 | 80 | 78 |
| World total | 2,201 | 3,262 | 3,131 | 3,197 |

Source: (1973, 1987) International Energy Agency; (1988, 1989) BP Statistical Review of World Energy 1990.

years (upon which many forecasts had been based) proved to be wildly overstated. Perhaps most significantly of all, the forecasts failed to take account of a slow-down of world economic growth, and hence energy demand, brought about by recession induced in turn (partly) by higher energy costs.

In these changed circumstances newly revised forecasts suggested a much lower increase in global coal demand. Fischer (1984: p. 24) anticipated that in the light of 1983 demand at 2,440 m tonnes, consumption would increase to 2,750 m tonnes by 1990 (against WOCOL's previous estimate of 3,300 m tonnes) and to 3,000 m tonnes by 1995 (against WOCOL's predicted 4,400 m tonnes by 2000). At the same time the new capacity opened up in anticipation of a booming market found instead a growing surplus of production over demand. In real terms, steam coal prices fell from $60/tonne in 1981/82 to $26/tonne in 1987.[1] The reasons for this dramatic price collapse were both complex and of crucial importance for understanding the nature of change in international coal supply.

Major growth in coal production capacity and in exports had taken place in the 1970s in established producer countries: the USA, Canada, Australia and South Africa (see Tables 1.2–1.6). In the course of the 1980s, these sources of supply were joined by newer projects in other nations, largely based on low-cost opencast operations. The most significant of these were in Colombia, China, Venezuela and Indonesia. These newly industrializing countries typically sought to earn foreign exchange from the export of a basic resource, and invited foreign companies to participate in return for taking a share of the initial investment costs (see Gordon 1987: pp. 87–103).

In Colombia, a joint venture was agreed in 1976 between

TABLE 1.3
*Coking coal exports by country, 1970–86*

| (m tonnes) | 1970 | 1975 | 1980 | 1985 | 1986 |
|---|---|---|---|---|---|
| Australia | 18 | 27 | 34 | 51 | 51 |
| USA | 42 | 38 | 52 | 48 | 44 |
| Canada | 3 | 11 | 14 | 22 | 21 |
| Poland | 6 | 10 | 6 | 6 | 7 |
| South Africa | – | – | 3 | 4 | 5 |
| Other | 6 | 6 | 5 | 10 | 12 |
| Total | 75 | 92 | 114 | 141 | 140 |

Source: Energy Committee, 1988 p. 131.

TABLE 1.4
*Seaborne international coking coal trade: imports and exports, 1986*

| (m tonnes) | Imports to: | | | | | |
|---|---|---|---|---|---|---|
| | Japan | EC | S.E. Asia | South America | Other | Total |
| Exports from: | | | | | | |
| Australia | 28 | 10 | 9 | 1 | 4 | 51 |
| USA | 10 | 20 | 2 | 6 | 6 | 44 |
| Canada | 16 | 1 | 3 | 1 | – | 21 |
| Poland | – | 3 | – | 3 | 1 | 7 |
| South Africa | 5 | – | – | – | – | 5 |
| Others | 7 | 2 | 2 | – | – | 12 |
| Total | 66 | 36 | 16 | 11 | 11 | 140 |

Source: Energy Committee 1988 p. 131.

TABLE 1.5
*Steam coal exports by country, 1973–86*

| (m tonnes) | 1973 | 1980 | 1986 |
|---|---|---|---|
| Australia | – | 9 | 41 |
| South Africa | 2 | 25 | 40 |
| USA | 2 | 15 | 21 |
| Poland | 13 | 14 | 8 |
| Others | 4 | 12 | 23 |
| Total | 21 | 75 | 133 |

Source: Energy Committee 1988 p. 132.

TABLE 1.6
*Seaborne international steam coal trade: imports and exports, 1986*

| (m tonnes) | Imports to: | | | | |
|---|---|---|---|---|---|
| | EC | S.E. Asia | Japan | Other | Total |
| Exports from: | | | | | |
| Australia | 11 | 13 | 15 | 2 | 41 |
| South Africa | 22 | 8 | 4 | 6 | 40 |
| USA | 13 | 6 | 1 | 1 | 21 |
| Poland | 5 | – | – | 3 | 8 |
| Others | 9 | 6 | 4 | 4 | 23 |
| Total | 60 | 33 | 24 | 16 | 133 |

Source: Energy Committee 1988 p. 132.

Intercor, a subsidiary of the US oil company Exxon, and Carbocol, the state-owned coal company, to develop and exploit vast reserves of coal (estimated as up to 3,600 m tonnes) at Cerrejon, in the interior of the country. After a feasibility study was conducted by Intercor, which incorporated the oil company's optimistic expectations of coal demand, the project was given the go-ahead in 1980. For an investment of $3,000 m, the two partners completed a whole new export infrastructure, including a 150 km rail link and an export terminal at Port Bolivar. The first exports of coal were made in 1985 at a price significantly lower than the feasibility study had forecast. By 1987, selling prices for the coal were down as low as $27–28/tonne against earlier forecasts of $89/tonne—scarcely profitable even given low operating costs, and a financial nightmare for the operators.

The volume of steam coal from this single mine was substantial; up to 15 m tonnes annually in the first phase with a possible expansion to 25 m tonnes per year (see Townsend 1988). It was not the only coal-based development planned in the north east of the country, either. A joint venture agreed between Carbocol and Drummond of the USA in 1988 sought to export steam coal from La Loma by 1992, building up to exports of 10 m tonnes annually. Colombian steam coal was regarded as high quality in the international market, being low in sulphur content, but impending new projects depended on decisions on investment in transportation facilities, which rested in turn upon higher coal prices. Nonetheless, Colombia's initial excursions into the coal export market—reaching 10 m tonnes in 1987—looked set to expand still further.

At one stage of the 1980s much the same could have been said of China. A major coal producer in its own right, historically virtually all of its output was destined for the domestic market. At the start of the 1980s, the Chinese government proposed to double coal output by 2000, up to 1,200 m tonnes annually, and scheduled an increasing proportion of output for export in a bid to earn foreign currency. By 1985, China had overtaken the USA as the world's biggest producer of coal. In that year also the first foreign involvement in Chinese coal extraction was confirmed in an agreement between Occidental Petroleum and the Chinese government, to open up a major coal mine at An Tai Bao, with a projected initial capacity of 15 m tonnes/year, possibly rising in successive equal stages to a massive 45 m tonnes/year. This mine was specifically geared for the export market, as part of a drive to treble Chinese coal exports to 30 m tonnes by 1990. The first exports from An Tai Bao were made in 1987, but rising domestic demand soon outstripped increased production, and forced an embarrassing reversal. In 1988 exports from An Tai Bao were one-third of target, cut back in favour of supplies to domestic consumers. In 1989 China even imported coal. This led to considerable disruption in China's anticipated export market: as one survey put it, "China has over the last six months achieved an unassailable reputation for unreliability, letting down almost every buyer with whom contracts have been signed" (Prior and McCloskey 1988: p. 71). With such notoriety, and following internal political upheaval, the future role of China as a major coal exporter seemed far from assured.

Other major projects saw the Venezuelan state-owned company Carbozulia sign an agreement in 1987 with Agip Carbone (a subsidiary of Italy's state energy company, ENI) and Arco of the US, to develop a $500 m, 6.5 m tonnes annual capacity steam coal export mine in Venezuela's Zulia province. For the Venezuelan government this provided an important hedge against variations in the price of its oil exports. In Indonesia, too, planned expansion of production to support domestic demand was supplemented in the late 1980s by a series of projects for the extraction of low-sulphur coal from the island of Kalimantan for export. These included Kaltim Prima (owned by BP Coal and Australian minerals group CRA), Arutmin (owned by Australia's BHP-Utah) and Adaro (50 per cent owned by a subsidiary of Australia's New Hope Collieries). The forecast export potential of the island was 20 m tonnes by 1994, rising to 38 m tonnes by 2000, from a location ideally placed to serve the growth markets of South East Asia.

These new and prospective projects, then, indicated the extent to which new sources of supply were being opened up. Whilst not always vast in relation to total world *output* they represented a notable addition to the volume of coal *traded internationally*. At the same time the longer-established exporting nations were also adjusting to changed circumstances. Australia, the world's biggest coal exporter, depended on the Japanese market for more than one-half of its total exports. In the early to mid 1980s, on the strength of optimistic demand forecasts from Japanese consumers of coking and steam coals, Australian mine companies invested heavily. Increased demand failed to material- ize though, and a situation of over-supply was compounded by the growth of alternative sources (see Gibson 1990). Similar problems befell the Quintette coking coal mine in Canada, a joint venture between Japanese steel companies and the Canadian company Denison Mines which was agreed in 1981. Japanese dependence on imports—reinforced by closure of domestic mines, whose output fell from 50 m tonnes in 1960 to 15 m tonnes in 1986—was countered by its market power as the overwhelmingly dominant importer, and an aggressive pursuit of alternative sources of low-cost supply.

One such supplier, largely for political reasons, was South Africa. In the mid-1980s several European countries, notably France and Denmark, imposed total embargoes on the purchase of South African coal, in protest against the apartheid system. Whilst this partly resulted in some mine closures, the coal which had formerly been sold to Europe was instead marketed around the globe in search of a buyer, and ended up in Japan—at a considerable political discount. This served further to undercut Australian coal, which in turn was shipped to seek a replacement market in Europe. Effectively this meant that a two-tier pricing system came into operation, with South African coal selling well below existing market rates and also serving to drag these down even further.

Thus, by the late 1980s four factors had conspired together to create a situation of considerable over-supply of low priced coal on the world market. First, the major oil companies had dramatically expanded their coal interests in the late 1970s, mostly in the established producer bases but also in Latin America.[2] Several newly industrializing countries had sought to capitalize on the potential to earn export revenues, throwing more coal onto the marketplace. Japan, as the world's major importer, cut back its domestic capacity and actively encouraged expansion in Australia and Canada in a search for diversity and security of supply. Finally, South African coal, embargoed in several European states, was sold at a political discount elsewhere in the globe.

Against this had to be weighed one further vital factor. The volume of steam coal traded internationally had historically been minute in proportion to total world output. The major producers had been the major consumers, and little was left for export. In 1973, just 20 m tonnes of steam coal and 87 m tonnes of coking coal were traded internationally by sea. Rapid expansion by 1986 saw seaborne trade increase to 133 m tonnes of steam coal and 140 m tonnes of coking coal (see Tables 1.3–1.6). This was still only a very small proportion of world hard coal consumption, which stood at roughly 3,000 m tonnes. Of this, 500 m tonnes was coking coal, so that 28 per cent was traded; but the 133 m tonnes of internationally traded steam coal represented only a mere 4 per cent of consumption (see Energy Committee 1986: p. 351). Even this amount of coal traded internationally by sea represented a sevenfold increase in just over ten years. So the new capacity coming onstream had to be placed into a context where a true "world" market for steam coal was only just beginning to emerge. A wholly new geography of coal production was being constructed, accounting in part for the tremendous scale of price disruption.

Most forecasts agreed that this growth in international steam coal trade was set to continue. Prior and McCloskey (1988: p. 69), for instance, anticipated that it would reach 210 m tonnes by 1995 and 310 m tonnes by 2005. They concluded:

> The dynamism of this growth cannot be over-stated. The irresistible rise of the seaborne steam coal trade has not been approached by any other raw material or commodity industry in the last fifteen years and yet this growth is not only going to continue with the same strength, it is going to accelerate. In short, the energy market has seen nothing yet from steam coal.

The combined impact of these developments on prices had, as shown above, been dramatic. But the huge discrepancy between the volumes of world production and trade meant that the price of internationally traded coal rested on a delicate balance. Towards the end of the decade coal prices began a recovery, reaching $37–38/tonne in 1988. Prior and McCloskey (1988: p. 71) argued that the low levels of the mid-1980s were wholly unsustainable in the long run. It is in this context that the UK's role in the international coal supply picture was highly relevant—especially as the UK was both major producer and consumer. Amongst European Community states, only West Germany produced even vaguely comparable tonnages; French and Belgian output was far smaller. With the exception of Denmark (which was dependent upon imported coal but used one-tenth of the energy of the UK economy) only the UK (at around 70 per cent), depended upon coal for more than one-third of its electricity generation.

One of the central features in the UK coal industry during the 1980s was a drive to cut costs, even if this meant dramatic reductions in capacity. As a result, UK coal production costs were the cheapest in Europe (see Steenblik 1987). Even in West Germany, the state heavily subsidized both coking and steam coal output.[3] On the other hand, UK coal production costs were totally incomparable to those of coal delivered into Europe from the international market. Prior and McCloskey (1988: p. 75) estimated export steam coal production costs (including 10 per cent return on capital) as $23.5/tonne in South Africa, $24.5/tonne in Alaska, $30/tonne in Indonesia, Venezuela and Australia, and $42.5—56.5/tonne in Colombia—all well undercutting the UK.

The evidence of such a disparity between UK and world coal production costs was not in dispute. What was under contention was the availability of sufficient *quantities* of traded coal, even in the prevailing market, to enable large-scale imports into the UK without markedly increasing the world price. During negotiations with the National Coal Board in 1986, the Central Electricity Generating Board suggested it could rapidly move to import up to 30 m tonnes annually without any substantial effect on the world price, and save £750 m a year on its fuel bills. But the NCB hotly contested this view. Arguing that such a move would add 25 per cent to the volume of world steam coal trade, and 50 per cent to the volume of steam coal imports into Western Europe, it concluded that the CEGB would substantially increase the world price of coal. The NCB also highlighted a further problem to coal trade: the expense of constructing import facilities, estimating that just one terminal on the Humber alone (far from adequate for such large-scale traffic) would cost £100 m. It concluded: "a firm long term commitment by the CEGB to import an increment of even 10 m tonnes in one year would be the biggest single consumer decision the world coal market has ever experienced" (see Energy Committee 1986: p. 355).

Whatever the rights and wrongs of this debate, it illustrated one fundamental point. Whilst the price of internationally traded coal had been driven downwards during the early to mid-1980s as a consequence of interrelated factors which combined to produce chronic over-supply, it still rested on a perilous equilibrium. The relatively small volumes traded belied the massive extent of consumer demand, and any sudden upsurge in demand would generate upward pressures on price. This tension was at the heart of the UK industry's fortunes.

## 1.3 The UK coal industry

The UK equivalent of the global oil companies' expansionary dreams for the coal industry was enshrined in two tripartite plans agreed between the National Union of Mineworkers, strongly backed by the 1974–79 Labour Government, and the state-owned producer, the National Coal Board.[4] The 1974 *Plan for Coal* envisaged annual capacity up by 1985 to the range 135–145 m tonnes (output in 1974/75 amounted to 127 m tonnes); in 1977 *Coal for the Future* forecast an output range of 135–200 m tonnes by 2000. To meet this demand after years of decline, it was anticipated that substantial additional deep-mined capacity would have to be constructed and opencast production expanded.

Just as in the world at large, though, UK energy demand, and demand for coal in particular, failed to grow at anything like the rate expected. Some markets for coal suffered a major collapse instead, especially iron and steel and domestic consumption. Yet at least some new capacity was constructed, both in existing mines and at wholly new complexes such as Selby, although a similarly vast development proposed for Belvoir was scaled down dramatically after a public inquiry heard growing disquiet over coal demand forecasts. It was this combination of new capacity and declining demand, in the face of world market pressures, which underpinned the UK coal industry's decline in the 1980s.

In 1981 the NCB produced 127 m tonnes of coal from 211 collieries which employed 231,000 people (see Table 1.7). In February of that year, it issued a list of 23 pits planned for closure, but withdrew this proposal in the face of a threatened all-out national strike. Instead, it undertook an "intensive review" of twenty pits which had resulted, by October, in the closure of half of those pits at risk in February. By July 1982, it was reviewing thirty pits, having already closed fifteen on the original list. In November of that year leaked documents suggested that there was a prospect of 75 colliery closures, and 50,000 job losses within a decade. Then, in June 1983, after an investigation by the Monopolies and Mergers Commission (1983) which pronounced 141 of the NCB's 198 pits "unprofitable", the NCB announced its intention to shed 70,000 jobs over five years. Coupled with a hostile government intent on breaking the power of the NUM, this effectively provoked the year-long miners' strike of 1984/85 which ended in bitter defeat for the miners. After it, the pace of closure accelerated dramatically. In just two years, employment at collieries fell from 171,000 to 108,000, as sixty pits were closed. By 1990, output had slumped to 95 m tonnes and employment at the remaining 73 collieries was down to 65,000, nearly one-quarter of its level at the start of the decade.

These changes were at first uneven across the coalfields, before a more generalized decline set in. Table 1.8 compares the situation region by region in 1982/83, on the eve of an overtime ban which preceded the lengthy national strike, with that in 1989/90. Over this period employment became slightly more concentrated in Yorkshire and Nottinghamshire, whilst the peripheral coalfields saw even greater contraction. In Scotland, south Wales and north east England, 50 collieries closed—a high proportion of the 118 closures across the country—and employment fell by

TABLE 1.7
*British Coal/National Coal Board: key statistics, 1947–90*

| | 1947 | 1974/75 | 1979/80 | 1980/81 | 1981/82 | 1982/83 | 1983/84 | 1984/85[1] | 1985/86 | 1986/87 | 1987/88 | 1988/89 | 1989/90 |
|---|---|---|---|---|---|---|---|---|---|---|---|---|---|
| Output (m tonnes) | 200 | 127 | 123 | 127 | 124 | 121 | 105 | 43 | 105 | 103 | 100 | 104 | 95 |
| – of which opencast (mt) | 10 | 9 | 13 | 15 | 14 | 15 | 14 | 13 | 14 | 13 | 15 | 17 | 18 |
| UK sales (m tonnes) to: | | | | | | | | | | | | | |
| – power stations | 28 | 73 | 89 | 88 | 85 | 81 | 82 | 43 | 86 | 82 | 86 | 81 | 82 |
| – coke ovens | 43 | 21 | 14 | 11 | 11 | 10 | 10 | 8 | 12 | 11 | 11 | 11 | 11 |
| – domestic | 37 | 15 | 10 | 9 | 9 | 8 | 8 | 6 | 9 | 8 | 7 | 6 | 6 |
| Number of collieries | 958 | 246 | 219 | 211 | 200 | 191 | 170 | 169 | 133 | 110 | 94 | 86 | 73 |
| Output per manshift (t) | 1.09 | 2.29 | 2.31 | 2.32 | 2.40 | 2.44 | 2.43 | 2.08 | 2.72 | 3.29 | 3.62 | 4.14 | 4.32 |
| Colliery industrial employment 1000s | 718 | 246 | 232 | 231 | 219 | 208 | 192 | 171 | 139 | 108 | 89 | 80 | 65 |
| Operating profit/loss £m | – | – | 45 | 98 | (23) | (79) | (336) | (1,545) | 625 | 369 | 261 | 498 | 133 |
| Overall loss £m [2] | – | – | (159) | (207) | (428) | (485) | (875) | (2,225) | (50) | (288) | (495) | (203) | (5,076) |

Notes: [1] Affected by strike action.
[2] The difference from operating loss largely reflects interest payments and exceptional costs to do with pit closures.
Source: British Coal Corporation.

TABLE 1.8
British Coal results by area: 1982/83¹ and 1989/90

| | | North Yorks | South Yorks | Notts | Central | Scotland | North East | North West | South Wales |
|---|---|---|---|---|---|---|---|---|---|
| No. of collieries | 89/90 | 13 | 16 | 15 | 8 | 1 | 7 | 7 | 6 |
| | 82/83 | 29 | 27 | 25 | 28 | 13 | 18 | 18 | 33 |
| Saleable output m tonnes | 89/90 | 13.9 | 11.1 | 16.8 | 10.9 | 2.0 | 10.3 | 7.0 | 3.4 |
| | 82/83 | 16.8 | 14.2 | 20.7 | 16.4 | 6.7 | 12.5 | 10.8 | 6.9 |
| Output/manshift, tonnes² | 89/90 | 5.01 | 4.14 | 4.69 | 4.09 | 4.36 | 4.09 | 4.34 | 3.04 |
| | 82/83 | | | | | 1.97 | 2.09 | 2.53 | 1.47 |
| Employment 1,000s | 89/90 | 11 | 11 | 14 | 10 | 2 | 10 | 6 | 4 |
| | 82/83 | 29 | 30 | 32 | 26 | 17 | 26 | 20 | 23 |
| Cost of production²³ £/GJ | 88/89 | 1.54 | 1.40 | 1.43 | 1.46 | 2.99 | 1.43 | 1.54 | 2.12 |
| | 85/86 | 1.86 | 1.67 | 1.50 | | 2.29 | 1.96 | 1.88 | 2.15 |
| Operating profit/loss £m (mining) | 89/90 | (90) | (13) | 47 | (49) | (15) | 66 | (18) | (72) |
| | 82/83 | (32) | (25) | 19 | (23) | (67) | (67) | (9) | (113) |

¹ 1982/83 was chosen in preference to the year immediately preceding the miners' strike since 1983/84 figures were affected by a prolonged overtime ban.
² In August 1985, the North Notts and South Notts areas merged to form one Notts area. In October 1985, the former N. Yorks area merged with the Barnsley area to form a new N. Yorks area, and the former S. Yorks Area merged with Doncaster to form a new S. Yorks area. In April 1987, the N. Derbys and S. Midlands areas merged to form the Central area. Most figures for 1982/83 have been restated to reflect these changes but the following ratios cannot be restated from the annual report:

TABLE 1.8 Contd.

| | Output/manshift (t) 1982/83 | Cost of production £/GJ 1985/86 |
|---|---|---|
| N Yorks | 3.01 | |
| Barnsley | 2.64 | |
| S Yorks | 2.35 | |
| Doncaster | 2.30 | |
| N Notts | 3.25 | |
| S Notts | 2.69 | |
| N Derby | 3.30 | 1.67 |
| S Midlands | 2.52 | 1.82 |

[3] Figures for cost of production were first published as £/GJ in 1985/86; these are produced here. In 1989/90, no reference was made to costs of production in terms of £/GJ. The most recently available figures (for 1988/89) are produced here, but it should be noted that they are not necessarily comparable to other indicators for 1989/90.

Source: British Coal Corporation.

76 per cent to 50,000. The central coalfields also saw very heavy job losses though, as part of a drive to increase productivity. As the 1980s progressed, regional variations in the incidence of decline were increasingly submerged in the overall pattern of downwardly spiralling output and employment. There seemed to be practically no end in sight to the process of cutback and job loss. As the following account goes on to show, much of this was due to some quite fundamental changes in the nature of *demand* for UK-produced coal.

## 1.3.1 Changing patterns of demand

British Coal's overwhelmingly dominant customer in the 1980s was the Central Electricity Generating Board.[5] Historically though, this had not always been the case. In 1947, when the NCB was formed, the power station market amounted to just 15 per cent of its total UK sales. As late as 1970, electricity generation accounted for only 50 per cent of total sales. By 1974/75 this proportion was up to 60 per cent, as other markets contracted (total power station deliveries remained practically constant); and, in the 1980s, sales to power stations (up sharply to 80–90 m tonnes annually—see Table 1.7) consistently accounted for over 70 per cent of British Coal's total UK sales. In recognition of this strong interdependence between customer and supplier, a series of informal deals was struck which effectively regulated the volume and price of coal deliveries to the CEGB.

The first Joint Understanding between the two parties was signed in October 1979. This was extended in 1983 to run originally until 1987. Under these revised terms, the CEGB agreed to buy at least 95 per cent of its coal from the NCB, and undertook to attempt to purchase at least 70 m tonnes annually (the previous deal incorporated sales of at least 75 m tonnes annually). In return, the NCB agreed to keep the average coal price increase below the rate of inflation, with a discount on any sales in excess of 65 m tonnes in each year. In 1986, under pressure from tumbling oil prices, the NCB agreed a new five-year deal with the CEGB. Under this agreement, the CEGB contracted to buy three separate amounts, or "tranches" of coal. A first 50 m tonnes would be sold at a price reflecting NCB production costs (against the previous deal's 65 m tonnes); a second reflecting the price of imported coal to the Thames estuary; and a third was to be equated both with the cost at which coal could be imported to inland power stations and with the price of oil. The second and third tranches together were to amount to at least 20 m tonnes annually, rising gradually over the duration of the agreement to 30 m tonnes, whilst the first tranche was to decline in compensating fashion to 40 m tonnes. Effectively, this immediately cut the cost of NCB coal to the CEGB by £3/tonne; it also contained provision for a continuing gradual reduction in price.

The main threat from the NCB's point of view, acting to drive prices downwards, was cheaper imported coal. CEGB assertions that it could import up to 30 m tonnes annually were, as indicated above, hostly contested by the NCB; but the prospect was certainly a tantalizing one for the CEGB, even if only as a negotiating tactic (see McCloskey 1986). Yet in the long term, a further factor also threatened coal's share of the UK energy market: competition from alternative fuels, including for a long time the nuclear industry.

The UK electricity supply industry already operated two generations of nuclear power stations. The older, Magnox reactors were commissioned between 1962 and 1971. Then, initially, five of the technically more sophisticated, higher-output, Advanced Gas-cooled Reactors (AGRs), were ordered in the mid to late 1960s: at Hinckley Point B, Dungeness B, Hartlepool, Heysham 1 and Hunterston B. The last three had spectacular construction delays and cost overruns, and were still being worked up to full capacity in the late 1970s when orders were placed for two more, Heysham II and Torness, due for completion in the late 1980s. In 1981, the CEGB made application to go ahead with a third generation of nuclear stations, the American-designed Pressurized Water Reactor (PWR), with the first plant to be constructed at Sizewell B.

Sizewell B was the subject of a mammoth public inquiry—lasting four years—and the final report, of eight volumes, was not produced by the Inspector, Sir Frank Layfield, until January 1987. In it he anticipated a slightly lower rise in coal and oil prices over the coming four decades than the CEGB case had indicated, but still a large enough increase to justify the nuclear option. Given this approval, the CEGB indicated its eagerness to proceed with a fresh round of nuclear plant construction, in an attempt to increase the proportion of power generated from nuclear stations.

With the re-election of a Conservative administration in 1987 which was committed to privatization of the entire electricity supply industry, however, future prospects became highly uncertain. The government's proposals for the structure of the industry in England and Wales (see Helm 1988; HMSO 1988) envisaged the creation of two new private sector generating companies, National Power and PowerGen, incorporating 70 per cent and 30 per cent respectively of the CEGB's existing capacity; the privatization of the twelve area distribution companies; and creation of a separate electricity transmission company. Similar changes were also proposed for Scotland. The larger generating company would receive the nuclear stations, and was charged with maintaining at least the current proportion of output from nuclear sources. Such plans threw the entire generating industry into some turmoil. The CEGB had already indicated its desire to proceed with three new coal-fired stations (the first for more than a decade) alongside existing stations at Fawley, Kingsnorth and West Burton. As privatization planning proceeded, it also identified sites for three further PWRs (Hinkley Point C, Wylfa C and Sizewell C) in a total nuclear programme estimated to cost around £7,000 m.

The impending choice between coal and nuclear fuel, and the legislative framework within which it was to be made, were of vital significance to the UK coal industry. The previous understanding between the CEGB and British Coal reflected a view that both bodies would remain in continuing public ownership. On this basis an integrated coal supply and electricity generating chain had developed over forty years with two-thirds of all coal delivered to the CEGB (representing one-third of its fuel use) being consumed at just ten sites in the central coalfields. There was no legally binding agreement between the parties, but rather a mutually agreed set of guidelines. British Coal argued that before privatization this should be replaced with a new energy supply contract (see Energy Committee 1988: pp. 120–5). Elsewhere in the world, it maintained, such arrangements were commonplace. In the USA, over 80 per cent of all coal delivered to power stations fell within the terms of one or other ten-year supply contract.

British Coal was concerned with the potential competition from both imported coal and nuclear capacity. Any supply deal should reflect what it saw as a realistic view of world coal prices, it maintained: up to $40—55/tonne by 2000. The government's decision in favour of Sizewell B had accepted even higher estimates of the cost of coal as one argument for the nuclear option. British Coal's view was that these prices should therefore be used consistently, as the basis for a ten-year supply contract with the privatized UK electricity industry from 1991. In other words, it still strongly challenged the CEGB's claim that it could expand coal imports dramatically without affecting the price of internationally traded steam coal. BC also complained that it would be "anomalous" for nuclear power generation to be accorded a guaranteed share of the UK market while coal production was left "wholly or largely exposed" to short-term market forces (see Energy Committee 1988: p. 249).

These two sources of competition—imported coal, and nuclear fuel—dominated BC's prospects. The CEGB's all-out coal import policy was strongly criticized by Prior and McCloskey (1988) who argued that it would result in the closure of UK production capacity which by 1995 would have been producing cheaper coal than the then prevailing world price. The claimed short-term saving of £750 m on 30 m tonnes imports, they indicated, was nearer £270 m (a not insubstantial sum). There were also considerable physical obstacles in the way of coal imports.

In 1987, the CEGB imported just 1 m tonnes of coal. Only three power stations had their own coal-importing capacity: West Thurrock, Kingsnorth and Tilbury, all on the Thames. These had a potential to handle up to 11 m tonnes annually but only in ships of up to 19,000 dwt the size of coastal vessels bringing coal from the north east coalfield—wholly unsuited to large-scale international trade. The proposed Fawley plant and import terminal on the Solent would be able to import 5 m tonnes annually for its own needs, with a further 2–3 m tonnes shipped in and carried by rail to the Didcot power station near Oxford, whilst the Kingsnorth proposal (an addition to the existing plant) also embraced new coal import facilities. The proposed West Burton plant looked to coal supplies from Nottinghamshire. Other proposed coal import terminals included two on Humberside (amounting to 10 m tonnes annual capacity) whilst BP Oil also offered for sale its Isle of Grain refinery site on the Thames estuary near Kingsnorth. During 1989, the CEGB ordered 1.7 m tonnes of coal from Colombia, China, Australia and the USA, and experimented with smaller volumes of trial shipments through a variety of port and rail links. But at the same time, it was forced to cancel indefinitely all three of the proposed new coal-fired stations, in the face of the area electricity distribution boards' refusal to sign long-term contracts for the purchase of their electricity.

Equally, the CEGB's determination (under government direction) to construct new nuclear capacity looked increasingly questionable. As a public inquiry into the Hinkley Point B PWR progressed, it became apparent that privatization would have a considerable impact which the government would not have intended. As a public company, the CEGB was only required to make a notional return on capital invested of 5 per cent (this increased to 8 per cent, in the course of the Hinkley Point inquiry).

53

As a private business, it would need to make, at the very least, a 10 per cent return. On this basis, and on the CEGB's own figures, the nuclear option appeared uneconomic against the coal-fired option: for nuclear stations were more expensive to build, costing £1,500 m against £770 m for an equivalent coal-fired plant of 1,100 megawatts (MW) capacity, and took longer to construct. The CEGB pro-nuclear case, in other words, rested on government direction to keep a certain nuclear share, and the need to build four PWRs to replace Magnox stations as they were phased out in the 1990s; not on comparative costs against coal. These choices were of course potentially decisive to British Coal for each PWR (if built) would displace 3 m tonnes of coal demand.

The contradictions at the heart of the government's policy on nuclear power came home to roost in 1989. In July, the seven remaining first generation nuclear reactors—the Magnox stations—were withdrawn from the electricity privatization programme, as it finally became fully apparent that the imminent decommissioning costs would represent a considerable disincentive to private investment in the industry (see Figure 1.1). Then, in November, in a further about-turn, the government revised its decision to continue with privatization of the remainder of nuclear generating capacity—seven AGRs and the half-built Sizewell B—in response to a view expressed forcefully by National Power that it would be unsaleable if forced to carry the costs and risks of a nuclear programme, including the expense of decommissioning. It had also become apparent that the Sizewell B PWR was already £170 m over its anticipated construction budget, and the government indicated that no further PWRs would be built until at least 1994. Lord Marshall, Chairman of the CEGB and firm proponent of nuclear power, resigned in protest—but the die was cast. National Power would now hold 55 per cent of generating capacity, PowerGen 30 per cent, and a state-run Nuclear Electric 15 per cent.

The true cost differential between coal and nuclear power had been clearly exposed for the first time. It was not what it had been proclaimed for so long. For, in addition to higher construction costs at nuclear stations, it was now apparent—contrary to the previous conventional wisdom from the government and the electricity industry—that if the true expenses of decommissioning were added to the equation, not the figures which had previously been used by the CEGB, then fuel or running costs were the same for the nuclear option as for coal—if not higher. In total this meant that power from the AGRs effectively cost up to 9p/kilowatt hour compared to 3p/kilowatt hour from coal-fired stations.

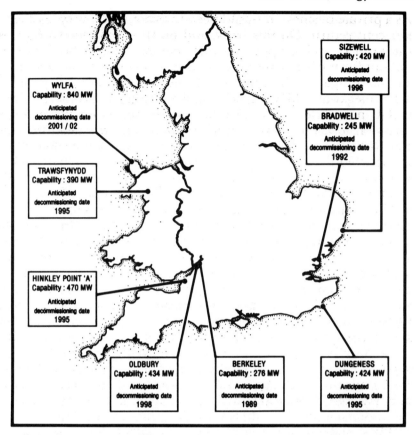

FIG 1.1. Anticipated dates of decommissioning of former CEGB Magnox reactors. (Source: *Financial Times* 25 July 1989. Note also that the South of Scotland Electricity Board is closing its Magnox station at Hunterston.)

These revelations were described as follows by the *Financial Times International Coal Report* (17 November 1989):

> For many years UK energy ministers and electricity consumers have been subject to an elaborate falsehood that nuclear was a cheap and cheerful way to generate electricity while coal was troublesome, dirty and, above all, expensive. It now turns out that British Coal's much-derided high-priced output has not only been keeping the CEGB in a handsome profit over the last decade but has also been used to fund a hopelessly loss-making nuclear programme.

In the midst of these changes the government was also forced to re-order its timetable for privatization, as it proved difficult to negotiate supply contracts between electricity production and distribution companies. One key factor in these discussions was the future of supplies from British Coal. In December, with the generating companies more keen to secure an agreement after removal of the nuclear burden, British Coal announced the conclusion of a three-year deal with National Power and PowerGen. This included a continued freeze on coal prices at around £1.70/GigaJoule (GJ) or £42/tonne, compared with the delivered cost of imported coal to Thames power stations estimated by British Coal at around £35 to £36 per tonne. In return, British Coal kept most of the existing market. The two generating companies agreed to purchase at least 70 m tonnes for the first two years, and up to 65 m tonnes in the third year. Perhaps paradoxically, one reason for these relatively high volumes was government direction, for privatization of British Coal had become a publicly stated objective and the government was suddenly keen to introduce a degree of protection for the coal industry from the threat of imports. As Gerard McCloskey, editor of the *Financial Times International Coal Report* put it:

> the power companies were shocked at the price they had to pay for British coal as well as the volume contained in the contract . . . . the large volume and price for the coal was dictated by the Energy Department back in November 1989. The imperative was to give British Coal a reasonable chance of successful operation to enable it to be privatised sometime in the early 1990s.

In the longer term too he speculated that such pressure might act to force a further deal on the new electricity generators:

> the power companies may well find themselves obliged to sign much longer contracts with British Coal. Without contracts it would be extremely difficult to accord British Coal its full value. (*Financial Times* survey on the electricity industry, 29 March 1990)

The decline in the final year of the 1990–93 coal supply contract was to allow the power companies scope to increase their imports of low-sulphur coals. As preparation for this, the new generating companies continued to experiment with ways and means to increase imports of coal, signing contracts for 6 m tonnes in 1990 from outside the UK. National Power began to investigate the possibility of using two new ports for large-scale coal imports—Milford Haven in Wales, and the Tees estuary—each potentially capable of handling up to 5 m tonnes annually.

Sulphur content had become an additional factor in the pressure for increased imports because coal was vulnerable to the growing environmentalist tide. When burnt in power stations, it contributed substantially both to the greenhouse effect and to acid rain (see Commission of the European Communities 1989; Energy Committee 1989). In 1988, European Community environment ministers agreed to cut sulphur dioxide emissions from power stations and industrial plant. For the UK this meant a reduction from the 1980 level by 40 per cent before 1998, and by 60 per cent before 2003. The CEGB said it would spend £2,000 m installing sulphur-scrubbing equipment (flue gas desulphurization, or FGD) at coal-fired stations with 12,000 MW capacity. By 1990, £600 m had been committed at the 4,000 MW Drax station but the successor companies to the CEGB argued strongly that they could not afford such a programme, preferring to reduce sulphur emissions in a different way—the increased purchase of low sulphur content imported coal. British Coal cautioned that such proposals would lead to an accelerated rate of job loss within the UK coal mining industry. The generating companies, it argued, would need to import 40 m tonnes by the early 2000s to cut sulphur emissions significantly this way, leading to severe cut-backs even in the previously relatively secure Nottinghamshire coalfield and the loss of 12,500 jobs there. The case put by National Power and PowerGen was partly accepted by the government when it allowed the two companies to curtail their plans, dropping £800 m of the original £2,000 m investment, so that only 8,000 MW capacity of plant would be fitted with FGD.

A second route to the reduction of sulphur dioxide emissions was rendered increasingly popular once the nuclear option was ruled out. Additional generating capacity would still be required, and it was more and more attractive to meet this from small-scale gas-fired power stations. Historically, gas had not figured strongly in the UK's electricity supply system, although it was a substantial contributor elsewhere in the European Community, especially in the Netherlands. Quite rapidly, small and relatively cheap gas-fired power stations came to be seen as less risky investments for the private sector, especially compared to the giant coal- and oil-fired stations of the past. By February 1990, twenty gas-fired projects, totalling 7,000 MW, were under active consideration by various private sector companies and consortia. In that month, National Power announced concrete plans for three new gas-fired power stations, costing about £700 m, with a combined capacity of 2,000 MW, to be onstream from around 1994. These were likely to lead to the loss of 3,500 jobs in the Nottinghamshire coalfield as older coal-fired power stations were closed more quickly than previously anticipated. In the same month, PowerGen outlined plans for a £350 m, 900 MW gas-fired station at Killingholme on Humberside.

Even more far-ranging plans were also being laid. National Power discussed the prospect of developing whole new gas fields, possibly from the Norwegian sector of the North Sea, specifically for power station use. Other gas-fired projects were announced, typically involving one or more of the area distribution companies looking to introduce alternative sources of electricity supply to the market. Thames Power proposed to develop a £500 m, 1,000 MW plant at Barking Reach on the Thames (with CU Power and Scottish Hydro). A £120 m 350 MW station was unveiled for Corby by East Midlands Electricity and Hawker Siddeley. A £700 m, 1,725 MW project at Wilton on Teesside involved ICI, Enron Power Corporation of the USA and several area distribution companies. The first independent licensed generator, Lakeland Power, announced plans for up to four stations. A vast array of supply possibilities was under investigation—almost wholly dependent on gas as a fuel, creating still more potential problems for the UK coal industry.

This twin response to the growing environmental pressures in electricity generation—imported low sulphur coal and the construction of gas-fired stations—was strongly criticized by the National Union of Mineworkers. It argued that such a strategy was incapable of satisfactorily reducing the levels of emissions and was dependent upon questionable assumptions about the likely future level of gas prices. As for imported coal, it envisaged great upward pressure on price as more and more consumers chased finite reserves of low-sulphur coal:

> The reality is that a low sulphur strategy based on imported coal, to be later supplemented with gas-fired units, is simply unsustainable. Demand stimulated by such an approach here and in the USA will rapidly drive lower sulphur grades of coal to premium prices. (NUM 1990)

Nonetheless, government policy was clearly set on restricting the level of FGD investment in coal-fired stations and encouraging the development of alternative sources of electricity supply—casting natural gas in the strategic role once held by nuclear power.

By March 1990, the new electricity generating structure in England and Wales was at least established, with the formal creation of three new generating companies, twelve area distribution companies and a transmission company, National Grid Co. (see Figure 1.2). A timetable was also laid out for the flotation process: the sale of the distribution companies was scheduled

FIG 1.2. Main power stations of National Power and PowerGen.

for late 1990, the generating companies for early 1991 and the Scottish side of the industry for mid-1991 (the South of Scotland Electricity Board was to be replaced by Scottish Power, and the North of Scotland Hydro Electricity Board by Scottish Hydro, whilst the nuclear plants remained in a state-owned Scottish Nuclear). The overriding impression in the industry though was still one of unpredictability, something which continued to impact very heavily on British Coal's planning horizons. The extent of future uncertainty was reflected in its 1989 estimates for future coal sales in the UK—in the range of 90–110 m tonnes by 1995 and 85–120 m tonnes by 2000 (Table 1.9). To many commentators (for instance, Prior and McCloskey 1988; CICS 1989) these forecasts appeared on the high side. Where, in the wide range of predictions, future coal production actually did emerge was subject not just to dramatic changes in terms of UK demand, but also in the pattern of coal supply.

TABLE 1.9
*British Coal market forecasts, 1989*

| (m tonnes) | 1995 | 2000 |
|---|---|---|
| Power station demand | 75–90 | 75–95 |
| Total UK demand | 105–120 | 105–130 |
| Imports | 15–10 | 20–10 |
| BC sales in UK | 90–110 | 85–120 |
| World steam coal trade | 160–255 | 190–305 |

Source: British Coal, reproduced in Monopolies and Mergers Commission 1989 p. 66.

## 1.3.2 New sources and means of supply

In 1985, the NCB announced a wholly new strategy for coal (reported in Energy Committee 1986 pp. 26–9), finally supplanting the long-discredited *Plan for Coal*.[6] This no longer emphasized fixed output targets, but rather stressed the need to produce coal at minimum cost. To this end, it introduced the idea of "cost parameters" set not in terms of £/tonne, but £/GigaJoule (GJ). Use of the GJ unit—a measure of energy—reflected the differing calorific value of various coals, and their subsequent use to the energy industry. With average 1985 proceeds at £1.70/GJ, the NCB strategy set £1.65/GJ as an absolute upper limit for continued operation at an individual colliery, whilst long-life pits had to aim for costs of £1.50/GJ (about £38/tonne). Investment in new capacity would need to be justified by the opportunity of production at less than £1.00/GJ. To cut costs in this fashion, the strategy identified a number of objectives. These included improved capital utilization, in particular the greater use of "heavy duty" faces; more flexible working arrangements; and an increase in low-cost opencast output. These three elements are considered below.

Improved capital utilization depended in part upon maximizing output from the newer, larger and more capital-intensive collieries. Of these, the most important was the Selby complex, begun in 1976. It comprised five distinct mines, each with its own surface access, linked to a common underground transport network and one coal output point at Gascoigne Wood. Production began at the first mine, Wistow, in 1983, though it was temporarily interrupted by flooding problems. By 1988/89 Selby's output was up to 5 m tonnes, well on the way to the initial target of 10 m tonnes annually—although Prior and McCloskey (1988) indicated that it could possibly produce as much as 15–20 m tonnes annually with minimal further investment. The entire complex was geared to exploit reserves of over 2,000 m tonnes: at a cost of £1,400 m, it represented some 20 per cent of British Coal's capital investment over a ten-year period. It was described by Prior and McCloskey (1988 p. 32) as "the biggest and most complex underground coal mining operation in the world". Other wholly new collieries included Asfordby, approved in 1984 after a more ambitious three pit scheme for the Belvoir coalfield was turned down in 1982. This was due to produce coal in 1991/92, reaching an output of 4 m tonnes by 1993/94.[7] Finally, at Hawkhurst in Warwickshire, a public inquiry heard plans in 1989 for a further 4 m tonnes of capacity at another wholly new mine.

Such new collieries were of course the exception, but they epitomized British Coal's drive to increase the automation and mechanization of coal production. In particular, BC concentrated on the application of systems engineering principles to control the operation of the whole coal supply process through MINOS—the Mine Operating System (see Burns *et al.* 1985). The Barnsley West Side complex was the first to have the full MINOS system, and Selby was designed to use MINOS from the start. MINOS consisted of a number of integrated subsystems, all engineered to monitor and regulate the rate of production. One of its subsystems, for instance, was FIDO (Face Information Digested On-line). This gathered information from the coal face in an attempt to ensure maximum continuous productive operation and minimize "down-time". Effectively, it supervised operations, maximized machine running time, and reduced the number of men required at the face. Fully integrated MINOS collieries required roughly one-half of the labour of a non-MINOS pit for similar output.

Whilst MINOS concentrated on the organization of production, further enormous productivity gains were made from the increased use of "heavy-duty" faces. Progressive concentration upon such faces, with large-scale capital investment in equipment such as shield supports, power loaders and armoured face conveyors, brought down the total number of coal faces operated, and increased the average daily output from each face (Table 1.10). In 1982/83, fully and/or partly equipped heavy-duty faces only amounted to 6 per cent of the total 574 faces in operation. By 1987/88, they accounted for 48 per cent of the total of 246 faces in operation, and each heavy-duty face produced 1,500 tonnes daily against 1,000 tonnes daily from conventional faces. Similarly, an increased emphasis upon retreat faces (where

TABLE 1.10
*British Coal: heavy duty and retreat faces, 1982/83–1987/88*

|  | *1982/83* | *1985/86* | *1986/87* | *1987/88* |
|---|---|---|---|---|
| *Total no. of faces:* | 574 | 381 | 305 | 246 |
| – of which heavy duty | 32 | 87 | 119 | 117 |
| % HD to total | 6 | 23 | 39 | 48 |
| – of which retreat | 120 | 103 | 103 | 91 |
| % retreat to total | 21 | 27 | 34 | 37 |
| *Output/face/day (t):* |  |  |  |  |
| – conventional | 711 | 766 | 900 | 1,003 |
| – heavy duty | 1,390 | 1,393 | 1,459 | 1,496 |
| – advance | 710 | 809 | 984 | 1,106 |
| – retreat | 872 | 1,042 | 1,260 | 1,385 |

Source: Monopolies and Mergers Commission 1989 p. 36.

roadways were driven before coal was extracted) against advance faces (where roadways were driven along with coal extraction, entailing vulnerability to unexpected geological problems) had also acted to increase overall output per face.

Investment in new collieries, operating systems and productive machinery was notably concentrated in the central coalfields—both cause and result of these areas high labour productivity. The North Yorkshire area (which included the Selby complex) accounted for a mammoth 36 per cent of the total £3,700 m capital investment by British Coal from 1982/83 to 1987/88 (see Table 1.11). Together with the Nottinghamshire, Central, and South Yorkshire areas, this proportion rose to 75 per cent. The peripheral coalfields in north east England, South Wales and Scotland, by contrast, received only 5 per cent of the total each. This was a further clear indication of the continuing process of contraction outside the central coalfield belt, although even in supposedly long-life coalfields such as Nottinghamshire, the increasingly stringent colliery-level financial targets led to an accelerating rate of job loss and pit closures in the late 1980s.

A second component of BC's drive to cut costs was to increase labour productivity (and improve capital utilization) via the adoption of flexible working procedures. In this it came into sustained conflict with the National Union of Mineworkers, which bitterly resisted changes to working conditions; although the Union of Democratic Mineworkers (UDM), formed after the 1984/85 strike, proved far more cooperative.

The key elements of flexible working were six-day coal production (against the existing five-day arrangement), and four

TABLE 1.11
*British Coal: capital expenditure by region, 1982/83–1987/88*

|  | £m at 1987/88 prices | % of total |
|---|---|---|
| North Yorkshire[1] | 1,354 | 36.4 |
| Nottinghamshire | 655 | 17.6 |
| Central | 402 | 10.8 |
| South Yorkshire | 385 | 10.4 |
| Western | 357 | 9.6 |
| North East | 196 | 5.3 |
| South Wales | 196 | 5.2 |
| Scotland | 169 | 4.5 |
| Kent | 7 | 0.2 |
| Total | 3,721 | |

[1] Includes the Selby complex.
Source: Monopolies and Mergers Commission 1989 p. 34.

nine-hour shifts for each miner in the week.[8] In the north east area, for instance, British Coal pointed to the time spent on travelling six or seven miles to the coal face at undersea collieries, estimating that flexible shift patterns would increase machine available time by 30 per cent and improve productivity by 10 per cent (see Energy Committee 1986 pp. 263–5). Such changes, though, would require legislative amendment, since the 1908 Coal Mines Regulation Act limited the amount of time any miner could spend underground to 7.5 hours per shift.

Historically, working hours had been highly significant to trade unions in the mining industry, and the NUM strongly contested British Coal's proposals. One of the first major tests came with apparent renewed interest in developing the last big deposit of coking coal in South Wales, at Margam. A new mine had first been planned there several decades earlier; in 1987 British Coal revived the proposal. It anticipated a £90 m project to extract 1.2 m tonnes of prime coking coal annually, employing 800 miners. British Coal insisted that the investment would be dependent upon an agreement on six-day coal production. Without it, BC estimated that Margam would have made a loss of £3.20/tonne; with it, a profit of £1.33/tonne. The national NUM disputed this, reckoning that even on five-day working a profit of £2.80/tonne could be achieved; but the South Wales NUM was less certain, and favoured negotiations on six-day working.

This was to become a pattern; new investment dependent on changes to working practices. In July 1987, British Coal identified thirteen collieries where new investment worth about £2,000 m was planned but subject to flexible working deals. Gradually, local agreements were struck, usually with little publicity, against the national NUM leadership's wishes and despite its insistence that 40,000 jobs were at risk. By contrast, the formal deals agreed between the UDM and British Coal were publicly paraded by both sides. In 1988, an agreement was reached under which new working patterns would be introduced at any mine receiving £50 m investment or more. Later that year agreement was made on this basis for the UDM at Asfordby, and in 1989 at Margam (although further postponement of this project subsequently delayed the impact of the deal).

In other ways, too, proposed changes in working patterns were highly contentious. The use of new techniques such as roof-bolting (in preference to higher cost steel supports) and free-steered vehicles was condemned by the NUM and NACODS on safety grounds, for instance. The whole issue of "flexibility"—in its many guises—was one of the most problematic labour relations issues of the late 1980s, and looked set to continue as such well into the 1990s.

These pressures on the workforce reflected British Coal's continuing drive to achieve profitability, and ultimately privatization. In 1988, Cecil Parkinson, Secretary of State for Energy, made his "historic pledge" to the Conservative Party Conference that, if the government were re-elected again, coal would be privatized. A number of commentators had already identified coal as a potential flotation prospect (see, for instance, Boyfield 1985; Robinson 1988; Robinson and Sykes 1987)—indeed, some of these earlier proposals had envisaged the sale of pits and power stations as integrated units. But in a real sense, the privatization of the industry was already gradually being achieved through the increasing incursion into low-cost opencast operations or small-scale underground mines by the private sector (see Beynon, Cox and Hudson 1990). Private deep mines were limited by law to employing fewer than thirty men underground at any one time (although in 1990 the government introduced measures to increase this to 150), but the opencast sector had tremendous scope for private operators. Thus, opencast production represented both the thin end of the wedge of privatization, and the key third element of British Coal's drive to cut costs and increase profitability.

Opencast mining began in the UK on an organized basis in 1942 as part of wartime efforts to supplement deep-mined production. It continued in this supporting role after the war, although cut-back after 1959 in line with the pressure on deep-mined coal from imported oil. In 1974, Plan for Coal forecast an expansion in opencast output from 9 m to 15 m tonnes as part of the general expansionary drive. This growth took place (see Table 1.7), but as deep-mined output contracted, there was no substantial decrease in opencast: if anything, it continued to increase. Effectively, opencast production was cast in a wholly different relationship to the deep-mined sector than had previously prevailed.

Opencast production took place in two distinct sectors. The bulk of output (17.5 m tonnes in 1989/90) came from sites run for British Coal by civil engineering companies, using non-mining employees. These were under the control of British Coal's Opencast Executive in England and Wales, and BC's Scottish Area in Scotland (although in 1990, with the disbanding of the Scottish Area, responsibility for opencast activities in Scotland reverted to the Opencast Executive). The contractor paid a fixed fee for each tonne of coal produced, which was marketed by British Coal, usually to power stations. The biggest contractors were specialist groups such as A F Budge, Crouch Mining and NSM Coal Contractors; and well-known construction companies such as Taylor Woodrow and Wimpey. A much smaller volume (1.1 m tonnes of the 2.1 m tonnes produced by the licensed sector in 1989/90) came from private opencast sites where companies paid a royalty to British Coal of about £14 on each tonne produced (the remainder of this licensed output came from private underground mines, which were limited to reserves of 25,000 tonnes, but with extensions could easily reach up to 100,000 tonnes in total; although in 1990, the government raised this figure to 250,000 tonnes, which with extensions could reach 500,000 tonnes). Opencast output was highly lucrative, with operating costs of £1.04/GJ against the deep-mined average of £1.54/GJ in 1988/89, producing a profit of £272 m. In 1989/90, British Coal reverted to costs in terms of £/tonne; in the opencast sector these amounted to £29/tonne against £43/tonne for the deep mines. Technical advances meant that opencasting could reach depths of up to 100 metres in UK conditions, so that some operators were working seams already partly recovered by the older deep-mined bord-and-pillar method which had left large pockets of coal.

During the 1980s, the legislative environment strongly favoured continued expansion of opencast output. Although the 1982 Flowers Commission report on coal and the environment recommended that it should be cut back for environmental reasons, the Department of the Environment's Circular 3/84 saw no case for setting a target opencast output. Instead, British Coal's National

Assessment in 1986 indicated that an increased level of up to 18 m tonnes annually was being sought. Despite repeated objections from local authorities, upheld at public inquiries, opencast output (and targets) continued to expand, with inquiry decisions frequently overruled by the government. In 1988, the Department of the Environment's Mineral Planning Note 3 accepted that there was a national need for opencast coal, one basis on which inquiries had challenged applications, and in 1989 British Coal indicated that opencast output could easily reach 20 m tonnes annually (Monopolies and Mergers Commission 1989 p. 39).

The issues around this expansion of opencast output were bitterly contested. British Coal maintained that opencast profits were necessary to balance the books against losses from deep-mined operations. From British Coal's viewpoint it was particularly attractive since, although opencast production was capital intensive, much of the investment was undertaken by the contractor. Thus, in 1988/89, British Coal's operating profit of £272 m from opencast production represented a staggering 158 per cent return on its own capital investment, against a deep-mined operating profit of £132 m, representing a mere 3 per cent return on investment. British Coal had moved to squeeze its capital investment in opencast production, which fell every year from 1984 to 1989, and to keep tight control of other costs, such as site restoration, which remained roughly constant despite a marked rise in opencast output (see Table 1.12). British Coal also argued that opencast coal was of a quality which could not be obtained elsewhere—citing, in particular, anthracite from South Wales, low chlorine coal, and coking coal. Both arguments were disputed by a range of groups allied in opposition, from the NUM to the Council for the Protection of Rural England, anxious about the environmentally destructive character of much opencast production. The profitability of opencast coal was challenged on the grounds that such output, at a time of over supply, displaced deep-mined output, sales and employment, whilst the quality of opencast coal was generally poor and could easily be supplied from deep mines elsewhere in the UK.

Whatever the rights and wrongs of the argument, there was no doubt that expansion of opencast output represented a substantial involvement by the private sector in the UK coal industry. In many ways, this underpinned what took place during the 1980s, especially after 1985. The drive to cut costs via intensive use of new capital investment, flexible working practices and expanded opencast output all mirrored a government-imposed pressure to produce profitably despite substantial restraints imposed on

TABLE 1.12
*British Coal: financial statistics, 1982–90*

| £m | 1982/83 | 1983/84 | 1984/85 | 1985/86 | 1986/87 | 1987/88 | 1988/89 | 1989/90 |
|---|---|---|---|---|---|---|---|---|
| *Deepmined operations* | | | | | | | | |
| Operating profit (loss) | (317) | (595) | (1773) | 232 | 41 | (67) | 132 | (149) |
| Average capital employed | 3633 | 4153 | 4839 | 5070 | 5106 | 5089 | 4824 | 5078 |
| Return on capital (%) | – | – | – | 3 | 1 | – | 3 | – |
| *Opencast operations* | | | | | | | | |
| Operating profit | 192 | 211 | 140 | 343 | 244 | 252 | 272 | 234 |
| Average capital employed | 277 | 319 | 379 | 316 | 205 | 187 | 173 | 202 |
| Return on capital (%) | 69 | 66 | 37 | 108 | 119 | 135 | 158 | 116 |
| Site restoration costs | (15) | (16) | (14) | (12) | (10) | (11) | (12) | (15) |
| *All operations* | | | | | | | | |
| Interest charges | (364) | (467) | (520) | (437) | (386) | (368) | (432) | (574) |

Source: British Coal Corporation.

British Coal by the structure of its debt to the government (which entailed interest charges of over £400 m annually throughout the 1980s—see Table 1.12), and its historical legacy of under-investment and low prices. These changes were also partly inspired by a market, power generation, in which coal was under substantial challenge from the threat of imported coal and oil and first nuclear energy, then natural gas. In one sense, then, there was no strategy for British Coal other than the rules of the market: but a very short-term market in which all consideration of longer-term strategies for coal was swept aside. Yet paradoxically, a government-imposed insistence on high-cost domestic nuclear generating capacity as safeguard against over-dependence upon one source—coal—posed further problems for British Coal. This inconsistency clearly indicated the politics of coal production; but as was increasingly recognized, the proposed use of relatively cheap (in the short-term) supplies of imported coal also contained a potential strategic dilemma (see Beynon and Hudson 1986; British Association of Colliery Managers 1986). This was the spectre of over-dependence upon imported energy in just the same fashion (albeit in a different form) as had precipitated the dramatic impact of the OPEC oil price increases in 1973 and 1974.[9] To compound matters further within the UK, the "market" strategy—in reality one heavily mediated by the government—had particularly serious consequences for other sectors of the economy which were dependent wholly or in part upon UK coal production. This issue is explored in the following section.

## 1.4 Energy supply and the UK electricity generating plant industry

The impact of developments in the UK energy supply sector—and coal's changing relationship to it—on the UK economy more generally was clearly apparent in the power station manufacturing industry. This suffered heavily in the late 1980s from delays in ordering new UK power stations. Power plant manufacture essentially encompassed four main product areas: boilers, turbines, switchgear and controls. The first two of these represented the major items of capital investment, and three companies dominated the UK supply picture in the 1980s. The main turbine makers were GEC and Northern Engineering Industries (based in the Midlands and on Tyneside respectively) and the main boiler-makers were NEI and Babcock, based in Scotland. The industry was a substantial one, with UK sales of £700 m and exports of £650 m in 1985; but highly dependent upon a flow of new power station orders. The tremendous uncertainty over new generating capacity engendered first by the lengthy Sizewell B inquiry, then impending privatization, had a powerful impact on the sector (see North East Campaign for Coal 1987).

After substantial orders in the 1960s, there had been a sharp tailing-off after 1973, with the only major orders placed being for the nuclear stations Heysham II and Torness in 1978, and the coal-fired Drax B station in 1977—the latter a deliberate attempt by the Labour Government to stimulate demand for the electrical engineering industry, expanding an existing plant located near the Selby coalfield to the point where it could meet on its own almost 10 per cent of electricity demand in England and Wales. No further orders were placed until the end of the 1980s. Faced with this lack of business, UK companies moved out into the export market, successfully earning major contracts in the late 1970s and early 1980s; but then this market too underwent a collapse. In 1974, world plant orders amounted to 75,000 MW; by 1985 this was down to 10,000 MW, and orders continued at this low level for the rest of the decade.

Under these conditions, the UK power plant industry faced a bleak future. It lobbied heavily for a new generation of coal and/or nuclear stations from the mid-1980s onwards (see, for instance, NEI 1986) and strengthened moves to diversify out of the sector. In the meantime, as order books dried up, redundancies became the order of the day. Babcock laid off one-quarter of the workforce at its Renfrew boiler plant in 1986. NEI was even more exposed, depending on power stations for 75 per cent of its turnover against GEC's 20 per cent. From 1978 to 1984, NEI shed 12,000 jobs; in 1986 it announced a further 6,000 job losses. These were heavily concentrated on Tyneside, where it was the largest private employer (see Tyne and Wear District Councils 1986). To compound the UK industry's difficulties, further problems were caused by impending privatization of electricity supply. In 1988, provisional orders were placed for the projected round of three coal-fired plants with GEC for the turbines and NEI for the boilers (leaving Babcock in the cold): but when these were cancelled, it left Sizewell B as the only firm UK order. For this, GEC had a contract to supply the turbines and Babcock the boilers, but Westinghouse of the USA was the prime contractor for the technically complex reactor core.

In the UK, new electricity generating capacity was clearly required in the 1990s, though there was little certainty as to how much. Estimates ranged as high as the CEGB's (contested) 15,500 MW. Elsewhere in the world a familiar pattern to the UK—heavy investment in generating plant in the 1960s, which was due for replacement in the 1990s—meant that an upsurge in new power station orders was far from an unlikely prospect. It remained to be seen, though, how much UK manufacturing capability would remain to meet that demand in the face of global competition.

Three Japanese companies—Mitsubishi, Toshiba and Hitachi —took 30 per cent of the world's export market in the 1980s, backed by a government-financed funding scheme for their customers in addition to a protected domestic market. GEC expanded its export business to the point where it became second only to Mitsubishi. Other major producers included General Electric and Westinghouse in the USA, Siemens in West Germany, and Brown Boveri in Switzerland. Additional competition in turbines and boilers came from India and China, and in turbines from South Korea. At the end of the 1980s, a series of strategic alliances took place. Brown Boveri merged with Asea of Sweden to form ABB; GEC with Alsthom of France; and Rolls-Royce acquired NEI. In the process of rationalization, the UK was uniquely handicapped by the low state of domestic order books and continuing uncertainty over the future structure of electricity generation, leaving UK producers dependent upon highly contested export markets.

Once it became apparent that the dominant power station technology in the UK, for at least the short term, was likely to involve gas-fired stations, further difficulties were also evident for traditional UK-based power plant manufacturers. For these companies were far from specialists in gas turbine technology—there had been no such demand in the UK before—whereas their competitors were long experienced in developing and installing gas-fired plant. This weakness in the UK's manufacturing capability was rapidly exposed as the first round of new power station orders was practically swept clean by overseas companies. Siemens won the contract to establish a 900 MW plant at Killingholme, the first large-scale non-nuclear station for well over a decade; Mitsubishi the contract for a 1,725 MW plant on Teesside; ABB for a 220 MW station for Lakeland Power (in which it had a significant stake). The move away from coal-fired power stations, then, had other implications besides those for the UK coal industry.

## 1.5 Concluding comments

This chapter has explored some of the implications of a changing international environment for the UK coal-mining industry. A temporary chronic surplus of world steam coal in the 1980s was utilized by national government policies in an attempt to stimulate radical change in UK energy supply. The pressures of international competition were mediated in a particular fashion which accepted some of the implications of short-term market forces, but not others—notably on the demand side through an emphasis on continuing nuclear generating capacity whilst denouncing any similar long-term concept for coal. In the process, the UK coal industry—the supply side—was dramatically restructured with marked implications for both capital and labour. The private sector, looking towards potential privatization of British Coal, benefited from an increase in low-cost (but environmentally destructive) opencast production; whilst labour in the industry was faced with a triple challenge—massive job loss, flexible working practices and increased mechanization at the pits which remained. These changes at British Coal, coupled with proposed privatization in the electricity supply sector, had implications elsewhere in the economy. Power plant manufacturers withered as UK orders were conspicuous by their absence.

Whether the overall benefits of state intervention, in terms of cheaper energy to the economy as a whole, outweighed the costs was a further point at issue, for the pursuit of cheap energy supplies had been a factor underpinning central government policies since 1945 and even earlier. Whilst highly tangible, the whole question of coal's contribution to UK energy costs was also a very complex one, dependent upon a range of assumptions. Divergent estimates abounded, especially over the cost of UK energy in a comparative international context.

The CEGB, for instance, compared its own performance relatively favourably with other major generators, despite what it saw as high coal costs and fuel oil duty (Energy Committee 1988 pp. 8–22). Electricity supply to industry was cheaper, it argued, than in most other European countries, with Japan, West Germany and the USA having electricity costs almost double those in the UK. By contrast, the Institute of Directors (1986 p. 43) suggested that British industry paid "twice as much for its electricity as its French competitors, and about the same as most of the other Community members". In terms of coal's contribution, similar uncertainty prevailed. To advocates of privatization (such as Robinson and Sykes 1987) coal had long been a high-cost monopoly supplier, causing UK electricity to be unnecessarily expensive. The National Union of Mineworkers (1987) argued instead that for many years coal had been kept at artificially low prices by government direction, causing the National Coal Board to lose more than £2,000 m in revenue from 1947 to 1970.

Clearly, evaluation of coal's performance depended on standpoint; but most parties accepted that the cost of coal to the energy supply industry declined in the 1980s. Future fuel decisions depended on supply contracts negotiated upon privatization of the CEGB, but coal had already gone a long way towards reducing its price. As the Chairman of British Coal put it in 1990, the cost of coal to the generating industry had fallen in real terms after 1986 by £850 m, and the three-year supply contract at fixed prices meant a further progressive income loss of £150 m each year, so that by 1992/93, British Coal would have made price reductions to the electricity industry amounting to £1,300 m annually. But whether this cutback was sufficient to drive off imports, and whether it made any appreciable difference to the cost of UK energy, was a debating point to lay alongside the certain impact of decline in UK coal production capacity and change in other sectors dependent upon UK coal production and electricity supply. What was also very clear was the way in which international market forces, once unleashed and supported by a national government intent on reducing the strategic power of labour in the mining industry—regardless of the significance of finite energy resources—could wreak wide-ranging havoc in the short-term, with so little regard for the longer-term.

At the same time, the impact of UK state policies towards the coal-mining industry in the particular context of electricity privatization produced a number of results which demonstrated again the deep and tangled involvement of successive governments in the question of UK energy, often blurring the distinctions between coal demand and supply (see Hudson and Sadler 1990). The gradual emergence of nuclear power's cost disadvantage against coal was described above (in section 1.3.1) and some of its implications considered. This reappraisal of the "economics" of energy—in reality a political fix—was highlighted further in a subsequent report from the Energy Committee (1990a) in what was described by the *Financial Times* (28 June 1990) as "one of the most damning accusations of incompetence in a government department ever issued by a select committee". It began with this observation:

> after years of official assurances that nuclear power was (or could be) the cheapest form of electricity generation, Parliament and the public are entitled to know why it was only when faced with the commercial

discipline of life in the private sector that nuclear power (from both existing and proposed reactors) suddenly became an expensive form of generation (pp. ix–x).

Using National Power's figures, it revealed that even electricity from the Sizewell B PWR would be relatively expensive, costing 6.25 p/kWh against 3–4 p/kWh for coal-fired power stations and 2–3 p/kWh from gas-fired sources. Three reasons were given for the increased cost of nuclear energy: the estimated costs of reprocessing spent fuel had risen; estimated decommissioning costs were up (in the case of the Magnox stations from £2.8 bn in the CEGB's 1988 accounts to £6.9 bn in 1989); and assumed required rates of return on investment had also increased. Criticizing the "systematic bias in the CEGB costings in favour of nuclear power" (p. xix), and the secrecy surrounding them, the report condemned the Secretary of State for Energy for policies for which "it is now known inadequate preparation had been made" (p. xxxiii). The report concluded with concern over the impending 1994 review: "given the recent history of nuclear power, it will never again be possible to take assurances as to the viability of any type of nuclear power on trust" (p. xxxvii).

Such concerns were only sharpened by news that the estimated cost of Sizewell B had increased once again, from the original £1.69 bn to £2.03 bn (at constant 1987 prices). Yet, despite the effective subsidy which was supporting the nuclear industry to the tune of about £900 m annually, resulting in a less than fully competitive electricity generating market, the government reaffirmed its commitment to Sizewell B and its favourable disposition towards nuclear energy, if only for security of supply. Such assurances highlighted again one of the key reasons why nuclear's high costs had been concealed for so long: government long-term commitment, in stark contrast to its policies towards the coal industry.

Once nuclear power was exposed as an expensive option, gas-fired generating capacity was heavily promoted instead, not only as an alternative energy source in its own right (albeit a premium fuel whose use in electricity generation had previously been constrained) but also for its lesser environmental impact in comparison with coal. This option also impacted dramatically upon the future of British Coal, for it presupposed minimal investment in alternative technologies which could remove sulphur dioxide from coal-fired power station waste gases (flue gas desulphurization, or FGD). This was introduced above (see section 1.3.1) and again, a government report (Energy Committee 1990b) outlined the full extent of these implications. Whilst recognizing that not all proposed gas-fired power stations would be built, it noted that some 10,000 MW of such capacity was provisionally planned which would displace 25 m tonnes of coal consumption annually. At the same time, the two main power generating companies planned to purchase increased volumes of low-sulphur content imported coal. These developments would effectively cut British Coal's sales from 70 m tonnes to 50 m tonnes by 1998 and 38 m tonnes by 2003, entailing 20,000 job losses in coal-mining by 1998 and 32,000 by 2003. British Coal argued that if only 8,000 MW of coal-fired capacity was fitted with FGD (as was planned) and if sulphur emission reduction targets were met, the maximum possible burn of relatively high-sulphur UK coal in 2003 would be 30 m tonnes.[10] To maintain annual consumption of 70 m tonnes of UK-produced coal in power stations would mean 20,000 MW of capacity fitted with FGD. Yet no readily available alternative to the current FGD technology was available, largely because of limited support for research:

> Whereas billions of pounds have been spent on nuclear research and development, giving rise so far only to a small, heavily-subsidised sector of the electricity supply industry, research and development which could have improved the efficiency of coal-fired generation has been starved of the comparatively small sums needed. (p. xviii)

These dramatic prognoses contrasted markedly with British Coal's earlier market forecasts (see Table 1.9), and there was no doubt that the gas-fired/low-sulphur imported coal strategy of the generators posed a major threat to British Coal's operations. In 1990, a further 7,500 redundancies were announced, to be spread at first over three years, then later reduced to eighteen months. The future for British Coal looked very grim indeed as the continued squeeze on its prices in the generating market, coupled with geological difficulties and small-scale labour disputes (especially in the Yorkshire coalfield), combined with restricted demand from the generating companies to produce dramatically poor financial results for 1989/90. Output dropped by nearly 10 per cent from the previous year's total to 95 m tonnes; deep-mined operations swung back into an operating loss; and even opencast profits were reduced. The overall deficit of over £5 bn for the year reflected also a (belated) financial reconstruction which took place under the terms of the Coal Industry Act 1990, writing off past losses and devaluing fixed assets in recognition of lower world coal prices. This would have the effect of reducing the burden of future interest repayments, but not even such a massive financial adjustment could conceal the very serious threat to the long-term viability of British Coal's continuing operations.

All of this further highlighted the significance of a final set of questions to do with the longer-term national strategic implications of coal's demise. Just 25 m tonnes of coal imported a year at £30 per tonne would raise the UK's annual import bill by £750 m, exacerbating balance-of-payments difficulties (Energy Committee 1990b, p. xx). Lack of concern for this problem at the Department of Energy squared oddly with its encouragement to alternative fuels. The government's continued obsession with the power (whether apparent or real) of the NUM also led to the further paradox of its ordering the new generating companies to hold between them coal reserves of 27 m tonnes at the start of each winter (22 m tonnes at the end) as an insurance against strike disruption, whilst still downplaying the threat of import dependence. This particular risk was even (somewhat belatedly) recognized by the Energy Committee, which reported the views of National Power's Mr Webster. He had argued in evidence as follows:

> I think the greatest safeguard we have is that there is a huge number of players in the international coal industry. It is fragmented, there is no threat of an OPEC or of large monopolies there. (Energy Committee 1990b p. xv)

The Energy Committee's report, though, cautioned the Department of Energy, recommending that it "monitor the effects of the UK generators' coal purchases on security of supply" (p. xvi). It further concluded in no uncertain terms that:

> private sector generators cannot be expected to take account of national interests, and pit closures are irreversible: deep-mined coal capacity cannot be turned on and off like a tap. We are not convinced that the government has yet faced up to the dilemma which confronts it over the future of Britain's coal industry. It is essential that these issues are not side-stepped. (p. xxi)

It was apparent in mid-1990 that the government was still set on a course of dramatic capacity reduction regardless of longer-term implications. Whether this represented a rational energy policy—either in terms of the relations between the UK and the world market, or of appropriate use of environmentally sensitive and finite UK energy resources—was another issue. There were all too many indications, though, that it did not.

# Notes

1. Given the great variability of different coal types, no single spot-market price existed in the way that it did for oil. One commonly used reference point though was a particular grade of South African coal, used by the authoritative *Financial Times International Coal Report* as its "spot marker price".

2. Malcolm Edwards, commercial director of British Coal, laid the blame on oil companies for "imprudent over-investment" in coal after the oil crisis of 1973. Speaking at an international coal conference in 1989, he went on:

   > Too large, too fast, too grand to listen, far too optimistic about the response of the market, all those overweight cuckoos crowded into a very small nest. When it became clear that the market for traded coal was not going to expand to order, the reaction of oil companies was what came naturally to them—to rely on their great cash flows to price down hard to drive out the competition . . . [but] all the resulting price war did was to drive out the other coal producers. (quoted in *Financial Times* 22 June 1989)

   His remarks came as one of the oil companies so indicted (BP—with sales of 29 m tonnes in 1988), announced plans to sell off most of its coal interests, beating a retreat from a problem it had itself helped to create.

3. In steam coal, West German power companies were committed under the *Jahrhundertvertrag* to buy 45 m tonnes of domestic coal until 1995. To compensate for the difference between the price of this coal and alternative imported energy, the power companies were permitted to levy an extra 7.5 per cent on electricity bills—known as the *Kohlepfennig*. In coking coal, the major steel companies were committed under the *Hüttenvertrag* to buy most of their supplies from the domestic producer, Ruhrkohle, until 1997, at prices subsidized by the state.

4. In the aftermath of the 1984/85 miners' strike, the National Coal Board was renamed British Coal Corporation. The two terms are used here interchangeably.

5. The sale of coal to the South of Scotland Electricity Board (SSEB) was covered by a separate agreement. This was subject to renegotiation in the late 1980s, but accounted for much smaller volumes (some 2–3 m tonnes annually) than the CEGB. The other major BC market, coking coal sales to BSC, is discussed in Chapters 2 and 4.

6. With considerable understatement, British Coal prefaced its revised strategy with the remark that "A great deal has changed since the launch of *Plan for Coal* in 1974".

7. The Monopolies and Mergers Commission (1989) was highly critical that the Asfordby pit had been developed, describing it as "marginal in financial terms" (p. 62).

8. The NCB's proposals on flexibility had a long heritage. Its history of mechanization and attempts to improve productivity stretched from the 1947 inheritance of worn-out pits to the gradual introduction of the shearer loader from 1958, the failed Remote Operated Longwall Face (ROLF) system in the 1960s, and the National Power Loading Agreement in the late 1960s. Early in the 1970s, Wilfred Miron, chairman of the East Midlands NCB, proposed six-day working, automation and pit incentive schemes to divide the NUM. These proposals were effectively restated by Albert Wheeler, Nottinghamshire Area Director of the NCB, in an address to the Institute of Mining Engineers in 1986. They subsequently formed the main basis of negotiations between British Coal and the unions.

9. It is perhaps instructive in this context to contrast the UK's policy to the coal industry with that of West Germany, where state support continued into the 1990s, albeit on a reduced scale, partly to guarantee security of supply (see also note 3 above). As the coal producer Ruhrkohle explained in its 1989 annual report:

> additional demand on the world coal market will require new sources in the long-term. The new capacities must be set up mainly on difficult deposits, and sometimes new infrastructures will be needed. Cost-induced price rises can be expected here. The relations on the world coal market underscore the long-term importance of domestic coal for reliable supply in the European Community.

10. The Energy Committee (1990b) report on FGD also raised the spectre (from the UK coal industry's viewpoint, at least) of still further restrictions on sulphur dioxide emissions. After complex negotiations, the UK's reduction of 60 per cent by 2003 from 1980 levels (as against 70 per cent for Belgium, West Germany, France and the Netherlands) was set in recognition of reductions achieved in the 1970s (due largely to decline in manufacturing industry) and the expectation that the required cutbacks would be achieved through the relatively costly option of FGD. As the Energy Committee put it.

> having obtained such limits by that means the UK now proposes to comply with them by cheaper methods instead.

Yet this was unlikely to find favour with the European Community, so that:

> A witness from National Power told us that the company had not taken account of the possibility of the [sulphur dioxide emission] limit in 2003 becoming stricter. In our view both generators would be wise to do so. (p. xx)

# 2

# Iron and Steel: Global Change and the Rise of New Producers

## 2.1 Introduction

In Western Europe and North America, the significance of iron and steel to nineteenth-century industrialization was matched only by its contribution to twentieth-century de-industrialization. After 1974, in particular, the industry encapsulated the decline of traditional manufacturing as hundreds of thousands of jobs were lost. For over a decade, steel companies struggled to come to terms with a radically new environment, meeting falling demand and sales with wholesale closures. Increasingly, national governments became involved in attempts to stem some of the consequences. It was not until the late 1980s that an upturn developed, though even then it was not clear how long this would last (for a review, see Hudson and Sadler 1989).

Yet steel was not necessarily an "old" industry. Its technology was relatively advanced and its products were used in a range of "modern" industries.[1] What was happening, in fact, was a wholesale shift in the geographical balance of production. Capacity and output were expanding in a few of the newly-industrializing countries such as Brazil and South Korea, as they became increasingly significant forces in the global market for manufactured goods. Declining demand in the industrialized countries reflected competition from alternative materials, and a growing shift out of manufacturing into less steel-intensive service sector activities. As one result of its intermediate position in the chain of production, in other words, steel very rapidly and very clearly expressed the changing balance of power in manufacturing industry between different nation-states.

This chapter documents these developments, starting in section 2.2 with an examination of the new global pattern of steel production and trade. It goes on in section 2.3 to consider the UK's role, stressing the changing balance between public and private ownership, and the implications of privatization in the course of the 1980s. Then section 2.4 describes the impact of steel's changing fortunes on raw material supply sectors such as iron ore and coking coal. The main conclusions and implications are evaluated in section 2.5.

## 2.2 World steel

Global steel production followed a steadily rising trend for most of the twentieth century, enduring cyclical economic slumps to return with strong annual growth rates. After 1945, output grew especially dramatically in response to demand from dynamic steel-consuming sectors such as motor vehicles—epitomized by the rise of Japan from practically nowhere to a global challenger in the 1950s and 1960s. From 1946 to 1974, total world steel output increased more than sixfold, from 112 m tonnes to 708 m tonnes. In only three years during this period (1954, 1958 and 1971) was there less steel produced than in the twelve preceding months. It was hardly surprising, then, that by the end of the 1960s steel producers envisaged a prospect of enduring world production growth.

In the event, however, the world's capitalist economies collectively plunged into a recession which dramatically depressed demand. For steel producers, the slump was aggravated by high levels of steel stocks built up by consumers in anticipation of threatened shortages, and by capacity expansion plans initiated before 1974 which took several more years to reach completion. In 1975, output slumped from the previous year's total by nearly 10 per cent, and did not recover again until 1978. Demand picked up in 1979 to sustain a new record output of 746 m tonnes; but this was to prove falsely optimistic as production slumped again to 645 m tonnes in 1982. On only two other occasions in the entire century (the great depression, 1930–32 and the rundown from wartime, 1944–46) had annual output dropped consecutively over a three-year period.

In the new global economic climate, divergent patterns of growth in steel production in different areas became increasingly significant. Within the developed economies, steel was vulnerable to substitution by other products such as plastics or aluminium.[2] These were less energy-intensive at the production stage, lowering overall costs significantly at a time of high energy prices; and lighter, giving rise to product improvements, such as increased fuel efficiency in motor vehicles (see, for instance, IISI 1983). Within the newly industrializing countries, on the other hand, production was growing in response to the demands of early stages of planned industrialization programmes and the ready availability of steel production machinery and technology, often supplied through subsidiary companies of established European or American steel producers.

In 1974, the newly-industrializing countries produced just 59 m tonnes of steel, amounting to 8 per cent of the world total. By 1988, this had almost trebled to 165 m tonnes, for a 21 per cent share of world output. Over the same period, the developed countries' share of world output plunged from 66 to 50 per cent (see Table 2.1). A small handful of countries dominated expansion: China, Brazil, South Korea, India, Mexico, Taiwan, Argentina and Venezuela. Of these, three (Brazil, South Korea and Taiwan) were by far the most significant exporters. With consumption in the NICs growing ahead of production for most of the 1980s, the real global trade battle (albeit a little-publicized one) involved competition between Japanese, American, European and some NIC producers for access to other, growing NIC markets.

This section expands on these remarks by considering the new pattern of steel production and trade. It examines output growth in first Japan, then several of the newly industrializing countries. This is contrasted with the picture of contraction in Western Europe and the USA. Finally, it considers how the geographical balance of production was mediated by the impact of international trade, and the growing role of government policies in regulating this trade.

## 2.2.1 Japan and the newly-industrializing countries

The early rise of Japan, followed by heavy investment in steel production in Brazil and South Korea, meant that by the late 1980s companies from these countries figured prominently amongst the world's biggest steelmakers (see Table 2.2). In the period from 1945 to 1974 the Japanese steel industry saw remarkable growth. Its output soared from 1 m tonnes in 1947 to 22 m tonnes in 1960 and 93 m tonnes in 1970, reaching 119 m tonnes in 1973. This supplied both domestic demand and a growing world export market, and was underpinned by a massive programme of support from the country's main financial institutions. New capacity was constructed in large coastal complexes with massive blast furnaces. Ten sites each had an annual capacity in excess of 8 m tonnes, whilst the developed world's largest, at Fukuyama City, had an annual capacity of 16 m tonnes. Japan became the developed world's biggest steel producer, exceeded only by the

TABLE 2.1
*World crude steel production, 1974–88*

| (*m tonnes*) | 1974 | 1979 | 1980 | 1981 | 1982 | 1983 | 1984 | 1985 | 1986 | 1987 | 1988 |
|---|---|---|---|---|---|---|---|---|---|---|---|
| Advanced economies | 464 | 442 | 407 | 401 | 338 | 344 | 376 | 374 | 352 | 361 | 393 |
| Newly industrializing countries | 59 | 95 | 100 | 100 | 103 | 109 | 121 | 131 | 139 | 150 | 165 |
| Centrally planned economies | 185 | 209 | 209 | 206 | 204 | 210 | 214 | 214 | 222 | 225 | 232 |
| *World total* | 708 | 746 | 716 | 707 | 645 | 663 | 711 | 719 | 713 | 736 | 790 |
| European Community (12) | 168 | 154 | 142 | 109 | 125 | 123 | 134 | 136 | 126 | 127 | 138 |
| USA | 132 | 123 | 102 | 102 | 68 | 77 | 84 | 80 | 74 | 81 | 91 |
| Japan | 117 | 112 | 111 | | 100 | 97 | 106 | 105 | 98 | 99 | 105 |
| Brazil | 8 | 14 | 15 | 13 | 13 | 15 | 18 | 20 | 21 | 22 | 25 |
| South Korea | | 8 | 9 | 11 | 12 | 12 | 13 | 14 | 15 | 17 | 19 |
| India | | | | | | | 11 | 12 | 12 | 13 | 14 |
| Taiwan | | | | | | 5 | 5 | 5 | 6 | 6 | 8 |
| China | | | | | | 40 | 43 | 47 | 52 | 56 | 58 |
| (% of world total) | | | | | | | | | | | |
| Advanced economies | 66 | 59 | 57 | 57 | 52 | 52 | 53 | 52 | 49 | 49 | 50 |
| Newly industrializing countries | 8 | 13 | 14 | 14 | 16 | 16 | 17 | 18 | 20 | 20 | 21 |
| Centrally planned economies | 26 | 28 | 29 | 29 | 32 | 32 | 30 | 30 | 31 | 31 | 29 |

Source: International Iron and Steel Institute.

TABLE 2.2

*World's largest steel producers (excluding centrally planned economies), 1987*

| Company | Country | Output (m tonnes) |
| --- | --- | --- |
| Nippon Steel | Japan | 26.0 |
| Usinor-Sacilor | France | 16.7 |
| Siderbras | Brazil | 14.1 |
| British Steel | UK | 13.6 |
| Finsider | Italy | 12.5 |
| Posco | South Korea | 11.3 |
| NKK | Japan | 11.3 |
| Thyssen | FR Germany | 10.9 |
| Bethlehem Steel | USA | 10.5 |
| LTV Steel | USA | 10.4 |
| USX | USA | 10.4 |
| Kawasaki Steel | Japan | 10.1 |
| Sumitomo Metal | Japan | 10.1 |

Includes all producers whose output exceeded 10 m tonnes.
Source: International Iron and Steel Institute.

USSR, and its largest steel company, Nippon Steel, dwarfed all other producers.

The success of the Japanese steel industry was based upon exports. Dramatic growth in the 1960s was expressly designed to feed world markets. The construction of steelworks on deepwater harbours was essential both for the import of raw materials and the export of steel. In 1960, the Japanese steel industry exported 14 per cent of its output; by 1975 exports accounted for 34 per cent of production. To this growth in the volume of direct steel trade, the proportion of steel traded indirectly should also be added, in the form for example of ships, machinery, motor vehicles or other consumer goods. On this basis, one estimate was that at least half of Japan's total steel output was ultimately destined for export (Hogan 1983 p. 83).

Within this dependence upon export markets lay the seeds of crisis. Just as in other advanced economics, Japanese steel companies initiated ambitious expansion programmes in 1973 and 1974 (on the eve of world recession) to add a further 22 m tonnes of capacity, which were completed by 1978. Yet as the recession intensified, key export markets, such as the USA, retreated behind trade barriers, with protection the new order of the day. Former NIC markets, such as Brazil and South Korea, were increasingly sourced from domestic production, not Japanese exports. When other sectors felt the brunt of recession and trade restriction, Japanese domestic steel demand also dropped.

In response, Japanese steel companies adopted a number of new strategies in the 1980s. All the major companies diversified into the manufacture of silicon wafers for the electronics industry. Kawasaki Steel anticipated that its non-steel business, centred on electronics, would generate 40 per cent of its income by the end of the century (compared to 20 per cent in 1985), whilst Nippon Steel estimated that electronics would provide 20 per cent of its turnover by 1995. The steel companies did not forsake their primary business activity, continuing with modernization investments to reduce costs and improve product quality. Partly as a defensive reaction against import quotas, some companies also invested in steel production overseas; for example, in 1984 Nippon Kokan took a 50 per cent stake in National Steel, then the sixth largest US steel company.

Yet even these measures did not prove sufficient to restore and maintain balance sheet profitability. In the half-year to September 1986, the five major companies sustained losses of £790 m. Within a matter of months they had all announced restructuring plans aimed at reducing their combined workforce by 44,000 to 132,000 by 1990. Even as these measures were being implemented, demand for steel began to pick up: but the central policy of diversification out of steel continued. In a very real sense, Japan had rapidly reached a position more common in the other advanced countries as its steel companies sought to cut back and reorganize during the 1980s.

This position had not yet been approached in Brazil, the biggest NIC steel producer. Siderbras, the state-owned company, was the third largest in the world in 1987, after rapid growth since the early 1970s. Yet the government-backed programme of expansion had run into a number of problems on the way. It was conceived at a time of rising domestic demand, in the context of a planned industrial growth strategy. Downturn in the economy in the early 1980s effectively wiped out several years' growth and forced the expanding steel industry to concentrate more and more upon export markets. This was most clearly manifest at the two newest works, Tubarao and Acominas.

Tubarao was inaugurated in 1983 at a cost of $3,100 m, with an annual capacity of 3.2 m tonnes. It represented a first for Brazil: a steel plant designed specifically for export (in this case of semi-finished slabs). The company which controlled the plant was an international conglomerate in which Siderbras held a controlling 51 per cent stake, but two foreign partners, Kawasaki Steel of Japan and Finsider of Italy held the remaining 49 per cent, and were each obliged to market one-fifth of its output.

By way of contrast, Acominas was originally conceived in 1976 as a plant to supply the domestic market, with an initial annual capacity of 2 m tonnes, to be built up to 10 m tonnes at a later date. Falling demand and major construction delays meant that the first stage was not completed until 1986. At a cost of $6,000 m, it was some $2,500 m over the estimated budget. Its output was completely re-orientated by the time it was finally completed, away from domestic sales and towards the export market.

Over-capacity and project delays, coupled with currency fluctuations and government control of some domestic prices, were partially responsible for the growing financial problems of Siderbras. By 1986, its total debt amounted to $15,600 m, including $6,800 m owed to foreign banks, $7,500 m to the Brazilian government and $1,300 m in short-term bank loans. In an attempt to meet the debt service burden, and given insufficient domestic demand, Siderbras turned more and more towards exports. In 1984, Brazil exported nearly 7 m tonnes of steel products, a far cry from the 4 m tonnes imported in 1974. Yet this led the country into another series of problems with regard to its trading relations with the USA. Anti-dumping complaints were lodged by US steel producers, plunging Brazil into the middle of a steel trade crisis. This was temporarily resolved at the end of 1984, when a five-year export restraint agreement was concluded, limiting Brazilian exports to 0.8 per cent of the US market for finished steel (approximately 0.8 m tonnes annually). A further 0.7 m tonnes of semi-finished steel slab exports annually were permitted (rising to 1.1 m tonnes over a fifteen-year period) from Tubarao, to supply California Steel, 25 per cent of which was owned by the Brazilian government and 25 per cent by Kawasaki Steel of Japan (which partially owned Tubarao); a graphic example of the growing internationalization of steel production and marketing arrangements as a means of at least partially overcoming international trade sanctions.

The second largest steel producer amongst NICs was South Korea. The state-backed company, Pohang Iron and Steel (Posco), produced 11.3 m tonnes in 1987, making it the sixth largest steel company in the Western world (see Table 2.2). Just as in Brazil, this was the result of a conscious growth strategy adopted during the 1970s in an attempt to foster domestic industry and reduce dependence on imports.

Posco's major works was the product of an ambitious expansion programme launched in 1970 and completed in 1981 at a cost of $3,300 m. Throughout the 1970s, the project was a major national priority. It was finished ahead of schedule and on budget, able to meet its central aim, supplying domestic demand at prices well below those prevailing for imports. By 1979, South Korean exports exceeded imports. As the 1980s progressed, the company came to rely increasingly upon these export markets as a means of utilizing capacity. Domestic demand did not stall to the same extent as in Brazil, though, ensuring that a planned second plant (on the south coast at Kwangyang), with an additional capacity of 2.8 m tonnes, was authorized in the mid-1980s. By 1988, the company was a highly efficient steel producer employing just 19,000 workers directly, along with 9,000 contract workers; and it planned to invest a further $6,400 m over four years on new steel capacity and increased diversification (on the regional impact in South Korea, see Auty 1990).

In different ways, South Korea and Brazil were illustrative of a number of tendencies amongst the NIC steel producers. They had rapidly become major producers, able to supply rising domestic demand and keen to expand an export market in both the developed world (especially Japan and the USA) and other NICs. The countries of the south-east Asian Pacific Rim figured prominently among their smaller, yet significant, steel trade flows. Yet these two producer countries (particularly Brazil) demonstrated the uncertainties, as well as the opportunities, of the global steel industry and the problems of attempting to follow the "Japanese model" in a changed economic climate. They were both acutely sensitive to domestic economic performance and that of the world's economy at large through the threat of trade sanctions within the European, American and Japanese markets; and to the competitive threat in other NIC markets posed by the diversion of surplus developed country output as an indirect result of the same trade sanctions. The path of NIC expansion was far from even or secure.

## 2.2.2 Decline in Western Europe and the USA

The recent performance of the steel industry in Western Europe and North America has been, by contrast, one of almost unremitting decline. After 1974, demand and output slumped, profits turned to losses and redundancy and retrenchment came to dominate the boardroom agenda. In the recession of 1982/83, all but four of the Western world's 37 major steel companies had at least one year with no profits (Keeling 1988 p. 52). Employment fell to one half of the 1974 levels (see Table 2.3). These problems increasingly drew in national governments and

TABLE 2.3

*European Community, USA and Japan: employment in steel production, 1974–88*

| 1000s | 1974 | 1979 | 1986 | 1988 |
|---|---|---|---|---|
| European Community (12) | 894 | 782 | 474 | 415 |
| USA | 521 | 479 | 221 | 213 |
| Japan | 324 | 282 | 251 | 207 |
| OECD total | 1,956 | 1,741 | 1,109 | 1,011 |

Source: Keeling 1988.

the European Community in an attempt to resolve a deepening over-production crisis.

The collapse of the US steel industry was particularly dramatic. In 1982, output slumped to 68 m tonnes, nearly 40 m tonnes less than in the previous year, and one-half of the output of 1974. Recovery was a slow and uneven process. By 1988, output had only climbed to 91 m tonnes (see Table 2.1). One of the most significant challenges to domestic producers came from a surge in imports which flooded into the USA in the early 1980s, taking up to one-quarter of the market against one-tenth in the early 1970s. In response, steel companies lobbied for trade protection, re-structured their operations, and focused increasingly on cost-cutting through labour contract re-negotiation.

The susceptibility of the US steel industry to imports had much to do with the early history and subsequent location of steel production capacity (see especially, Markusen 1985b pp. 73–100; 1986). From the later years of the nineteenth century, growth in steel was heavily concentrated in the north-eastern states, around Pittsburgh and Youngstown. After a short period of intense competition, a series of mergers resulted by 1900 in a near-monopolistic situation where one company, US Steel, controlled 65 per cent of output. At this time, the industry adopted a procedure for fixing prices known as "Pittsburgh plus", or the basing point system. Prices quoted by all suppliers, whatever their location, were the Pittsburgh rate plus the cost from Pittsburgh to the customer, effectively eliminating any advantage for a steel plant located nearer to the market than Pittsburgh. This system of oligopolistic pricing greatly favoured the continued prominence of Pittsburgh as a production centre. As late as 1945, over 95 per cent of all steel production was in the north-eastern states. In 1948, the industry abandoned multiple basing point pricing, replacing it with a system whereby all firms automatically followed US Steel's lead in pricing. During this era, companies were assured of a comfortable profit margin and faced little incentive to seek out new, more profitable locations; nor did they do so. Collusion between steel firms only began to break down towards the end of the 1950s as the USA's role in the world steel industry began to decline. Belatedly, a degree of decentralization occurred, but on the eve of recession this trend had had only a marginal impact.

As a result of this oligopolistic control of prices, the US steel industry entered the recession highly vulnerable to imports to serve the west coast and southern states' manufacturing capacity, and to closures within the increasingly antiquated north-eastern heartland (see, for instance, Buss and Redburn 1983). The early history of the industry therefore impacted on its later fortunes in a particularly concentrated phase of restructuring—especially after 1981—aimed at internal reorganization and diversification in the face of an import threat made particularly acute by the degree of global over-capacity. The largest company, US Steel, embarked upon a programme of closures which cut capacity in its most vulnerable areas (particularly long products such as bar, wire and rails), and concentrated resources upon flat rolled products. At the same time, it adopted a policy of diversification out of steel and into oil and gas, including the purchase of Marathon Oil in the early 1980s and of Texas Oil and Gas in 1986. The shift of direction was exemplified in the company's change of name to USX later in that year, symbolically dropping the "Steel". By then, more than half the group's sales came from its oil and gas business. LTV, the second biggest steel producer, also diversified out of steel, into aerospace and industries linked to defence. By 1986, however, the company faced an acute crisis, and it was forced to file for protection under Chapter 11 of the US Bankruptcy Code—indicative of the industry's continuing crisis.

The third biggest company, Bethlehem Steel, stuck to the sector and invested heavily, but cut its workforce equally dramatically. Over-capacity was not so much a problem as the variable costs of production, especially labour productivity. National Steel took this concern to raise labour productivity to unprecedented levels. In 1984, it sold off its Weirton steel plant under an Employee Stock Ownership Plan, securing an 18 per cent pay reduction in the process. In the same year, 50 per cent of National Steel was sold to the Japanese steel group Nippon Kokan. This brought an infusion of capital, technology and management which was to prove particularly transformative for the company's collective bargaining arrangements.

In 1986, after dissolution of the former national wage-bargaining committee for the whole steel industry and whilst other companies were imposing deals with wage and benefit cuts, National Steel completed negotiations with the United Steelworkers' Union (USW) over its innovative "Cooperative Partnership" (see Clark 1987). This was a wide-ranging agreement which encompassed collective commitment to improved labour productivity, wage and benefit cuts of $1/hour, flexible working and re-assignment across job classifications. In return, the company promised new investment and limited job guarantees. The deal provided for a Productivity Gain Sharing Plan, offering bonuses on the basis of labour productivity improvements, and a profit-sharing scheme. It also introduced joint management-labour problem-solving committees, effectively decentralizing control of day-to-day operations. Overall, it tied employees to the efficient functioning of the company in a clear imitation of the Japanese model of industrial relations.

In the meantime, wage talks at USX became deadlocked, and in 1986 the company faced a complete stoppage as the USW refused to cede the company's demand of a $3.30/hour wages and benefits cut. The strike lasted six months and ended in 1987, when the USW accepted a new four-year labour contract with a wages and benefit cut of $2.45/hour in the first year. USX made plain its determination to make further sharp cuts in steelmaking operations, with plans to axe capacity from 28 m to 19 m tonnes, close five plants indefinitely and shed 20 per cent of its steel workforce.

Clearly, despite an intense period of rationalization with its many manifestations of closure, merger, diversification and new patterns of collective bargaining, the US steel industry remained in crisis. In such circumstances, attention was increasingly drawn to the country's trade deficit in steel products, most especially by aggrieved domestic producers. At the same time, Japanese participation in the US steel industry continued to expand, with Inland Steel developing a joint venture with Nippon Steel in Indiana, and Kawasaki Steel taking a 40 per cent stake in Armco in 1988. In 1989, as market conditions began to improve, the USW sought to regain some of the ground its members had lost in the mid-1980s. Workers at Bethlehem Steel won a 20 per cent pay rise over four years, but a similar deal at National Steel was rejected in a ballot. Meanwhile, the steel companies and the USW together lobbied for further extension of US government-imposed trade restrictions. One major source of contention concerned imports from the European Community, where production had also been cut back heavily in the 1980s (see Table 2.1). Throughout the 1980s, the EC had consistently recorded a substantial trade surplus with the rest of the world, as producers sought to compensate for excess capacity in relation to domestic markets.

In response to deepening recession, the European Community had developed a series of measures aimed at facilitating a relatively orderly restructuring amongst steel companies.[3] These were first introduced in 1977 when the Commission (appointed by member states to further the Community's interests as a whole) approved a voluntary system of suggested minimum prices for certain steel products, which later became compulsory. During 1980, it became apparent that these measures were insufficient, and the Commission sought approval from the Council (comprising representatives of member state governments) to invoke Article 58 of the Treaty of Paris, which provided it with the power to establish a system of production quotas. Never before had the Council been willing to recognise "manifest crisis" (as prescribed by the Treaty of Rome) in this way: but on this occasion it was.

Under the newly installed quota system, the Commission allocated production to each steel company on the basis of an average output from the preceding three-year period in the light of short and long-term forecasts for demand. It had the power to inspect and monitor production levels and could levy fines on any producer which exceeded its quota. In 1981, to back up the system of controls, the Commission sought and received the Council's approval for a further series of measures, giving it the ability to order capacity closures by effectively linking Community approval of state aid to steel producers with Community plans for the reduction of production capacity. The ultimate intention was to eliminate state aid altogether by 1985. Steel had become distinctive amongst manufacturing industries in the extent and sophistication of regulation exercised by the European Community.

Proposals for capacity reductions (see Table 2.4) soon proved to be optimistic. In 1985, the Commission called for a *further* 27 m tonnes of capacity to be closed by the end of the decade, in addition to the 26 m tonnes already closed. In this context, it was politically impossible unilaterally to abandon the quota system (as had been the original intention for 1985), although the Commission was keen to phase out some controls as evidence that its system of regulation was at least partially resolving the problem of over-capacity. The West German government, which had initially opposed introduction of the whole system, now argued in favour of its retention. To remove regulation, it maintained, would invite

TABLE 2.4

*European Community proposals for steel production capacity reductions, 1980–85*

|  | Capacity 1980 (m t) | Total closures called for (m t) | Closures 1980–85 (m t) | Closures by 1985 as % of 1980 capacity |
|---|---|---|---|---|
| West Germany | 53.1 | 6.0 | 6.3 | 11.9 |
| France | 26.9 | 5.3 | 4.5 | 16.7 |
| Italy | 36.3 | 5.8 | 5.7 | 15.7 |
| Netherlands | 7.3 | 1.0 | 0.8 | 11.0 |
| Belgium | 16.0 | 3.1 | 3.1 | 19.4 |
| Luxemburg | 5.2 | 1.0 | 1.0 | 19.2 |
| UK | 22.8 | 4.5 | 4.6 | 20.2 |
| Eire | 0.1 | – | – | – |
| Denmark | 0.9 | – | – | – |
| Total | 168.6 | 26.7 | 26.0 | 15.5 |

Source: European Commission.

a price war with state-subsidized competition pitched against the private West German steelmakers. Other countries were more concerned to secure an increase in their quota under the existing system. At the end of October 1985, agreement was therefore reached to carry part of the system over for a further year. The West German delegation gained at least the substance of what it wanted in that state subsidies were only permitted to help plant closures. The Commission partially secured its way by removing some products from the quota system; and France and the UK benefited from two flexibilities in the method of allocating quotas.

During 1986, negotiations commenced over the structure of the steel quota regime from 1987 onwards. Initial Commission proposals envisaged the abolition of quotas on more of the industry's output and confirmed its desire to discontinue the whole quota system from the end of 1987. This was unpopular with the big integrated steel producers, and their association, Eurofer, put forward an alternative plan which entailed continuation of the existing quota regime until the middle of 1987 and its replacement by an (unspecified) alternative system of controls from July 1987 to 1990. Quotas were announced in December for the first quarter of 1987 which excluded some products. In March 1987, further capacity reductions were offered by the steel companies, amounting in total to 15.3 m tonnes. Crucially though, the revised plan offered no cuts in the production of hot rolled coil, where over-capacity was greatest and national state assistance most apparent. The scheme was dismissed as inadequate by the Commission.

Once it was apparent that the gap between the cuts sought by the Commission and those offered by the steel companies could be narrowed no further, the Community set in train the process of formulating new plans for the industry's future. By December, no fresh proposals had been made to break the deadlock, and the Commission prepared to abolish quotas on wire rod and merchant bar from the end of the year; on hot rolled coil from July; and on heavy sections and heavy plate from the end of 1990, but only if companies produced adequate guarantees of intent to close capacity. This was ultimately to prove an insurmountable obstacle for steel companies. When the deadline of June 1988 expired, no closures had been offered in hot rolled coils, and cutbacks proposed in other sectors were well short of the Commission's demands. The quota system was therefore wholly abolished with effect from 1 July. The shifting international coalitions which had prolonged a crisis management system for so long had finally fallen apart.

More fundamentally, the Community steel quota regime had also proved inadequate as a mechanism for resolving problems in the industry. In its 1990 review, *General Objectives Steel 1995*, the Commission of the European Communities pointed out that whilst by and large the immediate crisis was over, restructuring was by no means complete (see CEC 1990). In some sectors—particularly hot rolled coil and strip, heavy sheet, and heavy and light sections—it argued that "relatively small changes in demand together with a commensurate weakening of prices can once again place certain steel manufacturers in a difficult position" (p. 2). It went on to add (with specific reference to sheet and sections): "further significant cuts in capacity must be made to ensure the medium-term stability of undertakings making these products" (p. 7). Apparently, an embryonic supranational state was no more capable of managing a crisis of international dimensions in steel production than were the various national states in the Community. That the quota system was devised and implemented at all was testimony to the durability of the EC as an institution, the magnitude of the over-capacity and the increasing evidence of national government's inability to manage decline in a highly internationalized industry even through strongly interventionist policies such as nationalization. In response, the Community became keen to disengage from intervention as soon as practically possible; but this proved to be even more politically contentious than the process of applying quotas in the first place.

Other major non-EC producers in Western Europe included Sweden, and here also the limits to state intervention in a capitalist economy were gradually exposed. The Swedish industry was relatively unusual in that whilst total steel capacity was small (at around 5 m tonnes annually), an unusually large proportion (around 30 per cent) was of special grades, making the country's evolving special steel producers among the major European competitors. Retrenchment and reorganization throughout the industry, financially backed by the government, began well before most European steelmakers recognized the depth and severity of the crisis.

Rationalization in special steels was concentrated in four product areas. By the mid-1970s, the country's three leading tool steel producers had merged to form Uddeholm Tooling, the world's third biggest company in the sector after VEW of Austria and Thyssen of West Germany. In 1982, the high-speed steel producers joined forces as Klosters Speedsteel, a world leader with an annual output of some 15,000 tonnes and a 20 per cent share of the European market. Ball and roller bearing production was concentrated at SKF, whose low alloy special steel division was a market leader in bearing steel. In 1984, the four stainless steel companies merged to form two units, eliminating overlapping production. Avesta paid SKr230 m each to Uddeholm and Fagersta to leave the sector, concentrating into one large company European market shares of 40 per cent in stainless welded tubes and 30–35 per cent in stainless strip and hot-rolled plate. Sandvik created a wholly owned subsidiary, Sandvik Steel, to specialize in the production of seamless tubes, strip and wire. The Swedish government agreed to provide some Skr460 m in special financing to cover the agreements, whilst the costs of laying off some 1,500 workers because of capacity closures were borne between Avesta and Sandvik.

The state-backed stainless steel merger completed a reorganization of the industry into discrete product areas each controlled by major producers. So successful were the new ventures, however, that they were soon to fall foul of Sweden's position within the international system of trade. Sweden was heavily dependent upon export markets in countries whose own producers were themselves rationalizing and seeking a degree of protection from competition. During 1984, Swedish producers were forced to agree to reduce exports of tool steel to the USA by some 20 per cent. Partly in response, the Swedish steel industry began to internationalize production. In 1985, Uddeholm took a 20 per cent stake in a new, $15 m special steels plant at Pittsburgh in the USA, and in 1986 SKF Steel merged with Ovako of Finland to form one of the biggest special steel producers in Europe. Just as in the European Community, there was only a limited room for manoeuvre in steel production strategies within national frontiers.

### 2.2.3 New trends in international steel trade

From the mid-1970s, as steel production expanded in the NICs and faltered or declined in the more advanced economies, patterns of international trade took on a new and growing significance.[4] As the proportion of steel output traded internationally continued to increase, there was a substantial redirection of trade patterns, with an expansion in NIC exports (especially to other NICs) and a partial diversion of OECD exports to the NIC markets in response to growing protectionism within the developed countries. But easily the most significant single importer was the USA. Its massive steel trade deficit served to underline the political significance of a series of import restrictions in the USA, most especially on trade with the European Community.

There were several major periods of crisis in United States-European Community steel trade agreements (see Jones 1986; Walter 1979, 1983). Protectionist sentiment arose on each occasion as a result of surges in exports from a small number of easily identifiable countries. The US government formulated responses to mollify domestic producers, yet attempted to avoid generating similar retaliatory measures from other governments. Once such policy instruments were put in place, exports which had previously been destined for the US were switched to other markets, thereby generating a similar crisis elsewhere—part of a protectionist spiral in steel trade.

The first round of steel trade restrictions was negotiated in the wake of a slump in US domestic demand in 1967. This had the effect of making rising import penetration more readily apparent. Both the steel workers' union and the steel companies lobbied Congress, proposing comprehensive five-year bilateral import quotas on all supplying countries. US Steel filed a complaint against EC countries alleging that their exports were unfairly subsidized. The American government was caught in a dilemma, anxious to appease the still powerful steel interests but mindful of the long history of oligopolistic pricing practices of US steel companies. It was saved by an intervention from the Japanese Iron and Steel Exporting Association, which was fearful of the potentially restrictive effects of a bilateral deal. The Japanese exporters proposed Voluntary Export Restraint (VER), and EC producers quickly agreed this was the best arrangement possible in the circumstances. Under VER, exporters were allowed a role in setting their own quotas. The first formal agreement ran from 1969 to 1971, limiting Japanese and EC exports to the US to 5.75 m tonnes annually from each party.

In 1971, prices fell in the EC and Japan whilst those in the USA rose, leading to a further surge in imports. A second round of negotiations began, leading to a new VER agreement for the period 1972–74, which set new limits of 7.3 m tonnes annually from the original EC members plus the UK, and 5.9 m tonnes annually from Japan. It was generally a more stringent set of controls, but was never really put to the test since devaluation of the dollar in 1971 and 1973 caused all import prices to the USA to rise; and high domestic demand in Japan and the EC reduced the potential surplus to be exported elsewhere.

Such profitable market conditions proved to be short-lived and several developments led the way to a second crisis in US steel trade policy. As global over-capacity became increasingly apparent, producers in Japan and the EC turned once again to the US export market. Japanese exports were particularly concentrated on the USA after a deal was concluded limiting Japanese exports to the EC. Just as in 1967, US steel companies and the steel workers' union advocated some form of protection, and, in 1977, US Steel filed an anti-dumping complaint, this time against the Japanese exporters. Along with the EC companies, Japan proposed in turn a new VER agreement; but this proved unpopular in the US in the light of the record of the previous voluntary agreements. The protectionist lobby eventually gained its way, with a new system, the Trigger Price Mechanism (TPM), implemented from March 1978. This induced "voluntary" restraint from exporters by establishing a system of dumping reference prices, sales below which would lead to an investigation by the US government, with the threat of sanctions to follow. It was a policy more powerful than the old system, yet still within US anti-trust legislation.

The TPM was introduced into an increasingly difficult market environment, and proved gradually to be inadequate to the task set for it. In 1980, US Steel filed an anti-dumping complaint against several EC producers; since this breached the terms of the agreement between US steel companies and the US government, the latter immediately suspended the TPM. It was temporarily reinstated later that year when US Steel withdrew the suit, but proved increasingly unpopular throughout 1981. The system was finally killed off by a major export surge from the EC. In 1982, as US steel output slumped to below one-half of capacity, fresh anti-dumping suits were filed and the TPM suspended indefinitely. A major political row ensued between the US and the EC, which was resolved only towards the end of that year.

Under this new agreement, the EC agreed to limit exports to the USA in ten specific product categories, in exchange for a withdrawal of 45 charges of dumping levied by eight US steel companies. It was initially intended to run until December 1985. Almost immediately, though, the EC announced new limits on imports into the Community, further continuing the protectionist cycle. US companies argued that the EC's fresh move would divert other countries' exports to America; they therefore pressed for additional import controls with countries such as Japan, Taiwan, Brazil and South Korea. In the wake of huge steel company losses, a massive protectionist lobby developed, culminating in the announcement of new measures in 1984. These included a limit on imports from all sources set at 18.5 per cent of the domestic steel product market, with a further allowance of 1.7 m tonnes of semi-finished steel annually. This was to be achieved through five-year agreements on a product and country basis. Most significantly, with the installation of a new licensing system to monitor imports, the process of restraint could no longer be labelled "voluntary". The barrier was further strengthened the following year when new products, especially special steel grades, were added to the list of those facing restraint.

The cycle of protectionism had therefore taken another turn, with a fresh import surge generating government trade restriction, retaliatory measures and export displacement, and leading to further, more stringent controls. As the five-year programme drew near to a close, considerable pressure developed within the USA for a further extension of import controls on the 29 countries affected by bilateral agreements. In 1989, the government unveiled its proposed Steel Trade Liberalization Programme; a two-and-a-half year renewal at roughly the same level of quotas with a gradual increase of around 1 per cent annually, dependent upon agreement to curb unfair practices in steel trade. This was an attempt to appease the steel lobby whilst laying down the preconditions for a gradual relaxation of trade barriers. The EC and Japan protested against any continuation of trade controls, whilst the American steel companies argued for an extension of five further years. After lengthy bargaining sessions, the EC concluded an important agreement leaving it with a practically unchanged share of the US market in return for a gradual phasing-out of its controls on imports from other countries. Other major exporters to the US—Japan, South Korea, Brazil, Mexico—signed similar "bilateral consensus agreements", tying quotas to the elimination of government aid to steel producers and the removal of trade barriers.

The significance of the EC-US deals was far-reaching, not just for other steel trade agreements but also in stimulating and fostering cooperation between US steel companies and the steel unions. Equally, the growing importance of NIC exports to the USA epitomized the changing geographical balance of the global steel industry and the increasing interconnectedness of the world economy—for many NIC producers were forced to export in a bid to earn foreign currency as one consequence of their growing indebtedness to the developed countries. Only by the late 1980s was there any sign of respite for the steel producers in the advanced economies—one reason why the US government's proposals on steel trade liberalization were accepted, at least in principle. Even then it was clear that, exposed to cyclical swings in the construction and engineering industries, the good times could not last for ever. Once installed, trade barriers proved highly durable, posing further questions over the future of the industry in countries dependent upon exports and casting a shadow in those where steel producers anxiously awaited a fresh downturn in demand. These worries were clearly apparent in the UK, where the newly privatized British Steel Corporation had just emerged from a traumatic period of closures and redundancies.

## 2.3 Privatization in the UK steel industry: preconditions and implications

The state-owned steel producer in the UK—British Steel Corporation (BSC)—was the object of major planned growth in the mid-1970s based on forecasts which proved to be extremely short-lived in their usefulness. As closures, rather than growth, became the order of the day, a wholesale restructuring of the industry was initiated based upon creating the opportunity for private capital to invest profitably in steel production in the UK. This strategy entailed the partial privatization of steel production and fabrication alongside sweeping changes in areas such as industrial relations and work organization, culminating in the eventual return of the remaining bulk steel operations of BSC to the private sector in 1988. This section examines these processes of change in the UK steel industry and considers some of their implications.

The 1970s expansion programme was expected to cost around £3,000 m and was concentrated on the five "heritage sites" of Llanwern and Port Talbot in South Wales, Scunthorpe and South Teesside in England, and Ravenscraig in Scotland, in an attempt to mimic the Japanese model of large coastal complexes (HMSO 1973). Under this "Ten Year Development Strategy", annual capacity was expected to increase from 27 m tonnes to 33–35 m tonnes by the late 1970s and to 36–38 m tonnes by the early 1980s. One-third of the investment was to be allocated to South Teesside creating a giant, modern coastal works with an annual capacity of some 12 m tonnes. These supremely optimistic forecasts were soon overtaken by events (see Bryer *et al.* 1982).

As recession deepened, BSC's steel production dropped and profits were replaced by larger and larger losses (see Table 2.5). A

TABLE 2.5
*British Steel: key statistics, 1967–90*

|  | Profit (loss) £m | Crude steel output m tonnes | Capital expenditure £m (net of grants) | Employment at year end 1000s |
|---|---|---|---|---|
| 67–68 | (22) | 22.9 | ND | 254 |
| 68–69 | (23) | 24.2 | ND | 254 |
| 69–70[1] | 12 | 12.3 | ND | 255 |
| 70–71 | (10) | 24.7 | ND | 252 |
| 71–72 | (68) | 20.4 | ND | 230 |
| 72–73 | 3 | 24.2 | 154 | 227 |
| 73–74 | 34 | 23.0 | 155 | 220 |
| 74–75 | 70 | 20.8 | 273 | 228 |
| 75–76 | (268) | 17.2 | 462 | 210 |
| 76–77 | (117) | 19.7 | 494 | 208 |
| 77–78 | (513) | 17.4 | 401 | 197 |
| 78–79 | (357) | 17.3 | 267 | 186 |
| 79–80[2] | (1,784) | 14.1 | 261 | 166 |
| 80–81 | (1,020) | 11.9 | 148 | 121 |
| 81–82 | (504) | 14.1 | 164 | 104 |
| 82–83 | (869) | 11.7 | 122 | 81 |
| 83–84 | (256) | 13.4 | 164 | 71 |
| 84–85 | (383) | 13.0 | 210 | 65 |
| 85–86 | 38 | 14.0 | 220 | 54 |
| 86–87 | 178 | 11.7 | 269 | 52 |
| 87–88 | 410 | 14.7 | 253 | 52 |
| 88–89[3] | 461 | 15.4 | 307 | 52 |
| 89–90 | 399 | 14.4 | 450 | 51 |

[1] Six-month trading period from October 1969 to March 1970.
[2] Figures affected by strike action, January–March 1980.
[3] The company was privatized in the course of the year.
Source: British Steel *Annual Reports* 1967–90.

drive to cut public expenditure which had been initiated by International Monetary Fund pressure in 1976 intensified, and BSC's policy of expansion switched to one of savage retrenchment. Formally announced in 1978 (HMSO 1978), the new strategy had in fact begun in 1976. From 1979 onwards a concerted assault was made on reducing capacity, which was cut from 21 m tonnes to 14 m tonnes by 1982. Employment fell even more dramatically, from 186,000 to 104,000. Some of the closures, especially at Consett and at Corby, were fiercely contested (see, for instance, Hudson and Sadler 1983; Maunders 1987). By 1982, even the future of the previously apparently secure integrated heritage sites seemed to be uncertain. Concern, especially at Ravenscraig, was only partially alleviated by successive three-year guarantees that steel making would continue at all five sites, given in 1982 and again in 1985.

Cut-backs at BSC in the 1980s were accompanied by government encouragement to private sector steel production.[5] Steel was targeted very early on by the Conservative administration as a candidate for privatization, partly because it had a relatively weak tradition of trade unionism, which was taken on and defeated in a three-month strike at BSC in 1980. The Iron and Steel Act of the following year allowed for the sale of assets to or joint ventures with private capital by BSC, and exempted the company from its previous statutory obligation to provide a full range of steel products—creating a clear opening for private capital (see Morgan 1983). Joint ventures were formed between public and private sector, codenamed "Phoenix", to designate an industry rising from the ashes.

Seven major Phoenix companies were created from 1981 to 1986 (see Table 2.6; Hudson and Sadler 1987a, 1987b). These

TABLE 2.6
*The "Phoenix" companies*

| Company | Date of formation | Initial shareholdings |
|---|---|---|
| Allied Steel and Wire | 1981 | 50% BSC, 50% GKN |
| Sheffield Forgemasters | 1982 | 50% BSC, 50% Johnson Firth Brown |
| British Bright Bar | 1983 | 40% BSC, 40% GKN, 20% Brynmill |
| Seamless Tubes | 1984 | 75% BSC, 25% TI |
| Cold Drawn Tubes | 1984 | 75% TI, 25% BSC |
| United Merchant Bar | 1984 | 75% Caparo, 25% BSC |
| United Engineering Steels | 1986 | 50% BSC, 50% GKN |

Source: NEDO 1986b.

were significant in a number of ways. They were formed with government support. Sheffield Forgemasters represented no saving to the public purse and Allied Steel and Wire cost more to establish than if the existing BSC businesses had been maintained (Public Accounts Committee 1985). They were active in introducing new patterns of industrial relations into the steel industry. Sheffield Forgemasters imposed new collective bargaining arrangements in 1985 which were bitterly contested during a sixteen-week dispute. United Merchant Bar was the first company in which BSC had a stake to introduce a single-union, no-strike agreement. But the most significant effect of reorganization into Phoenix companies was the closure of existing works. This was most apparent in the largest venture, Phoenix II.

Negotiations between BSC and GKN over Phoenix II, later called United Engineering Steels, commenced in 1980 but were not completed until 1986. Throughout this period, other private sector producers closed capacity, effectively clearing the stage for the new joint venture. Main markets for engineering steels, especially vehicle components and drop forgings, were in a state of severe decline. In 1981, Duport closed its works at Llanelli after heavy losses. In 1982, Round Oak Steel Works (formerly jointly owned by TI and BSC) was closed. In 1984, Hadfields of Sheffield closed with the loss of 800 jobs as the company's parent, Lonrho, was bought by BSC and GKN. FH Lloyd also shut its Dudley steel works, leaving only BSC and GKN in the engineering steels sector.

In that year, BSC and GKN finally presented draft proposals to the government. UK engineering steels capacity, at around 2.6 m tonnes a year, exceeded demand by 45 per cent. The plan embraced GKN's Brymbo works in north Wales, and four BSC plants in the South Yorkshire area. Approval was delayed, however, pending appraisal of the rationalization costs expected to be met by government. Then, in 1985, BSC closed its Tinsley Park works in Sheffield, and the newly formed United Engineering Steels began trading in April 1986, grouping three ex-BSC works in South Yorkshire, GKN's Brymbo plant and a range of GKN's smaller forging companies.

The Phoenix ventures—especially the largest, United Engineering Steels—were significant as a means of re-introducing private capital into the steel industry. By 1987, this had been accomplished. BSC was confined to the production of bulk steel and a range of increasingly profitable activities had been spun-off to the private sector. At the same time, BSC made its first profits for a decade (£38 m in 1986, £178 m in 1987 and £410 m in

1988). The process of reorganization in the sector, along with contraction at BSC, resulted, by the late 1980s, in a greatly slimmed down corporation with a workforce of just over 50,000 (less than one-third its level at the start of the decade) producing roughly as much steel.

Inside this smaller business, a number of vital changes to do with labour relations had been wrought. In the 1970s, BSC had been amongst the pioneers in the adoption of worker-directors as an attempt to incorporate labour participation in the running of industry (see Brannen *et al.* 1976; Jones 1979). This pattern was thrown into reverse after 1979, most especially during Ian MacGregor's chairmanship and in the course of the three-month national strike in 1980. Targeted, isolated and defeated, the steel unions, accommodative at the best of times, were in no position to resist dramatic changes, especially given the continuing threat of further closures. From 1981 to 1985, there was no national pay rise at BSC. Instead, pay increases were totally dependent upon locally agreed bonuses at works level in return for increased productivity, job losses and, from 1985, works-level profit. At the same time, substantial numerical and functional flexibility was introduced among the workforce with the greatly increased use of multi-skilling, short-term contracts, and subcontractors (see, for instance, Fevre 1987). Through this process, managerial control was dramatically re-asserted.

BSC had become a highly profitable concern. On one estimate, the UK steel industry (in which BSC was dominant) had the lowest pre-tax costs per tonne of steel produced of any steel industry in the world in 1987, just beating renowned low-cost producers such as South Korea (see Table 2.7). Although two-thirds of its sales were concentrated in the UK market, it had invested heavily, spending £1,165 m on new plant and equipment from 1983 to 1988. And in 1988, after a capital reconstruction which wrote off £642 m of accumulated losses, the company was returned to the private sector. A share issue valuing the company at £2,500 m was three times oversubscribed: 42 per cent of the stock went to the UK public, 33 per cent to UK industry and 25 per cent to overseas investors, including a 7 per cent Japanese holding.

One pressing question for the newly privatized company concerned its future plant configuration. The distribution of actual and planned capital expenditure provided a significant pointer to the shape of the company and, especially, the future of Ravenscraig. Since 1982 BSC had been trying to close this works, and was only prevented from doing so by government intervention on several occasions. In that period, there was marginal

TABLE 2.7
*World steel production costs, 1987*

| US$/tonne | Operating costs | Financial costs (depreciation, interest) | Pre-tax total |
|---|---|---|---|
| UK | 390 | 25 | 415 |
| South Korea | 319 | 100 | 419 |
| USA | 430 | 40 | 470 |
| West Germany | 468 | 45 | 513 |
| France | 445 | 70 | 515 |
| Japan | 460 | 95 | 555 |

Source: Paine Webber, quoted in *Financial Times* 9 November 1988.

investment at Ravenscraig: £15 m in major projects against an actual and planned investment of £288 m at Port Talbot, £193 m at Teesside, £118 m at Llanwern and £60 m at Scunthorpe (Table 2.8). Ravenscraig was regarded by British Steel as surplus capacity (see Table 2.9), producing hot rolled coil and strip (the product in greatest over-supply within both the European

TABLE 2.8
*Major capital investment projects at individual British Steel works, 1983–89*

| Works | Facilities | Cost £m | Total £m |
|---|---|---|---|
| Port Talbot | Hot strip mill modernization | 171 | |
| | Hot strip mill reheat furnace | 16 | |
| | Blast furnace re-line | 31 | |
| | Second continuous casting plant | 70 | 288 |
| Teesside | Coke ovens rebuild | 44 | |
| | Beam mill reheat furnace | 17 | |
| | Blast furnace rebuild | 50 | |
| | Ladle arc furnace | 13 | |
| | Beam mill modernization | 69 | 193 |
| Llanwern | Continuous casting plant | 47 | |
| | Vacuum degassing facility | 12 | |
| | Hot dip galvanizing line | 59 | 118 |
| Shotton | Hot dip galvanizing line | 30 | |
| | Electro-galvanizing line | 32 | 62 |
| Scunthorpe | Sinter plant | 45 | |
| | Ladle arc furnace | 15 | 60 |
| Trostre | Continuous annealing line | 48 | 48 |
| Ravenscraig | Blast furnace coal injection plant | 15 | 15 |

Source: Compiled from British Steel Prospectus 1988.

TABLE 2.9
*British Steel works capacity and output, 1987*

| Works | Crude steel production capacity[1] (m tonnes) | Output of crude steel (m tonnes) |
|---|---|---|
| Llanwern | 3.3 | 2.1 |
| Port Talbot | 3.0 | 2.2 |
| Ravenscraig | 2.9 | 1.9 |
| Scunthorpe | 3.6 | 3.6 |
| Teesside | 3.7 | 3.2 |
| | 16.5 | 13.0 |

[1] Theoretical maximum production assuming full manning; in practice manned to a lower level as required by sales.
Source: British Steel Prospectus 1988.

Community and the UK) in competition with similar mills at Port Talbot, Llanwern and Teesside.

When the privatization of BSC was first announced, Chairman Sir Bob Scholey gave a guarantee that "subject to market conditions . . . there will continue to be a commercial requirement for steelmaking and continuous casting at the Corporation's five integrated plants for at least the next seven years" (i.e. to 1994). He went on though to add that there was "surplus hot strip mill capacity" so that all present mills, "including the Ravenscraig mill", could be guaranteed to operate only until 1989. Whilst the seven-year guarantee was hedged with conditions, the threat to the strip mill at Ravenscraig was clearly apparent, especially when allied to further comments from Scholey that privatization would bring the "freedom to deal with problems" including options which were "not always politically acceptable" (quoted in *Financial Times* 4 December 1987).

Such indications were bound to provoke reaction from Scotland, and in January 1988 (before privatization) this crystallized in a novel proposal from Motherwell District Council, in whose area the Ravenscraig works was located. It suggested that rather than dispose of BSC wholesale (as had been widely foreshadowed), the company should be split into constituent parts. One of these would incorporate Ravenscraig with the coated strip and sheet mill at Shotton in North Wales, to which much of its output was delivered and in which BSC had invested heavily. This attempt to forge a new future for the Ravenscraig works by allying it in a new company structure with one of BSC's more profitable end-product activities prompted a fierce response, not just from the South Wales sites at Port Talbot and Llanwern (which also supplied Shotton) but also from workers at Shotton, who had no wish to be drawn into what they saw as Ravenscraig's problems. Chairman of the joint union committee at Shotton, Vernon Kindlin, sent an uncompromising message to Ravenscraig: "Back off and leave Wales alone. Stand on your own feet—we won't be part of your fight" (quoted in *Western Mail* 9 January 1988). Such sentiments were by no means new to BSC: in 1984, Llanwern union leaders had submitted evidence to a House of Commons committee comparing "their" profits to Ravenscraig's losses, and claiming greater customer satisfaction for the quality of "their" product (see Trade and Industry Committee 1984). They reflected above all else the weakness of the main steel workers' union, the Iron and Steel Trades Confederation, and the largely parochial character of steel works trade unionism; and they were a revealing insight into the impacts of and conditions for cutbacks and privatization (see also Sadler 1990a).

Elsewhere in the private sector, reorganization continued, as some at least of the Phoenix ventures became increasingly profitable. Allied Steel and Wire had made a loss of £13.9 m in its first eighteen months trading to 1982, but steadily improved the performance from its works at Cardiff and Scunthorpe to produce a profit of £34.2 m in 1988 (see Table 2.10). In that year, it became a publicly quoted company (slightly ahead of BSC). United Engineering Steels, the UK's second biggest steel producer (behind British Steel) also saw steadily rising profits, reaching £45.7 m in 1988 (see Table 2.11). It took over the activities of

TABLE 2.10
*Allied Steel and Wire, 1981–89*

|  | Operating profit (loss) £m | Employment average (1000s) |
|---|---|---|
| 1981–82[1] | (13.9) | 4.6 |
| 1983 | 1.2 | 4.2 |
| 1984 | 5.9 | 3.9 |
| 1985 | 15.2 | 3.3 |
| 1986 | 19.9 | 3.2 |
| 1987 | 24.2 | 3.1 |
| 1988 | 34.2 | 3.1 |
| 1989 | 42.0 | 3.1 |

[1] First eighteen months' trading.
Source: Allied Steel and Wire.

TABLE 2.11
*United Engineering Steels, 1986–88*

|  | *Operating profit £m* | *Employment at year end 1000s* | *Crude steel output (m tonnes)* |
|---|---|---|---|
| 1986[1] | 10.0 |  |  |
| 1987 | 29.6 | 9.8 | 2.1 |
| 1988 | 45.7 | 11.0 | 2.3 |

[1] First nine months trading.
Source: United Engineering Steels.

another of the Phoenix schemes, British Bright Bar, and planned capital investment amounting to £200 m in the period to 1992.

In the newly created Phoenix ventures, then, and in the privatized BSC, increased profitability was the main feature of the late 1980s as the restructured industry responded to strong demand conditions within the UK and from selected export markets. The sector was scarcely recognizable from that of the late 1970s and early 1980s, dramatically changed by a fierce wave of wholesale closures and writing-off of fixed capital. The apparent weakness of the main steel workers' union, the ISTC, was freshly epitomized in 1990 when it agreed to end national wage bargaining with British Steel, and to negotiate instead over wages and conditions in each of the four operating divisions. Yet the sheer dominance of steel in many towns and communities, and the lack of alternative employment, meant that in the early 1980s especially, there was bitter social and political conflict over the future of the industry. This was only resolved by heavily state-subsidized early-retirement packages and extensive state intervention in the form of promises for (and incentives to the creation of) new forms of employment (whether these were, or even could be, fulfilled is discussed in Chapter 5), a further measure of the impact of state policies in the UK steel industry.

At the start of the 1990s, it was apparent that even these sweeping changes were insufficient to restore long-term profitability, and that the upturn of the late 1980s rested heavily on favourable short-term market conditions. In separate, but closely-timed, moves further closures were announced which brought back echoes of the early to mid-1980s round of restructuring. UES planned to close its Brymbo works in north Wales with the loss of 1,100 jobs, in response to a downturn in motor vehicle sales from the peak levels of the late 1980s. British Steel intended to

FIG 2.1. Location of major British Steel production sites in the UK, 1990.

close the Ravenscraig strip mill in 1991 with the loss of 770 jobs, throwing even more uncertainty over the future of the remainder of the plant. Its main function would be to supply steel slabs to the South Wales rolling mills, but only until new capacity came onstream there in 1993. Clearly, cutbacks in UK steel making were far from complete.

Many of the changes described above were similar to those experienced in the UK coal-mining industry. The parallels were both striking and real: national industrial disputes (in 1980 and 1985/85) which were (arguably) provoked, and in any case definitely acted severely to weaken effective trades union representation; wholesale closures and job loss; and changes to working practices. These took place in the context of a political commitment to encouraging private capital to re-invest in coal and steel, either in more profitable peripheral activities (opencast coal, special steels) or wholesale (the privatization of British Steel matching neatly with promises to privatize British Coal once electricity was sold off). In the process, of course, any sense of rationally planning for these sectors for the longer-term was cast aside. This was nowhere more evident than in the encouragement of imports and the breaking of ties between UK coal and steel producers. It is to the nature of these linkages between sectors that we turn in the following section.

## 2.4 Steel in the production chain: raw material supply

This section focuses on four key raw materials supplied to the iron and steel industry: iron ore, coking coal, scrap and alloy metals. Each experienced a number of changes after 1974 as the pattern of global steel production altered and the UK's role increasingly dwindled.

The iron ore industry was characterized by a high degree of control from the steel companies, either directly through ownership linkages, or indirectly through purchasing power. Prices were negotiated annually between the major mines and the largest steel companies. Since the USA and the USSR had adequate indigenous reserves, the major buyers were Japanese and Western European steel producers; the major sources of supply were Brazil and Australia. In the early 1980s, growing over-supply led to a dramatic price fall, reaching 20 per cent over 1983–84. By 1987, exceptionally sensitive negotiations led to five leading iron ore companies—CVRD and MBR from Brazil, BHP Iron Ore and Hamersley Iron of Australia and Sweden's LKAB—warning the Japanese steel producers not to press their claim for a 10 per cent price cut. If implemented, it would, they argued, lead to a "fundamental destabilisation of the world iron ore industry" (quoted in *Financial Times* 19 February 1987). The urgency of their response, and the final terms of settlement—a 5 per cent cut—demonstrated both the growing fragility of the iron ore supply industry and the continuing supremacy of purchaser over raw material producer in an over-supplied market. Only later in the decade did iron ore producers secure some increase in price, as demand from the steel companies recovered sufficiently to affect all the available alternative sources of supply.

The collapse of the steel industry in the advanced economies was mirrored by a decline in the traditional iron ore exporters, especially France and Sweden (see Bradbury 1982; also Table 2.12). The output of the Swedish state-owned company LKAB halved from 27 m tonnes in 1979 to 13 m tonnes in 1982

TABLE 2.12
*World iron ore exports by country, 1974–87*

| (*m tonnes*) | 1974 | 1979 | 1987 |
|---|---|---|---|
| Brazil | 59 | 76 | 97 |
| Australia | 84 | 78 | 81 |
| USSR | 43 | 45 | 45 |
| Canada | 38 | 49 | 30 |
| India | 22 | 24 | 29 |
| Sweden | 33 | 26 | 17 |
| Liberia | 26 | 19 | 14 |
| Venezuela | 26 | 13 | 12 |
| Mauritania | 12 | 9 | 9 |
| South Africa | 3 | 14 | 9 |
| Chile | 9 | 7 | 5 |
| France | 20 | 10 | 4 |
| Peru | 10 | 5 | 4 |
| Total | 407 | 396 | 367 |

Source: International Iron and Steel Institute.

as a consequence of the collapse of the European Community steel industry. The Canadian industry, too, suffered, despite the negotiation of a number of long-term contracts in the early 1970s. In 1975, for instance, British Steel Corporation had joined with Sidbec, the Government-owned steel company, to develop a new iron ore mine, Sidbec-Normines, at Fire Lake. The intention was to secure access to this key raw material at a time of potential shortage. Yet the mine began production in 1979 when world demand, and prices, had slumped. Under the terms of the deal, BSC was obliged to take some of its output at fixed prices well above the newly prevailing world market levels. The 2.5 m tonnes supplied annually from Fire Lake cost BSC an extra £20 m each year. In 1984, therefore, it renegotiated the agreement and, at a cost of £103 m, closed the mine completely. Not only had it been an expensive miscalculation; it also graphically demonstrated the changing balance between supply and demand in the iron ore industry.

From the point of view of the iron ore producers, this imbalance was exacerbated by the expansion of Brazil to rival Australia as an exporter. By 1987, the two countries accounted for just under one-half of all exports. Both were heavily dependent on the Japanese steel industry, which took one-third of all iron ore imports (see Table 2.13). The Australian iron ore mining industry

TABLE 2.13
*World iron ore trade, 1987*

| (m tonnes) | To: Western Europe | North America | Japan | Other | Total |
|---|---|---|---|---|---|
| *Exports from* | | | | | |
| Western Europe | 21 | – | 1 | 3 | 25 |
| North America | 18 | 14 | 3 | – | 35 |
| South America | 48 | 7 | 35 | 29 | 119 |
| Africa | 24 | 1 | 6 | – | 31 |
| Oceania | 17 | – | 47 | 19 | 83 |
| Other | 3 | 1 | 20 | 50 | 74 |
| Total | 131 | 23 | 112 | 101 | 367 |

Source: International Iron and Steel Institute.

grew on the strength of demand from Japanese steel companies, formalized by a series of contractual commitments in the 1960s. The availability of alternative sources was also encouraged by Japanese consumers, anxious to prevent over-dependence upon one supplier. In Brazil, the state-owned mining company CVRD developed several major new sites, including Carajas in the Amazon basin, which came into operation in 1986. For an investment of $3,600 m, this had the potential to produce 35 m tonnes annually of high grade, easily mined ore, shipped out via a new 500 km rail link from a new port at Sao Luis which was capable of accommodating ships of up to 280,000 tonnes capacity. With total reserves estimated at 18,000 m tonnes, a potential output equal to one-tenth of total annual world exports and low operating costs, this single site alone was capable of exerting a strong influence on the world price of iron ore.

By the end of the 1980s, a slight upturn in the market outlook for iron ore producers led to a gradual shifting of concern on the part of some of the major consumers. In the European Community in particular, the closure of domestic iron ore mines had led to heightened dependence upon imports, while steel companies had also lessened their involvement in other supply operations given that output exceeded demand for much of the previous decade. Only four sources of supply were contractually tied to the EC via steel company holdings—Liberia, Canada, Brazil and India—and these only accounted for one-quarter of total EC consumption. Yet the Community took in almost two-fifths of world seaborne iron ore imports, leading to some fears of dependence and price rises. These were made more acute because of the long-term nature of new supply contracts. In its *General Objectives Steel 1995*, the Commission of the EC warned:

> The steel industry should be aware of the dangers of such a policy of supply security, for such contracts are generally concluded with undertakings possessing large, rich deposits. However, this leads to increased dependence as the number of such rich deposits is limited. This would result in the market for iron ore becoming something of an oligopoly. (CEC 1990 p. ix/3)

After years of glut, then, the balance between iron ore producer and consumer—at least in the European Community—looked to be shifting (if only slightly) in the former's favour.

The influence of Japanese steel companies in encouraging expansion in coking coal has already been noted (see Chapter 1). In the UK, this over-supply decimated domestic coking coal capacity after 1979 in a fashion which the CEGB and its privatized successors hoped to emulate in steam coal in the 1990s—albeit with far larger volumes at stake. In 1979, BSC was granted freedom by the UK government to purchase coking coal on the world market. Despite later protestations that quality was at stake, price was clearly a determining factor: BSC initially proclaimed that it was losing £135 m a year in purchasing UK coking coal, as justification for its intention to import 25 per cent of its supplies. In 1980/81, BSC imported 2.7 m tonnes of its 7.3 m tonnes requirements (see Table 2.14). In this new situation, BSC

TABLE 2.14
*British Steel's purchases of coking coal, 1980–89*

| (m tonnes) | British Coal | Overseas | Total[1] |
|---|---|---|---|
| 1980/81 | 4.6 | 2.7 | 7.3 |
| 1981/82 | 5.5 | 3.1 | 8.6 |
| 1982/83 | 3.8 | 2.0 | 5.8 |
| 1983/84 | 4.2 | 2.6 | 6.8 |
| 1984/85 | 0.3 | 6.8 | 7.1 |
| 1985/86 | 2.8 | 5.9 | 8.7 |
| 1986/87 | 2.6 | | |
| 1987/88 | 2.7 | | |
| 1988/89 | 2.4 | | |

[1] In addition, BSC purchased 3.8 m tonnes of coke from 1981 to 1986, as the Redcar coke ovens were rebuilt. Of this, 2.2 m tonnes was imported and 1.6 m tonnes purchased in the UK.

Source: Energy Committee 1986 p. 133; British Coal (1986–89)

and the National Coal Board agreed a deal in 1981 under which BSC prices were determined by direct comparison to the price of equivalent quality overseas coking coal (see Energy Committee 1986 pp. 133–5). This held imports down for several years until the 1984/85 miners' strike forced BSC to look elsewhere for coking coal. In that year, it imported nearly 7 m tonnes, practically all of its requirements. Thereafter, imports accounted for the bulk of British Steel's coking coal purchases.

Modern steel production technologies did not rely just on these raw materials but wholly (in the case of electric arc furnaces) or partly (in the case of basic oxygen converters) on steel scrap inputs. Patterns of trade in the scrap industry arose from a complex balance between production (including scrap arising in the steel production process itself) and consumption. In the UK, the relationship between scrap production and trade demonstrated again the impact of international forces on the economy. During the late 1970s, more than 90 per cent of scrap handled by British merchants was sold inside the country. In 1979, the UK government lifted (but did not abolish) an export quota and licensing system which had governed scrap exports for nearly twenty years. Thereafter, the rise of the scrap merchant as exporter almost exactly paralleled the decline of the UK steel industry and the rise of foreign producers, especially in Spain. Between 1979 and 1982, the amount of Spanish steel produced in electric arc furnaces rose by 20 per cent. The producers needed more scrap, but the two traditional European exporters, West Germany and France, were tied to supply contracts with Italian plants. Britain's big four merchants, 600 Group, Bird Group, Coopers (Metals) and Mayer Newman, filled the gap. They spent £10 m equipping deep-water berths at Tilbury, Cardiff and Liverpool with scrap handling equipment and in 1983, UK exports of scrap (at 3.8 m tonnes) exceeded home sales of 2.9 m tonnes for the first time. Over 3 m tonnes of these exports went to Spanish steel producers which increasingly competed with the UK steel industry.

The alloy metals required by the steel industry were in a very different category; available from very few sources, and of great strategic significance. They included chrome, vital for stainless steels; manganese, used in refining bulk steels; and vanadium, incorporated originally in tool steels but also in high strength low alloy steels (see IISI 1983). In 1978–79, South Africa had an 18 per cent share of world manganese output, 26 per cent of chrome production and 35 per cent of vanadium output, giving it a strong global position. Yet as Bush *et al* (1983) argued, the dependence of many Western countries upon South Africa was by no means necessary or complete. It was as much a function of the strategies of multinational mining corporations as of the lack of adequate reserves elsewhere. There was, therefore, a complex web of economic and political power surrounding production of and trade in these minerals.

The key raw material industries, then, displayed a range of trends. In the bulk sectors of iron ore and coking coal, new producers emerged, with the decline of the old mirroring the new patterns of the consuming industry; whilst over-capacity since the mid-1970s served to emphasize the power of the consumer in a buyer's market. In the UK, the steel industry increasingly bought foreign coking coal and sold its scrap overseas, both to the detriment of domestic production. This was perhaps an appropriately poignant epitaph for much of UK industry closed in the 1980s.

## 2.5 Concluding comments

Two recurrent and interrelated themes have dominated this chapter: the shifting international pattern of production in steel, and the wide-ranging impact of state policies towards the industry. Globally, iron and steel experienced a dramatic decade-and-a-half of wholly divergent changes. Decline of almost unprecedented proportions in Western Europe and North America contrasted with modest growth in many NICs and powerful expansion in a select few countries such as Brazil and South Korea; whilst Japanese steel companies, having shot to world prominence in the 1960s, retreated and entered a new phase of diversification out of steel. The reasons for these differing patterns are various. In the advanced economies, steel became increasingly vulnerable to substitution by other products, and growth shifted to less steel-intensive service sector activities. In the NICs, capital intensive industrialization programmes consumed vast quantities of steel, and development of an indigenous iron and steel industry came to be seen as a key symbol of national economic independence—albeit one that came at a substantial and probably contradictory price in terms of foreign indebtedness. Overlaying this global mosaic was one of the deepest recessions in demand ever experienced, for steel—a highly energy intensive sector—suffered particularly badly in the post-1974 slump. This served not only to intensify the crisis in Western Europe and North America, and refocus Japanese producers' strategic horizons, but also to put the brakes on expansion programmes in many NICs (exacerbating their debt crisis still more) and to reinforce the significance of international trade as a means of exporting surplus capacity.

At the same time, national governments increasingly intervened in various ways in the industry, either in an attempt to seek a route out of the crisis or to underpin faltering expansion programmes. Iron and steel production became and to some extent remains a heavily state-supported activity. From 1980 to 1988, the European Community authorised state aid to steel producers amounting to 40,000 m ECU, or around £25,000 m. National government financial subsidy also underpinned growth in practically all NICs, whilst many advanced country producers were wholly or partly state-owned. This was largely in response to the perceived economic and political strategic significance of iron and steel. In Western Europe and the USA, the very scale of capacity cutbacks and closures, especially in the early 1980s, led to reverberating opposition and unrest which encouraged further state intervention in the form of re-industrialization policies and support for early retirement or retraining packages. The apparent inadequacy of such responses in turn became a further focus for dissatisfaction. So great was the extent of over-capacity that within the European Community "manifest crisis" was declared under the terms of the Treaty of Paris for the first time in three decades, giving the EC as an embryonic supra-national state institution considerable powers over production via the setting of quotas. Even these though proved insufficient to order the reorganization of the industry. In terms of trade, too, governments became highly interventionist, as a succession of EC-USA trade agreements (essentially trade barriers) set the tone for a period of highly protectionist trade policies.

By the end of the 1980s, it was apparent that after over a decade of turmoil, a brief upturn in global steel demand and production had developed, although it did not look to have many enduring characteristics—especially in North America and Western Europe. In this environment, steel companies continued to search for new ways of making profits. One increasingly popular strategy involved international mergers, which took place on a large scale for perhaps the first time in the industry's history. In the USA, all the big integrated steel producers except Bethlehem forged alliances with the five leading Japanese steel producers, seeking to exchange access to the US market—in particular to the growing tide of Japanese-owned vehicle assembly operations—for investment in technologically advanced production processes. In the European Community, several steel companies concluded cross-border mergers—for instance, the French company Usinor-Sacilor took over the German company Saarstahl in 1989 followed by the American company Jones and Laughlin in 1990—but national rivalries were proving harder to shed. British Steel became particularly geared towards expansion into other countries. In 1990 it spent £107 m on its first manufacturing venture outside the UK, purchasing Klockner-Werke's sectional steels division based at Troisdorf in West Germany. It intended to supply these mills—which in 1989 made 200,000 tonnes of special sections and 120,000 tonnes of tubes—with semi-finished steel from Scunthorpe and Teesside in the UK. This was followed by an attempt to purchase a stake in the Spanish company Aristrain which specialized in structural sections for the construction industry. Equally, many European steel companies—including British Steel—made great efforts to buy up steel stockholders in bids to strengthen position in domestic markets and ensure access to other outlets. Diversification proved to be increasingly popular too. Many of the West German steel producers were really engineering companies; the Dutch company Hooghovens moved into aluminium; whilst the diverse interests of Japanese "steel" companies ranged from electronics to theme parks.

The UK steel industry was also drastically refashioned in the 1980s. Cutbacks turned British Steel from a company which once produced the biggest loss in UK business history to a rising star on the stock exchange, although it had a continuing need for substantial capital investment and was likely to look to close at least one, possibly two of its five integrated steel plants.[6] In other words, one of the most sweeping programmes of closures ever in the UK was not necessarily complete, a clear indication of the extent of the crisis of the early 1980s. This, in turn, was one product of a half-completed expansion programme followed by the abandonment of any hope or pretence at rationally planning for particular sectors, as the UK economy was thrown open to the short-term logic of international market forces. Problem and solution were intertwined, neatly illustrating the constraints on "national" economic policies in a globally competitive market.

## Notes

1. The main production routes in the industry were either via the blast furnace (which smelted the iron ore to iron using coke and limestone) and the basic oxygen converter, which oxidized impurities in a mix of hot iron and scrap with a blast of oxygen, to produce steel; or the electric arc furnace, which used electricity to re-melt scrap steel. There were different *grades* of steel, dependent on chemical composition: special steels typically

contained more alloys and were of higher value added. There were also different types of steel *product*. Semi-finished steel came in the form of slabs, blooms or billets, often continuously cast. These could be further re-rolled into a range of shapes: long products such as beams, bars and wire which were used (for instance) in construction and engineering, and flat products, such as plate or strip, used in a range of manufactured goods from ships to car bodies and household goods.

2.  For instance, in 1984 GKN announced the successful completion of tests on a glass fibre and epoxy resin composite as an alternative to steel in the production of springs used in commercial vehicles. The new material produced 50 per cent weight savings and GKN embarked on a £6.4 m investment programme to install a plant at Sankey near Telford in the UK, capable of making 500,000 springs a year, for a world market of some 20 m commercial vehicle springs annually. In 1986, GKN also announced that it was to develop and produce plastic composite suspensions for cars, up to 70 per cent lighter than conventional steel systems, to be commercially available within five years.

3.  The European Coal and Steel Community, forerunner to the EC, was founded in 1951 to oversee postwar reconstruction of these basic industries. As national economies boomed during the growth years of the 1950s and 1960s, and demand for steel seemed to be on an inevitably upward path, the ECSC offered concrete support for investment programmes in new production capacity, acting as an intermediary in the procurement of low-interest loans on the global currency market. With the onset of crisis in steel production in the early 1970s, however, the European Community was faced with a new problem. It gradually expanded the scope of its measures, beginning to employ powers available since 1951 which had previously remained unused.

4.  Not all steel was traded in an easily measurable form. Indirect trade in steel—in the shape of manufactured goods—was also of considerable significance. The International Iron and Steel Institute (see IISI 1985) took a sample of fourteen major countries which accounted for over 90 per cent of the Western world's engineering exports by value, and 78 per cent of its steel output by volume. In 1982, these countries produced 261.7 m tonnes of steel, of which 94.9 m tonnes was exported directly and a further 56.6 m tonnes indirectly. The motor vehicle industry played a dominant role in this indirect steel trade, amounting to 23.4 m tonnes, or 41 per cent of the total.

5.  When BSC was created in 1967, it only included the fourteen largest (and least profitable) steel companies. Other, smaller firms producing lower volumes of special steels remained in profitable private ownership. This divide between public and private was a constant source of tension.

6.  One analyst assessed the state of BSC at the end of the 1980s as follows:

    > There is no question that it is now a leading, well-run producer. However, for basically a one-product company, with its operating base in a somewhat fragile domestic economy, British Steel inevitably

confronts a series of difficult short and long term issues. Its plant configuration is unsatisfactory. Through the 1990s, this will almost certainly result in closure of one or more of its integrated sites. Five sites are probably two (possibly three) too many. (*Financial Times* 19 December 1989)

# 3

# Automobile Production

## 3.1 Introduction

It is difficult to over-emphasize the true economic and political significance of the world motor vehicle industry. In the late 1980s, over 30 m cars were produced annually in a sector which employed several million people directly across the globe, and many more indirectly in the production of components and parts. Motor vehicle manufacture had an enormous impact on many individual economies in terms of output and employment, especially through its linkages to other sectors, typically accounting for around 5 per cent of Gross National Product (GNP) and 5–10 per cent of all manufacturing employment in developed countries, and a growing proportion in some developing countries. It was also overwhelmingly dominated by a handful of giant multinational companies; the top five corporations controlled over 50 per cent of all output, and the top ten over 75 per cent of world production. These companies were vast players on the international stage. Of the world's thirty largest industrial groups in terms of sales in 1986, no less than nine were motor vehicle manufacturers. Their income was such as to place them on a par with many major national economies. The largest, General Motors (also the world's biggest industrial group) had a sales revenue equal to the combined GNP of Greece and Taiwan; Ford's sales were equal to the GNP of Austria; and those of Toyota equal to the GNP of Greece (see Pemberton 1988 pp. 9–10).

Production was orchestrated globally by these multinationals, for the very nature of the assembly process enabled sourcing from a variety of different locations. National governments sought long and hard to reap some of the benefits, often resorting to protectionist trade policies in an attempt to support domestically established manufacturers, or offering substantial subsidies as inducement for multinationals to locate particular projects in their country. At the same time, these companies strived continuously, by a variety of means at their disposal, to ensure productivity improvements and control over the labour process, often using the practice or the threat of relocation to spur workers on to even greater efforts. In this fashion, the industry graphically demonstrated the tensions of international economic activity: with companies vying against each other for market share, governments competing frantically with each other to attract, foster or guide investment, and workers and their trade unions (where such existed) caught in an uncomfortable position in the middle—often exacerbated by apparent (sometimes real) competition between groups of workers in different places and countries.

This chapter examines these tensions through an analysis of the UK's changing position in this international market. One important definitional point should be clarified at the outset: motor vehicles, strictly speaking, includes not just passenger cars but also commercial vehicles such as trucks and buses. For the purpose of simplicity and convenience, however, most of this chapter is confined to the production of passenger cars. It is organized as follows. In section 3.2, the history of the industry is sketched out, and the main features of production changes, especially in the 1980s, are examined. Different ways of theoretically understanding such changes are also introduced. This is followed in section 3.3 by consideration of the important Western European market, focusing in particular on those key producers with no assembly bases in the UK, demonstrating the diverse strategies of European producers. The position of the UK within an overall global and Western European picture is then examined in section 3.4 through the lens of the strategies of companies actually producing cars in the UK. These vehicles are assembled from a bewildering variety of components and, in many senses, the purchasing and sourcing of these is as important as the actual process of assembly. Section 3.5, therefore, considers the significance of the motor vehicle component industry to changing patterns of production organization. In the final section, 3.6, the main implications are evaluated and some possible future developments in the industry are introduced.

## 3.2 Global challenge: the rise and rise of Japan

In its first century of existence, the motor car as a concept has hardly changed; but the motor car industry has gone through a number of dramatic transformations (see Altshuler *et al.* 1985 pp. 11–47). Each has followed a similar pattern. A creative breakthrough in some aspect of production or product in one country or group of countries led to rapid growth in the domestic market and an export threat to producers in other countries. A consequence was that a new region or country seized the initiative in shaping the world industry. At least three such major transformations could be identified, in which first the USA, then Europe, then Japan took the driving role.

The first passenger cars were made on a custom-built basis in France and Germany at the end of the nineteenth century. Around 1910, American producers began the switch from custom-building to mass production which was to mark the first major transformation of the industry. Ford led the way with the introduction of its standardized car, the Model T, in 1908, and the completion of the assembly line in 1914. Along with the development of the work measurement systems of scientific management, and the refinement of management in large corporations by Alfred Sloan at General Motors (GM) in the early 1920s, such innovations gave the USA a seemingly impregnable world lead. Ford's US production grew from 1,700 in its first year (1903) to 1.9 m twenty years later. By then, the company produced 44 per cent of the world's annual car output from its factories in America; together with GM, it accounted for nearly nine-tenths of world output.

Throughout the 1920s and 1930s, this overwhelming dominance of the world industry continued. But shipping problems, later coupled with increasingly strict trade barriers imposed by national governments (a tariff of 33.3 per cent was levied on all imported cars in the UK, for instance) drove both companies to set up overseas assembly operations. By 1929, Ford had established plant in 21 countries, GM in 16. Major new complexes were established in this era by Ford at Dagenham in the UK and Cologne in Germany in 1931, whilst GM bought out existing companies such as Vauxhall in the UK in 1925 and Opel in Germany in 1929. Internationalization would have proceeded even faster and further had not some European governments kept the American companies out in an attempt to preserve their domestically owned producers: GM was excluded from France, and GM and Ford were both prevented from investing in Italy.

After 1945, a second major transformation began in which the focus of dynamism switched to these European companies. In the early 1950s, they were a disorganized collection of relatively small producers (by world standards). However, as tariff barriers in Europe began to fall with the creation of the European Community and the European Free Trade Association, this diversity became a source of strength. Each manufacturer could sell its specialized products widely within Europe, and adequate market size to achieve economies of scale became a reality. Domestic sales also grew rapidly in the postwar boom, so that the Western European market equalled that of the USA by the early 1970s. Under these favourable circumstances, European companies prospered and developed new models which were exported to the USA, taking up to 10 per cent of the market there. In this phase, the dominance of the American companies was challenged, if not quite assailed by the Europeans.

But it was the third major transformation which had the most wide-ranging repercussions during the 1980s and into the 1990s: the rise of the Japanese companies. From the late 1960s onwards, these made dramatic changes in production organization which yielded much lower cost and higher quality products. Ironically, the motor industry had first been established in Japan by Ford and GM in the 1920s, and even in the early post-1945 years, Ford had a site at Yokohama on which it hoped to re-establish production. The dynamism of the Japanese motor industry, though, owed much to Japanese state support. By 1952, the Japanese government had affirmed its opposition to foreign ownership in the sector and initiated a major programme of low-cost credit to support expansion by its domestic producers. After initially slow progress, this was by any standards remarkably successful.

In the 1950s, there was bitter industrial conflict in the Japanese motor industry, most especially at Nissan but also at Toyota (see Okayama 1987). By 1960, though, a new labour relations model was securely installed based on right-wing company-centred unions. New manufacturing systems incorporating "just-in-time" production and "total quality" began to spread, leading to dramatic reliability and productivity improvements. By the 1970s, Japanese car exports had become a recognizable feature of the industry, but one which caused no great alarm to other companies. Until, that is, the oil price increases of 1973/74 pushed demand in the USA into the smaller car sector in which the Japanese producers specialized. For the first time, a "Japanese challenge" was really evident for all to see. A new round of government intervention followed, as in the 1930s. The UK government, for instance, made a deal with Japan to limit exports "voluntarily" to 11 per cent of the UK market. Other countries imposed much more severe measures, such as France's 3 per cent limit. By 1980, virtually every major car market in the world had some form of external trade restriction.

Faced with these barriers, the Japanese response in the 1980s was relatively simple: to invest in car production overseas. First the USA, then Western Europe saw a wave of Japanese companies investing in new plant. In the process, the productivity imbalance between Japanese and other producers became increasingly evident. It is far from dramatizing the issue to speak of this third transformation as the Japanese challenge. In terms of production and sales alone, Japan had become a major world power—and this (temporarily, at least) ignores the deeper impact of Japanese production systems. From being rank outsiders in 1960, Toyota and Nissan now challenged GM and Ford's dominance in the producers' league (see Table 3.1). From a bare 1 per cent of world output in 1960, Japan produced practically as many cars as the other, longer established areas of the USA and Western Europe—just over one-quarter of the world total (see Table 3.2). Yet despite rapid domestic sales growth to over 3 m annually, the Japanese market was still dwarfed by those of Western Europe and the USA, which each accounted for 11 m to 12 m sales a year (see Table 3.3). Much of Japan's expanded production was sold as exports: up to 4 m in 1980, accounting then for nearly one-quarter of the US market and one-tenth of the West European. This trade imbalance was made even more acute by the very low levels of imports into Japan's heavily protected home

TABLE 3.1
*Major car manufacturers, 1988*

| Company | Country of origin | Car production (m) |
| --- | --- | --- |
| General Motors | USA | 5.7 |
| Ford | USA | 4.2 |
| Toyota | Japan | 3.1 |
| Volkswagen | West Germany | 2.7 |
| Peugeot | France | 2.2 |
| Nissan | Japan | 2.0 |
| Fiat | Italy | 1.8 |
| Renault | France | 1.8 |
| Honda | Japan | 1.5 |
| Chrysler | USA | 1.2 |
| Mazda | Japan | 1.0 |
| Lada | Czechoslovakia | 0.7 |
| Mitsubishi | Japan | 0.6 |
| Daimler-Benz | West Germany | 0.6 |
| Hyundai | South Korea | 0.6 |

Source: Motor Vehicle Manufacturers Association, USA, quoted in *Financial Times* 18 September 1990.

TABLE 3.2
*Regional shares of world car production, 1946–85*

| (%) | 1946 | 1960 | 1970 | 1985 |
|---|---|---|---|---|
| USA | 79 | 51 | 28 | 26 |
| Western Europe | 13 | 40 | 40 | 28 |
| Japan | – | 1 | 18 | 27 |
| Eastern Europe | 3 | 2 | 5 | 8 |
| Others | 4 | 3 | 9 | 11 |
| Total (m cars) | 2.6 | 12.8 | 22.9 | 32.2 |

Source: Pemberton 1988 pp. 11, 12.

TABLE 3.3
*Car sales by major market area, 1960–90*

| (m) | 1960 | 1965 | 1970 | 1975 | 1980 | 1985 | 1990 |
|---|---|---|---|---|---|---|---|
| Western Europe | 3.6 | 6.2 | 8.0 | 8.4 | 10.0 | 10.6 | 12.5 |
| USA | 6.6 | 9.3 | 8.4 | 8.3 | 8.8 | 11.0 | 11.2 |
| Japan | 0.1 | 0.6 | 2.4 | 2.7 | 2.8 | 3.1 | 3.3 |
| Total | 12.0 | 18.5 | 22.0 | 24.7 | 28.2 | 31.3 | 35.2 |

Note: 1990 figures estimated.
Source: Pemberton 1988 p. 5.

market, accounting for just 1–2 per cent of sales. By the end of the decade, the volume of exports from Japan to the USA had declined somewhat as Japanese-owned US-based assembly plants came into production instead; but effectively this only underlined the threat to US producers like Ford and GM in their own home ground (see Figure 3.1). Similar tensions were also evident in Western Europe.

The basis of Japanese dominance, though, is by no means fully apparent from such figures alone. Another aspect rested in the proclaimed success of the management techniques and production systems installed in Japanese industry generally, and in motor vehicles in particular, in the 1960s. A tightly controlled system of industrial organization evolved then which effectively tied numerous dependent companies to the major giants like Toyota and Nissan in a symbiotic relationship. The number of these companies ran into many thousands, and a distinct layering existed among the subcontractors (see Sheard 1983). Within this

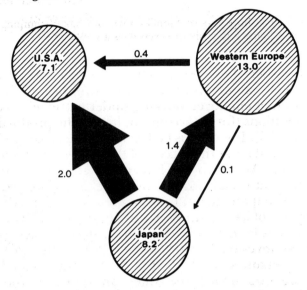

Fɪɢ 3.1.  Major world centres of automobile production and trade
flows, 1988 (n vehicles).

pyramid-shaped structure, the suppliers and parent company
were bound together by the *kanban* system. In Japanese *"kanban"*
literally means "small card": these cards were used to monitor and
ensure tight control over the flow of components, so that the stock
of materials awaiting processing or further manufacture was kept
to the barest minimum and topped up by regular (even hourly)
delivery (see Hall 1982). In itself, this minimum inventory cut
down on the vehicle assemblers' costs. At the same time, the
suppliers were also integrated with product development, so
that much of this work was done by them, externalizing risks
and costs for the assembler and further ensuring dependence.
Many of the major subcontractors were effectively owned by the
vehicle builders. The *kanban* system was also underpinned by a
distinctively Japanese conception of the nature of work, with
relatively secure employment in the major companies (albeit on
terms which left the worker highly dependent on output and
quality, and with trade unionism rigidly controlled) contrasting
strongly with much more insecure and unregulated conditions in
the subcontracting companies. As Hill (1989 p. 466) put it,

> Japan's auto production chain interlinks the most highly automated
> engine and final vehicle assembly plants in the world with crowded

backyard workshops where families turn out small stampings on foot presses ten hours a day, six or seven days a week.

Taken together, Japanese production systems represented a highly efficient way of producing more cars per given worker, at the cost of that employee working under extremely taxing and arduous conditions (for an account of life on the production line, see Kamata 1983). It is on this bedrock that the Japanese "model" was founded, and it was the success of this model which sent senior executives from American and European companies scurrying to Japan to find out exactly how it was done. So impressed was the Ford Motor Company that it re-ordered its calendar. After a visit to Japan by one of its executives in the late 1970s, an "After Japan" programme was launched to compete against the new rivals. As the Japanese invested heavily in the USA in the early 1980s, American companies also looked in turn to transplant Japanese ideas and organization into the American context. In the process, much of the basis of the Japanese system—in particular its rigid control over organized labour—became particularly apparent.

The first wave of Japanese investment in the USA took place in the early 1980s, led by Honda at Marysville, Ohio, closely followed by Nissan at Smyrna, Tennessee, and a joint venture between GM and Toyota at Fremont, California. In a second wave in the mid to late 1980s, Honda and Nissan each moved to expand capacity to around 400,000 cars annually, Toyota opened an additional wholly owned plant at Georgetown, Kentucky, and Honda at East Liberty in Ohio, and the big three were joined by others, including Mazda (25 per cent owned by Ford) at Flat Rock, Michigan; Mitsubishi, in a joint venture with Chrysler in central Illinois; and Subaru with Isuzu in Indiana. Additionally, new plants were built in Ontario, Canada by Honda, Toyota, and Suzuki in partnership with GM. By the end of the decade, Japanese plant (wholly or partially owned) had a capacity in excess of 2 m cars annually, expected to rise rapidly to 2.5 m (see Figure 3.2). Honda had started exporting some of its production to Japan and was planning to export to Western Europe, and others looked to follow this path.

The immediate threat, though, was to American producers in their own domestic market, for much of the Japanese production in the USA was intended to displace sales by Ford and GM, with few signs of any further cutback in exports from Japan to the USA, the reverse flow only a token gesture and the total US market relatively static. American companies moved gradually to counter the problem, closing capacity, laying off workers and

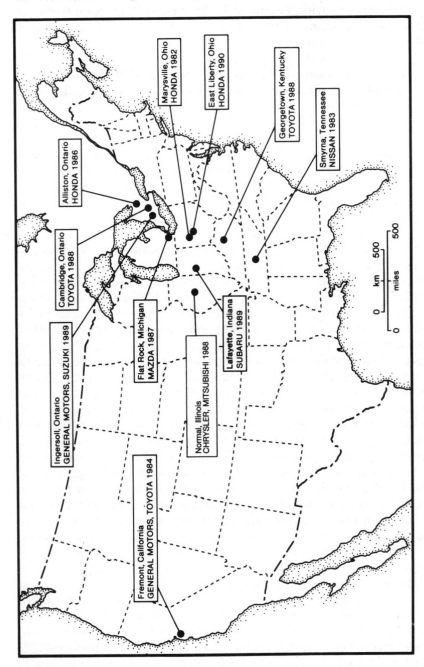

FIG 3.2. Japanese-owned automobile assembly plants in North America.

Marysville, Ohio
HONDA 1982

East Liberty, Ohio
HONDA 1990

Georgetown, Kentucky
TOYOTA 1988

Smyrna, Tennessee
NISSAN 1983

Alliston, Ontario
HONDA 1986

Cambridge, Ontario
TOYOTA 1988

Ingersoll, Ontario
GENERAL MOTORS, SUZUKI 1989

Flat Rock, Michigan
MAZDA 1987

Normal, Illinois
CHRYSLER, MITSUBISHI 1988

Lafayette, Indiana
SUBARU 1989

Fremont, California
GENERAL MOTORS, TOYOTA 1984

km    500    500

0     miles

0

seeking to develop their own new small car ranges. GM undertook its joint venture with Toyota at Fremont partly to learn from the Japanese, and many of these lessons were evident in its "Saturn" project, announced in 1985. This was a clear attempt to counter the Japanese threat by redesigning the production process. The plant, built at Nashville, Tennessee, borrowed three features of the Japanese system. A separate management unit was established with a streamlined structure, totally different to the systems first devised at GM by Alfred Sloan in the 1920s. Advanced technology was incorporated, partially supplied by GM's newly purchased subsidiary, Electronic Data Systems. Labour relations and organization, too, were closely modelled on the Japanese system, although in contrast to the Japanese-owned plants, these changes were introduced with the involvement of the unions (see Clark 1986; Meyer 1986).

GM secured acceptance of these changes by the unions through open threats to relocate production overseas. Ford also considered such moves: in 1984, for instance, it announced plans to invest 500 m $ in a plant in Mexico which would export to the USA, just as it was embarking on capacity cutbacks in the USA. These responses to the Japanese presence were also mirrored in negotiations with the main car workers' union, the Union of Auto Workers (UAW), over pay and conditions. In 1984, GM negotiated a radically different wage contract which borrowed heavily from the Japanese model. The (previously regular) cost-of-living increase was supplanted in importance by a series of bonuses dependent upon company profitability and labour force productivity. In return for limited job guarantees, the UAW negotiators accepted proposals for an extensive re-training programme and greater flexibility (see Katz 1987). GM and the union had begun to forge a more consultative style, sealed with the big prize from the UAW's standpoint: a promise to build the Saturn range in the USA. Ford rapidly followed suit, securing guarantees on new production methods from the UAW in return for an agreement for the union to participate in its new small car project, Alpha.

At GM and Ford, at least the UAW still had negotiating rights. At several of the new Japanese plants, a conscious non-union policy was adopted. Indeed southern locations such as Marysville and Smyrna had deliberately been selected partly for their distance from the traditional heartland of the US car industry around Detroit, and for their relatively acquiescent workforces. Honda and Nissan did not recognize the UAW. At Marysville, in 1986, the UAW was forced to concede defeat in its attempts to ballot workers on whether they even wanted union recognition. In 1989, at Smyrna, the UAW secured the statutory 30 per cent of signatures from the plant's 2,400 hourly paid employees required by US labour law to gain a ballot on union recognition, but then suffered a crushing defeat—only 700 voting in favour of unionization, and more than 1,600 against. Nissan had waged a strident campaign against the UAW and, from its own point of view, the company had clearly screened applicants for employment at Smyrna to good effect.

Whilst the US giants were struggling to come to terms with the threat in volume car sales, the Japanese companies were refining their latest strategic shift into the high-performance luxury car market which had previously been the preserve of companies such as BMW, Jaguar and Saab. The ground was carefully prepared by five years' development work before Honda led the way, launching its Acura luxury car range in the USA in 1987, followed by Nissan with its Infiniti range and the Toyota Lexus range in 1989. One of the reasons for this new shift was a growing awareness of the challenge in the volume car range from several newly industrializing countries.

In South Korea, for example, output soared from just 37,000 in 1975 to 0.1 m in 1980, 0.3 m in 1985 and 0.9 m in 1988. Initial expansion proceeded far from smoothly: in 1980, a major collapse in demand caused by deep domestic recession forced the government to restructure the industry by ordering one of the vehicle companies, Kia, out of car production until 1985. But in the second half of the 1980s, dramatic expansion policies were implemented, with two-thirds to three-quarters of output aimed at the export market. Hyundai (15 per cent owned by Mitsubishi) had an annual capacity of 0.75 m cars at its single plant at Ulsan, and began exporting to the US in 1986. Daewoo's joint venture with GM, and Kia (8 per cent owned by Mazda) followed Hyundai into the US market in 1987, whilst, in 1989, production began at Hyundai's plant opened in Quebec, Canada. In the same year, Ssangyong Motor, the fourth largest car maker, agreed tentative terms on a joint production and development deal with Volvo—a significant step for the motor industry in South Korea, for it was the first real attempt to develop new technology with a foreign company.

These and other new sources of supply, such as Indonesia and Malaysia, added fresh complexity to the global pattern, although the development of new production technologies represented a strong barrier to the growth of an indigenous motor vehicle industry in many newly industralizing countries (see Jones and Womack 1985). In interpreting the overall picture, three main features stand out. The first, and historically most significant, is the ability of giant multinational corporations like GM, Ford, Toyota, Nissan and Volkswagen (to name the biggest five alone) to relocate production and assembly away from their core market areas to take advantage of a range of factors and to open up access to new markets or to penetrate markets blocked by trade barriers (see Table 3.4; also Beynon 1984a, on Ford's global strategy; and Bloomfield 1981, for a review of international changes in the 1970s). One factor in such decisions is undoubtedly labour costs (see Table 3.5). Spain and the UK[1] (recipients of the bulk of inward investment by Japanese and American companies) had by far the lowest labour costs in Western Europe in the 1980s, almost one-half those in West Germany. The Japanese had a major labour cost advantage at the start of the decade but by its close, rapid appreciation of the yen had pushed comparative labour costs up to within a fraction of those in the USA and high-cost European countries. The diminishing labour cost differential was one factor in Japan's relocation of production to the US (although cause and effect were clearly intertwined). As one analyst for the US government put it:

> it may be cheaper to manufacture a car in the US than in Japan. The Japanese companies are dismantling one of the most efficient production machines the world has ever seen and are moving it off-shore. (quoted in *Financial Times* 14 September 1988)

A second significant element in understanding the pattern of production in the global vehicle industry derives from the growing adoption of Japanese production systems (see, for instance, Schoenberger 1987). With an emphasis upon regular deliveries of components, companies like Toyota and Nissan recreated Ford's integrated Rouge complex, but in a wholly different fashion. At Rouge in Detroit, a whole range of components was produced inhouse. Iron ore went in at one end and cars came out at the other. This left Ford heavily dependent on its own labour force, and bitter industrial conflict at Rouge in 1942 was one key factor underpinning the company's subsequent decentralization of component production. All of Toyota's main plants in Japan were located at Toyota City 150 miles west of Tokyo on the outskirts of Nagoya, along with a spatially concentrated cluster of most of its major suppliers (see Hill 1986). But the whole operation depended upon a radically different conception of both production organization and the labour process. For Ford and GM, the emphasis into the 1980s was on de-skilling; for Toyota, the corporation was the community, both literally and figuratively.

TABLE 3.4
*Automobile production, 1988: major countries and manufacturers*

*m cars*

| Japan | 8.2 of which: | Toyota | 3.0 |
|---|---|---|---|
| | | Nissan | 1.7 |
| | | Honda | 1.1 |
| USA | 7.1 | GM | 3.5 |
| | | Ford | 1.8 |
| | | Chrysler | 1.1 |
| | | Honda | 0.4 |
| | | Mazda | 0.2 |
| | | Nissan | 0.1 |
| | | Toyota | 0.1 |
| West Germany | 4.3 | VW-Audi | 1.8 |
| | | GM | 0.9 |
| | | Ford | 0.6 |
| | | Daimler-Benz | 0.6 |
| | | BMW | 0.5 |
| France | 3.2 | Peugeot-Citroen | 1.8 |
| | | Renault | 1.4 |
| Italy | 1.9 | Fiat-Alfa Romeo | 1.9 |
| Spain | 1.5 | VW-Seat | 0.4 |
| | | GM | 0.4 |
| | | Ford | 0.3 |
| | | Renault | 0.3 |
| | | Peugeot-Citroen | 0.2 |
| USSR | 1.3 | | |
| UK | 1.2 | Rover | 0.5 |
| | | Ford | 0.4 |
| | | GM | 0.2 |
| Canada | 1.0 | Ford | 0.5 |
| | | GM | 0.4 |
| | | Chrysler | 0.1 |
| South Korea | 0.9 | Hyundai | 0.6 |
| | | Daewoo | 0.2 |
| | | Kia | 0.1 |
| Brazil | 0.8 | VW | 0.3 |
| | | GM | 0.2 |
| | | Fiat | 0.2 |
| | | Ford | 0.1 |
| Sweden | 0.4 | Volvo | 0.3 |

Source: SMMT.

Toyota-owned dormitories at Toyota City housed up to 20,000 workers, whilst the employment ethic depended on subservience to corporate goals. The immense problems associated with transferring this "community" overseas held Japanese companies back

TABLE 3.5
*Labour costs in the world motor industry, 1980-88*

| DM/hour | | | |
|---|---|---|---|
| | 1980 | 1985 | 1988 |
| West Germany | 26.9 | 34.0 | 38.5 |
| USA | 24.8 | 55.8 | 37.6 |
| Sweden | 28.6 | 36.3 | 36.6 |
| Japan | 14.5 | 27.4 | 33.4 |
| Belgium | 28.1 | 30.9 | 32.1 |
| Netherlands | 23.3 | 28.6 | 30.4 |
| Italy | 17.1 | 25.2 | 27.8 |
| France | 19.7 | 25.1 | 24.9 |
| UK | 15.0 | 21.4 | 22.6 |
| Spain | 12.6 | 20.3 | 22.0 |

Source: West German Motor Industry Association.

from direct investment for a long time. Only restricted access to markets caused by government trade policies forced the new trend; narrowing labour cost differentials reinforced it. Once this move was underway, Japanese companies sought to establish similarly interlinked production complexes in the USA. By the end of the decade some 300 component suppliers had followed the vehicle assemblers there, developing new concentrations of production.

This is not to argue that the two processes—decentralization and reconcentration—were mutually exclusive. A further strand of the emerging picture rested upon an increasingly complex web of interlinkages between global producers, in particular products and specified markets. GM and Toyota operated a joint plant at Fremont in California. In Brazil and Argentina, Ford and VW merged their operations in 1986 to create a new venture, Autolatina. In 1988, Ford and Nissan agreed on the joint development of a new multi-purpose passenger vehicle in the USA. Such operations demonstrated the growing inter-dependence between producers, and yet again the increasing irrelevance of national frontiers. Whilst a degree of reconcentration was taking place, companies were nonetheless seeking to broaden their activities (where profitable) over the globe.

This section, then, has outlined the dimensions of the Japanese challenge and introduced explanations for the current restructuring in the global automobile industry. In a highly competitive environment, the USA and Western Europe looked increasingly like a market battleground, not just because of the arrival of the Japanese and the continuing struggle between Ford and GM, but also because of hard-fought encounters between European producers. The following section goes on to consider in detail the key Western European market, and the strategies adopted by companies based there but not producing cars in the UK to cope with the arrival of the Japanese manufacturers.

## 3.3 The Western European market

The Western European car market saw record sales in 1989 for a fifth successive year, up to 13.5 m units—reflecting one of the longest ever periods of sustained growth (see Table 3.6). VW just beat Fiat to first position, each company selling 2 m cars, amounting to almost 30 per cent of total registrations between them. Behind these came Peugeot, Ford, GM, and Renault. These six companies dominated the Western European market, accounting for 75 per cent of sales against a total Japanese presence of 11 per cent. In the following section, we go on to consider the strategies of the major European, Japanese and American companies with bases in the UK; but here we briefly examine the three major European companies with no assembly facilities in the UK—Volkswagen, Fiat and Renault—and describe the response of one company faced with markedly different constraints, Volvo of Sweden.

TABLE 3.6
*West European new car registrations by manufacturer, 1989*

|  | m units | % share |
|---|---|---|
| VW-Audi-Seat | 2.02 | 15.0 |
| Fiat | 1.99 | 14.8 |
| Peugeot-Citroen | 1.70 | 12.7 |
| Ford | 1.56 | 11.6 |
| GM | 1.49 | 11.0 |
| Renault | 1.39 | 10.4 |
| Mercedes | 0.43 | 3.2 |
| Rover | 0.41 | 3.1 |
| Nissan | 0.39 | 2.9 |
| BMW | 0.38 | 2.8 |
| Toyota | 0.34 | 2.6 |
| Volvo | 0.27 | 2.0 |
| Total | 13.48 | |
| of which Japanese | 1.46 | 10.9 |

Source: *Financial Times* 22 January 1990.

VW, the market leader in Europe, was probably the nearest thing to a truly European multinational motor manufacturer. Based at Wolfsburg, the dominant domestically owned vehicle producer in West Germany sold widely in the European market, and also had production facilities in several other states and continents. As early as 1955, VW purchased a site in the USA for installation of a new car factory, but the company subsequently rapidly changed course and sold off the land it had acquired. In the late 1950s, it invested in car production in Brazil instead, whilst, in the 1960s, it expanded production operations in Mexico (see Dombois 1987) and grew in West Germany, partly through merger, acquiring both Audi and NSU in this way. VW finally established a US production base in the 1970s when, despite opposition from the West German trade unions, it invested in a new plant at Westmoreland, Pennsylvania, which came onstream in 1978 (see Krumme 1981). In 1988, it pulled out of this operation, to concentrate instead on re-organizing the Spanish company Seat, which it had acquired in 1986 (after the collapse of a previous alliance between Fiat and Seat). In 1989, it announced a ten year, £3.3 bn investment programme, including a wholly new factory at Martorell near Barcelona, in an attempt to reap the benefits of lower labour costs in Spain and expand capacity there for the production of small cars. VW's strategy for the 1990s was to offer three differentiated "marques": Seat in the lower range, VW in the middle ranges, and Audi in the upper market.

The second major European company, Fiat, derived much of its strength from dominance of a heavily protected Italian market, where it captured over 60 per cent of all sales. In the early 1970s, Fiat tackled serious labour problems at its Turin plants by relocating production into new bases in southern Italy (see Amin 1985) and Brazil. After a series of dramatic labour disputes in the late 1970s in Italy (see Revelli 1982), it again moved to re-organize production there, introducing technologically sophisticated methods as at the computerized engine plant at Termoli in southern Italy. In 1980, Fiat pulled out of its participation in the Spanish company Seat after almost thirty years, saving it from the need to make further investment, but also reinforcing its dependence upon Italy as a production base. Attempts to diversify further the geographical spread of its operations failed when merger talks with Ford broke down in 1985, but the following year it strengthened the stranglehold on Italian sales when it acquired the up-market Alfa Romeo. Fiat's dominance in Italy was both a strength and a weakness, for its large domestic market was increasingly threatened by European Community anti-protectionist measures. During 1989, therefore, under pressure to install new capacity, the company actively reviewed the possibility of building a new factory at any of three locations—the UK, Spain and Italy.

Whilst Fiat dominated in Italy, Renault (along with Peugeot—see below) depended heavily on the French domestic market. In contrast to Peugeot, Renault was state-owned; but in the 1960s and 1970s both companies followed a similar strategy of decentralizing production away from the increasingly congested Paris region and into the north and east of France (see Oberhauser 1987). At the end of the 1970s, Renault also followed VW's attempt at gaining entry to the US market, acquiring a controlling 46 per cent stake in American Motor Corporation in 1980. During the early part of the following decade though, Renault registered heavy losses, and it was forced to initiate a dramatic restructuring programme from 1984 onwards, entailing a reduction of its workforce of one-quarter in just two years. The stake in AMC (which had made a loss for Renault in every year except 1984) was also sold off to the US company Chrysler in 1987.

In that same year, Renault recorded its first profit since 1981 and, by the end of the 1980s, the company was in an improved financial position. This led it into other difficulties, however, for the European Community, which had granted sizeable state subsidies from the French government only on the condition that capacity and employment were cut so as to make the company viable, argued that insufficient closures had taken place to ensure long-term profitability. Renault responded by announcing the complete closure of its oldest factory, Billancourt in Paris, to be completed by 1992. Despite this, in 1990, the Commission of the European Community demanded that Renault repay to the French government one-half of a previously agreed £1,200 m state aid package.

At the same time, having withdrawn from the US, Renault sought to reorganize within Western Europe. In 1979, it had purchased a small stake in Volvo and signed a potentially far-reaching cooperation deal. This folded in 1985, and the stake was bought back by Volvo, in the light of Renault's poor financial results. In 1990, though, Renault and Volvo re-opened cooperation with a wide-ranging "share swap" and joint development and production agreement. Renault took 25 per cent of Volvo's car subsidiary and 45 per cent of its truck and bus operations, agreeing to purchase 10 per cent of the parent company on the open market. In return, Volvo took 20 per cent of the Renault parent and 45 per cent of its truck and bus subsidiary. The deal created Western Europe's largest production group in commercial vehicles, overtaking Daimler-Benz. In car manufacture, it offered Renault access to Volvo's production systems and technological capability, whilst giving Volvo easier access to the European Community market.

Within Western Europe, Volvo was significant not so much for the volume of cars it produced, as for the way in which they were manufactured (see Berggren 1989). For, in its base of Sweden, Volvo suffered from a particularly acute problem which was highly uncommon in other states with their much higher levels of unemployment—that of recruiting and retaining sufficient skilled employees. As the company's annual report for 1988 explained:

> There continued to be problems in recruiting new employees—qualified craftsmen and certain categories of skilled white collar workers in particular—in the Swedish labour market. Absenteeism among blue-collar workers continued to rise, amounting to 24% in the Swedish sector of the group.

Such long-standing problems posed considerable difficulties for Volvo and were key factors behind its decision to open a new plant at Kalmar in 1974 based not on an assembly line, but on a work team approach, with computer-guided carriers bringing supplies of components to groups of workers involved in a far broader range of tasks than on an assembly line. The intention was that this would improve the quality of the working environment and hence reduce absenteeism. In the latter at least it was successful, one reason why Volvo chose to develop such strategies even further in its new plant at Uddevalla in the late 1980s. There, workers were grouped in relatively autonomous teams of eight to ten, responsible for the complete assembly of the car including quality control and, within company-set monthly production targets, the volume of output from each shift. Such production systems were a clear reflection of the Swedish model of industrial cooperation. Uddevalla also demonstrated the high level of Swedish state support for industry, for the government not only granted Volvo considerable financial subsidies to locate in Uddevalla so as to compensate for a shipyard closure there, but also agreed to complete a motorway link between Uddevalla and Volvo's main production base at Gothenburg (see also Auer 1985; Malmberg 1989).

Whilst Volvo developed new and innovative systems of production specifically tailored to Swedish labour market conditions, other Western European manufacturers evolved a range of strategies to keep up with rapidly shifting market conditions, entailing tactical moves into and out of particular countries and product ranges, and occasional forays into the USA and Latin America. Even before the arrival of the Japanese, the Western European market was intensely competitive. Such pressures also applied to the other group of manufacturers, those which had or were in the process of establishing assembly plants in the UK.

### 3.4 A new role for the UK?

Within the UK, the 1980s represented a dramatic decade for car production. At the depth of recession in 1982, just 0.9 m cars were produced (for a review of prospects at the start of the decade, see Manwaring 1982). By 1989 this figure had rebounded to 1.3 m, the highest level since 1977—although much below the previous (1972) peak of 1.9 m. But with major new investment projects by Nissan, Toyota and Honda amounting to a projected capacity of 500,000 units, it was confidently being predicted that the UK would produce around 2 m cars a year by the mid-1990s. In terms of sales, too, the UK market boomed, growing every year from 1984 to 1989, with total registrations over 50 per cent up on the start of the decade. This section first considers the nature of the UK car industry in aggregate in the 1980s, then identifies precisely how such changes came about through a consideration of the strategies of the major companies.

In terms of *output*, Rover and Ford dominated, with Vauxhall (GM) a close third (see Table 3.7). Other companies making

TABLE 3.7
*UK car production by manufacturer, 1980–88*

| 1000s | 1980 | 1981 | 1982 | 1983 | 1984 | 1985 | 1986 | 1987 | 1988 |
|---|---|---|---|---|---|---|---|---|---|
| Rover | 396 | 413 | 383 | 445 | 383 | 465 | 405 | 472 | 475 |
| Ford | 343 | 342 | 307 | 319 | 274 | 318 | 346 | 387 | 376 |
| GM | 55 | 70 | 113 | 127 | 117 | 153 | 162 | 184 | 176 |
| Peugeot | 125 | 117 | 56 | 121 | 95 | 67 | 58 | 46 | 82 |
| Jaguar | –[1] | –[1] | 22 | 28 | 33 | 38 | 41 | 48 | 52 |
| Nissan | – | – | – | – | – | – | – | 29[2] | 57 |
| Others | 5 | 13 | 7 | 5 | 7 | 7 | 8 | 6 | 9 |
| Total | 924 | 955 | 888 | 1045 | 909 | 1048 | 1020 | 1143 | 1227 |

[1] Included in Rover total.
[2] Not included in the UK total.
Source: SMMT.

substantial numbers of cars in the UK included Peugeot, Jaguar (floated off from British Leyland in 1984) and Nissan. Ford dominated the *sales* market with Rover and GM fighting for second place; GM finally displaced Rover to third place in 1989 (see Figure 3.3). In the early 1980s, GM's share increased from 9 to 17 per cent, mainly on the strength of one new model, the Cavalier. This was largely at the expense of Ford, whose share fell from 31 to 27 per cent. Rover's share also continued on a steady decline from the 40 per cent level of the early 1970s, to 20 per cent at the start of the 1980s and 14 per cent by the end of the decade. Peugeot increased its share in the later 1980s from 4 to 9 per cent on the back of new models such as the 309 and 405 (produced partly in the UK), and more than recovered ground lost earlier in the decade. The three major European companies not established in the UK—VW, Renault, and Fiat—took proportions of between 3 and 6 per cent each, along with Volvo's 3–4 per cent and Nissan's regulated 6 per cent.

These sales patterns depended largely on the success or failure of particular models within their market range (see Tables 3.8 and

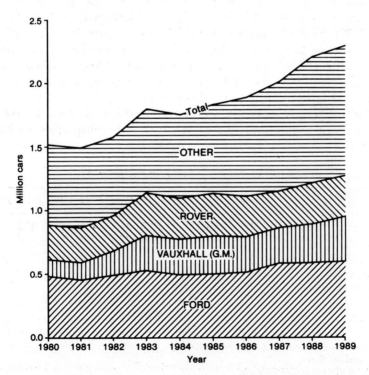

FIG 3.3.   UK car sales by manufacturer, 1980–89. (Source: SMMT.)

TABLE 3.8
UK car market by type, 1988

|  | % of sales |
| --- | --- |
| Mini | 2 |
| Supermini | 26 |
| Lower medium | 33 |
| Medium | 26 |
| Executive/luxury | 10 |
| Sports | 2 |
| Four-wheel drive | 1 |

| "Supermini" includes: | Austin Metro, Ford Fiesta, Vauxhall Nova (also Peugeot 205). |
| --- | --- |
| "Lower medium" includes: | Austin Maestro, Ford Escort, Vauxhall Astra (also VW Golf). |
| "Medium" includes: | Austin Montego, Ford Sierra, Vauxhall Cavalier (also Peugeot 405 and Nissan Bluebird). |

Source: Robertson 1989 p. 61.

3.9). Ford's success was based on its strength *across* these ranges, with the Escort, Sierra and Fiesta gaining the first three places in the ranking of UK car sales by model in every year from 1986 to 1989. The Cavalier's success was evident in its second place, pushing the Sierra into fifth in 1984 and 1985. In the small car class, the Metro shone through as Rover's best-selling model.

One consequence of the sales boom from 1984 onwards was to suck in an ever-increasing volume of imported cars. At the start of the 1970s, imports accounted for only one-quarter of sales. In 1979, imports exceeded UK-produced sales for the first time and, from then until 1986, imports never accounted for less than 56 per cent of UK sales. This reflected both the decline of the domestic producer (Rover), and an increasing reliance upon imports by multinationals like Ford, GM and Peugeot. One consequence was to push the UK's motor trade balance into deficit for the first time in 1982. From then onwards this deficit grew strongly to reach chronic imbalance (see Figure 3.4). By 1988, the £6,000 m deficit amounted to 30 per cent of the total UK visible trade gap. Public criticism focused in particular on Vauxhall. In 1985, government statements urged the company to increase both UK production and sourcing of components. The UK content of its UK-built models was as low as 50 per cent against around 70 per cent for the Ford range and 90 per cent for Rover. By 1988,

TABLE 3.9
*UK top ten car sales by model, 1980–89*

| 1000s | | | |
|---|---|---|---|
| | *1980* | | *1985* |
| Ford Cortina | 190 | Ford Escort | 157 |
| Ford Escort | 122 | Vauxhall Cavalier | 134 |
| Ford Fiesta | 92 | Ford Fiesta | 124 |
| Austin Mini | 61 | Austin Metro | 119 |
| Morris Marina | 60 | Ford Sierra | 102 |
| Vauxhall Chevette | 46 | Vauxhall Astra | 77 |
| Vauxhall Cavalier | 41 | Austin Montego | 74 |
| Austin Allegro | 40 | Ford Orion | 65 |
| Ford Capri | 31 | Vauxhall Nova | 61 |
| Renault 18 | 31 | Austin Maestro | 58 |
| | *1989* | | |
| Ford Escort | 181 | | |
| Ford Sierra | 176 | | |
| Ford Fiesta | 149 | | |
| Vauxhall Cavalier | 131 | | |
| Vauxhall Astra | 115 | | |
| Austin Metro | 99 | | |
| Vauxhall Nova | 71 | | |
| Ford Orion | 69 | | |
| Rover 200 | 68 | | |
| Austin Montego | 58 | | |

Source: SMMT.

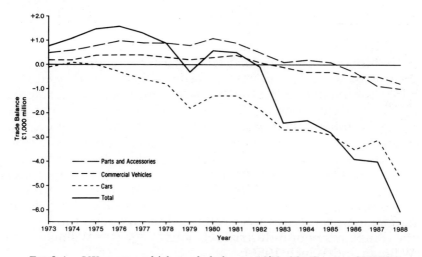

FIG 3.4.   UK motor vehicle trade balance, 1973–88. (Source: SMMT.)

137

Vauxhall had gone some way to relieve this criticism by raising total output within the UK, and Ford emerged as the "culprit" instead with imports rising to 43 per cent of sales against 30 per cent the previous year, one consequence of industrial action at its UK factories. Such figures were but one reminder of the extent to which the UK economy was dependent upon decisions taken elsewhere—not just in the USA, but increasingly (as the UK received the first major European car assembly investments by all three leading Japanese companies) in Japan.

This aggregate picture, of course, conceals the extent of variation in the production strategies of car producers. The remainder of this section therefore focuses on these companies and the ways in which they used the UK as a base for production to varying degrees and differing effect. It considers in detail the experience of the Rover Group and its Japanese partner Honda, Ford, Vauxhall, Peugeot, Nissan, and Toyota.

### 3.4.1 Rover

Rover (until 1986, British Leyland), the biggest producer of cars in the UK and the only major UK-owned manufacturer, had a troubled history. Its predecessor, the British Leyland Motor Corporation, was formed by merger in 1968, and stumbled through difficult times until it was nationalized in 1975. Under new chairman Don Ryder, a massive state-supported programme of capital investment was proposed to replace an out-dated model range and antiquated production methods (see HMSO 1975). Within two years, though, this new corporate strategy was faltering as the company's share of the UK market fell from 32 to 24 per cent—all the more acute when compared with a 40 per cent share at the start of the 1970s.

In this crisis situation, Michael Edwardes was appointed as new chairman. He sought to trim capacity in line with reduced sales, whilst continuing the product replacement programme. Potential output was cut from 1.2 m units in 1977 down to 0.75 m, with many peripheral sites closed altogether in the UK along with the company's only major overseas base in Belgium. Production was concentrated instead at Longbridge in Birmingham and Cowley in Oxford. In his five-year term of office, employment fell from 172,000 to 84,000. Efforts were made to introduce new working practices alongside new technologies, and collective bargaining procedures were reformed in an attempt to improve the company's poor industrial relations image (see Willman 1984; Willman and Winch 1985).

Edwardes was succeeded as chairman in 1982 by Austin Bide. Under his guidance, the new model programme was completed. The Metro (which had been launched in 1980) was followed by the Maestro in 1983, Montego in 1984 and Rover 800 in 1986. But, crucially, the hoped-for product-led recovery failed to materialize, and the company's share of the UK market stubbornly refused to depart from its downward trend. The reasons for this failure are complex. Williams *et al* (1987) attributed it to a series of management miscalculations about the company's room for manoeuvre in an increasingly competitive market. The Motor Industry Research Unit (1988 p. 17) blamed the UK economy. Despite the cutbacks initiated by Edwardes, the company

> was still battling against a severely depressed economic climate. In fact, from the beginning of the Edwardes era just about everything in the economic background that could have gone wrong did so. This was the primary reason for BL's disastrous profit record.

Under Bide, the company continued to develop the working relationship with Honda begun by Edwardes in 1979. The Honda Ballade was made under licence in a slightly modified form as the Triumph Acclaim from 1981 (succeeded by the Rover 200 in 1984), whilst, from 1986, small volumes of the Ballade itself were produced for Honda at Longbridge. The Rover 800/Honda Legend was also developed jointly under Project XX. For Honda, such moves represented tentative steps into the European market. It announced in 1985 that it intended to develop its own engine plant at Swindon, possibly followed later by a full car plant. An alternative was for Austin Rover (the volume car division of BL) to subcontract its underused capacity to Honda. Agreement on this and other matters was made difficult by UK government hesitancy over the size of future financial aid to the state company. Pressing BL to buy in the engine and gearbox for a planned Metro replacement, the government sought to save £250 m from £1,500 m scheduled over five years. This, for BL, raised questions over its future capability to develop new models independently, and it fought—ultimately successfully—to retain this part of the investment programme.

Concern over future state funding was entwined with the government's continuing attempts at privatization. The luxury car maker Jaguar was sold off separately in 1984. In February 1986, it emerged that Ford was in negotiation with BL over a possible purchase of Austin Rover whilst GM was similarly considering the acquisition of Leyland Vehicles (the commercial vehicle manufacturer) and Land Rover. A furious House of Commons debate saw a number of West Midlands based Conservative MPs express strong disapproval at the possibility of the loss of control to an American multinational. Later that month, and in the light of such revolt, government pressure forced the talks with Ford to be abandoned. Negotiations with GM collapsed the following month.

Into this situation a new chairman, Graham Day, was appointed, with effect from April 1986, in an attempt further to boost privatization prospects. One of his first acts was to change the group's name to Rover, dropping the British Leyland title with its historical connotations. In 1987, he achieved part of the objective set by the UK government, when in return for a debt write-off of £750 m, Leyland Vehicles was merged in a joint venture with DAF of the Netherlands. Then, in 1988, the rest of the business was finally sold to the private sector in a deal with British Aerospace (BAe) which achieved both privatization and (crucially, for some Conservative MPs) maintenance of UK ownership.

Under the original terms of this agreement, British Aerospace was to pay £150 m for Rover whilst the UK government offered £800 m in support of new investment. Some £1,100 m of Rover's tax losses was eliminated; the remaining £500 m could only be offset against any future Rover profits, not those of British Aerospace; and the UK government eliminated its guarantees on Rover's £1,600 m debt. British Aerospace undertook not to sell the business again within five years. After investigation by a European Community anxious to minimize state support, the cash injection was cut from £800 m to £547 m (comprising £469 m capital injection plus £78 m regional aid for new investment), but a further £500 m of tax-avoiding losses was made available to British Aerospace, worth an estimated £17–25 m annually. The rest of the package remained unchanged, although it subsequently became the subject of furious political debate over the extent of state subsidy amidst accusations that the Government had not received anything like a true value for the company.[2]

As parts of Rover's new corporate plan emerged, further closures appeared imminent. These included Cowley South works (employing 2,500) by the early 1990s, and Llanelli Pressings (employing 900) by 1990. Overall reaction to the takeover was mixed. The Motor Industry Research Unit (1988 p. 36) predicted that

> by the early 1990s Rover Group will achieve substantial profits. Rover Group is a potentially profitable asset for British Aerospace obtained at a very reasonable price.

From the UK government's point of view, it had disposed of a business with accumulated losses of £2,700 m which had absorbed £3,000 m of state aid since 1975. Questions remained, though, over Rover's future strategy, for its central dilemma continued: too small to be a volume producer, it still attempted to produce the full range of models. In the mid-1980s, it required production of 435,000 cars annually just to break-even and 650,000 to finance new investment internally. Whilst touching on the former, it never even approached the latter. One alternative scenario was suggested by the Motor Industry Research Unit (1988 p. 45): that Rover might aspire to a luxury car maker's image, perhaps paralleling Volvo or Saab, with strong domestic sales and selected niches in export markets—but it also cautioned that this would require dramatic improvements in quality and reliability.

Some of this uncertainty surrounding Rover's future was clarified in 1989 when Honda finally announced far-ranging plans both to invest in UK vehicle production and to maintain and deepen its relationship with Rover. Following the earlier examples of Nissan and Toyota, the other major Japanese vehicle manufacturers (see below), it was to invest £300 m in a full-scale, 100,000 cars/year capacity plant at Swindon, alongside its engine plant there. Production of vehicles was to start in 1991 with the assembly of kits imported from Japan, building up to full output by 1994. These cars were not to be collaborative ventures with Rover (unlike the 40,000 Honda Concertos being produced annually from Longbridge using engines at Swindon from later that year), but—and crucially for Rover—Honda did intend to extend its partnership in the UK by taking a 20 per cent stake in Rover.

Bolstered by this gesture of confidence (and under new ownership), Rover began a new strategic offensive later that year, launching the first products of its ongoing investment programme. These included the Rover 200/400 range (based on the Honda Concerto); the Land Rover Discovery (first new Land Rover product since the Range Rover was launched in 1970); and the K-series engine, to be produced in a new plant at Longbridge. This was the first new engine developed by Rover since 1978 and had been the source of contention with the UK Government in the mid-1980s. These new launches were crucial to the company's emerging strategy of going up-market, away from competition with the volume producers and into more specialized or differentiated sales openings so as to maintain an overall output of around 500,000 cars annually.[3]

These new products depended heavily upon Japanese technological support made available through the link with Honda. Rover also looked increasingly to reform its working practices in line with the Japanese model being installed in the UK by Honda and its rivals Nissan and Toyota. At the new engine plant, for instance, Rover sought 24 hour continuous production so as to get maximum return on the £200 m investment. It offered manual workers an extra £20/week in return for agreement on a four-week cycle of thirteen shifts of 11–11 1/2 hours (against the previous norm of 20 eight-hour shifts per month), with a guarantee of seven consecutive days holiday in each month and no more than three consecutive night shifts. This was rapidly followed by a call for continuous production on the Longbridge vehicle assembly line—the first 24 hour assembly in Western Europe since GM introduced it at Zaragoza in Spain in 1988 (subsequently followed at its Bochum plant in West Germany) and the first in the UK. In 1990, the trade unions offered outline agreement on these changes, in return for a two-hour cut in a standard working week to 37 hours for manual workers. In the wake of this, Rover subsequently announced plans to recruit up to 1,200 extra workers to meet a third shift's production at Longbridge. In a second workplace ballot (after a first resulted in opposition and was met by Rover with a threat to impose change), the new working practices were accepted by a majority of two to one. This was a clear reflection of the extent and character of changes at Rover since the 1970s.

### 3.4.2 Ford

Ford—the second biggest producer, but clear leader in terms of market share—had a substantial presence in the UK, with major car plants at Halewood on Merseyside and Dagenham in London, a Transit van assembly plant in Southampton, and major components plants at Belfast (carburettors), Bridgend (engines), Enfield (instruments) and Swansea (axles and gears). Just as elsewhere around the globe, Ford's international strategies within Europe enabled it to take full advantage of a range of differing conditions offered by national governments and trade unions, especially after the creation of Ford Europe in 1967 brought together strategic management of its European operations.

In the early to mid 1980s, Ford Europe's corporate planning focused on the threat of Japanese imports and new Japanese assembly plants in an industry troubled by over-capacity. Production programmes at the six major assembly plants—Cologne and Saarlouis in West Germany, Genk in Belgium, Valencia in

Spain, Halewood and Dagenham in the UK—were all put under intensive review, and European governments were called upon to monitor the local content of new Japanese assembly plants. Leaving aside for one moment the irony of an American company seeking government protection in European markets from Japanese companies, the threat was real enough. So too was the implication that competition between Ford's European sites would be intensified. As Bob Lutz, chairman of Ford Europe, insisted:

> If we find we have major assembly facilities, regardless of the country involved, which for one reason or another—perhaps uneducated government action (giving longer holidays, a shorter working week) or union intransigence—cannot be competitive, we would not shy away from a decision to close them. (quoted in *Financial Times* 30 October 1985)

In this context, four events encapsulated problems for Ford in its UK operations: two re-directed investment proposals and two lengthy disputes over new working practices and conditions.

In 1987, the AEU agreed a single union agreement with Ford for a greenfield electronic components plant which was to employ over 400, and which would be located at Dundee in Scotland, rather than the other initial potential sites in Spain and Portugal. This deal was wholly outside the existing multi-union bargaining arrangements which existed at the company's other sites in the UK. This angered other trade unions in the negotiating machinery, notably the TGWU and ASTMS. The Ford National Joint Negotiating Committee made clear that other unions would not handle any components moved from the proposed plant, and the TUC indicated that it would not support the AEU either. In 1988, by way of a reply, Ford withdrew from the investment proposal altogether, and even a delegation from a TUC hastily converted to acceptance of AEU single-union status, could not persuade the company to change its mind again. In August, it announced that the plant would instead be built in Spain (see Foster and Woolfson 1989).

In the meantime, from Ford's point of view, there had been further signs of the UK's increasingly problematic status as a base for production in Western Europe. In 1987, the company offered its 32,500 manual employees a radical three-year pay deal tied to stringent conditions. A two-year agreement in 1985 had brought some change to working practices, but the company now proposed to establish work teams of eight to twelve employees run by group leaders recruited from the factory floor, and area foremen with a wider range of responsibilities than the existing supervisors (who covered up to eighteen employees). Within these new work teams, skilled and unskilled workers would be more interchangeable. These changes were an attempt to tackle labour productivity which was up to 65 per cent lower than in Ford's West German plants, and they were a clear attempt to mimic the example being set by the Japanese companies. They were heavily rejected in a ballot, and, in February 1988, the first national strike for ten years began. It quickly demonstrated the problems to Ford from increased interdependence between plants, and low stock levels. At first, some 2,000, later 10,000 workers at the Genk plant (which was short of components produced at Dagenham) had to be temporarily laid off. In the UK alone, Ford lost some £200 m worth of production. After two weeks, workers in the UK voted to accept a revised two-year offer under which Ford won national union approval for new, flexible work teams but agreed not to implement them until local agreement was secured as well.

This served to highlight the disparity in work practices and labour productivity between Ford's UK operations and those elsewhere in Europe. Team working and multi-skilling had already been introduced at Genk, Cologne and Saarlouis; the group leader concept there, and in Valencia. The implications of this failure to improve productivity at the UK assembly plants were not only evident in cancellation of the Dundee plant; but also in more far-reaching fashion in 1989, when a review of European car assembly operations left Dagenham very much out in the cold. Ford announced that it was to cease making the Sierra there, with the loss of 500 out of 11,000 jobs, concentrating Sierra production at Genk, where 2,000 new jobs would be created. This plant had introduced quality circles in 1979, employed some 2,300 temporary workers, and had simplified negotiating procedures—all bitterly resisted in the UK. It also, perhaps not coincidentally, had double the number of robots as the Dagenham Sierra line. This move, though, left Dagenham dependent on just one model, the Fiesta, also produced at Valencia and Cologne (see Figure 3.5). With a decision impending on location of a replacement model to the Sierra much in their minds, union leaders at Dagenham now urged workers to cooperate with management to improve quality and productivity. The TGWU took the unusual step of sending letters to its members arguing that quality and productivity had to be improved to secure the future of the plant, warning that:

> There is a real danger that Ford will decide to close a plant in the early to mid 1990s. The plant most likely to close at the moment is Dagenham. (quoted in *Financial Times* 21 October 1989)

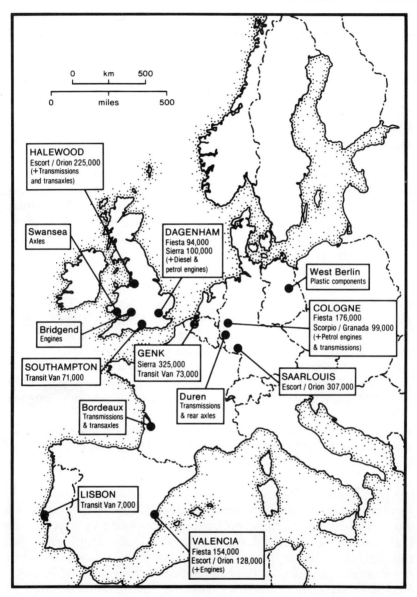

0    km    500

0    miles    500

**HALEWOOD**
Escort / Orion 225,000
(+Transmissions
and transaxles)

**Swansea**
Axles

**DAGENHAM**
Fiesta 94,000
Sierra 100,000
(+Diesel &
petrol engines)

**West Berlin**
Plastic components

**COLOGNE**
Fiesta 176,000
Scorpio / Granada 99,000
(+Petrol engines
& transmissions)

**Bridgend**
Engines

**GENK**
Sierra 325,000
Transit Van 73,000

**SOUTHAMPTON**
Transit Van 71,000

**SAARLOUIS**
Escort / Orion 307,000

**Duren**
Transmissions
& rear axles

**Bordeaux**
Transmissions
& transaxles

**LISBON**
Transit Van 7,000

**VALENCIA**
Fiesta 154,000
Escort / Orion 128,000
(+Engines)

FIG 3.5.   Ford: major operations in Western Europe, 1988 (Source: *Financial Times* 25 January 1989. Note Ford Europe vehicle production in 1988 was 1.8m units.)

Even increased production of the new generation Fiesta could not allay the acute threat to Dagenham's future.

Not that productivity was uniformly low in the UK. In engine

145

manufacture, the UK plants at Bridgend and Dagenham performed relatively better. In 1988, Ford announced a £725 m programme on an extension of its Bridgend plant. The projected capacity of 850,000 units a year confirmed Ford's intention to make the UK its European centre for engine production, creating about 3,000 jobs, some 700 of these at Bridgend and the rest at other sub-component plants. Production was scheduled for 1991, supported by some £30–40 m of UK government aid. These issues were temporarily submerged in industrial unrest over a new two-year pay agreement. Just as in 1985 and 1987, Ford sought to introduce new working practices in exchange for pay increases; just as in 1987, this proved to be a stumbling block which ultimately disrupted production and threatened investment plans. In exchange for a 10 per cent wages increase in the first year, Ford wanted to establish integrated manufacturing teams in the most advanced assembly operations, offering a 5 per cent bonus to these employees; a further 5 per cent for those undergoing electronics training; and a new multi-skilled craftsman grade, ending the distinction between electricians and mechanical engineers. For Ford, such issues were crucial in overcoming labour cost disadvantages, especially at Dagenham. It estimated that the labour cost of building a Fiesta there in 1989 was $1,400; a Sierra, $1,600. This was compared with $800 for a Fiesta at Valencia, and with $1,000 for a Sierra at Genk. Other factors clearly played a part in such comparisons: but the point being made by Ford was clear enough.

As negotiations dragged into 1990, a second ballot resulted in a narrow margin in favour of the company's revised offer; but unofficial action which had affected output throughout the discussions escalated instead, involving the skilled workers most affected by the proposals. At Halewood, 550 maintenance staff—mostly AEU members—began an indefinite unofficial walk-out. This rapidly led to the complete closure of the plant, since machinery which had broken down could not be repaired. As supplies of parts ran out, the effects of the dispute spread to cause a shutdown of Transit van production at Southampton and at Genk in Belgium. Separately, 1,600 electricians, members of the EETPU, also refused to accept the offer and went on official strike. This ended after three weeks; the Halewood dispute after seven.

These strikes caused the lost production of some 80,000 vehicles. They also pointed again to the extent to which Ford, in an integrated European production system, was dependent upon deliveries from its UK bases to other European plants. One consequence was made apparent when the company switched part of its planned engine plant investment away from Bridgend and to Cologne in West Germany instead. Blaming the unreliability of UK supplies, Ford removed the £225 m second stage of the project, shifting capacity for 300,000 engines annually (from the original planned total of 850,000) to an alternative source of supply. Other factors were also clearly at play—including changes in environmental legislation (entailing a re-think of Ford's engine-making strategy) and the potentially far-reaching implications of reform in Eastern Europe. Ford's propaganda campaign, and its message to workers and trade unions in the UK, were nonetheless acutely felt, and if anything, reinforced by the contents of a leaked Ford management document reported in the *Financial Times* (26 June 1990):

> By the late 1980s Dagenham had become unreliable and at times out of control. Continued labour disruption, poor quality and adverse cost performance were the product of an operation that required dramatic change if it was to survive into the 1990s . . . . It has been made absolutely clear to all our employees that if the agreed objectives are not met, then this plant can no longer expect to survive simply because of its historical importance.

Whilst an element of brinkmanship was clearly at work, both what Ford sought, and the implications if this was not forthcoming, were clear enough.

### 3.4.3 Vauxhall (General Motors)

Whilst GM eclipsed Ford on the global scene in terms of production at least, and the two ran close in terms of sales within Western Europe as a whole, it came a very poor second to Ford in terms of both production and sales in the UK. Its main car assembly plants at Ellesmere Port on Merseyside and at Luton relied to a much greater extent than Ford's upon imports of components from outside the UK. In part, this was a legacy of GM's reorganization of production within Europe in the mid-1970s, which gave Opel, its West German subsidiary, overall control of European operations in recognition of GM's strength in the West German market. That move, and the emphasis upon production in West Germany and then Spain, overshadowed GM's UK subsidiary, Vauxhall, in the early 1980s.

At the start of the decade, Vauxhall's market share was down to 8 per cent. The launch of new models, particularly the Cavalier (which sold to the UK's large company car sector) and an aggressive marketing campaign drove this share up to 17 per cent by

1985, closely challenging Rover for second place behind Ford. This big growth posed problems for GM, in two ways.

In the first place, it sucked in an increasing volume of imported cars and components, which drew considerable criticism within the UK of the company's sourcing policy. The TGWU threatened at one stage to block imports of the Astra, unless output was stepped up at Ellesmere Port. Politicians focused on GM's low domestic content in debates over the country's growing motor vehicle trade deficit. Vauxhall was even driven to mount a fierce advertising campaign in defence of its record, somewhat incongruously proclaiming General Motors (one of the biggest industrial groups in the world, with its headquarters in Detroit, USA), as "The name behind a great British family" (see Figure 3.6). This was GM's first such exercise in sixty years of UK operations—dramatically indicative of the pressure it felt itself under.

At the same time, Vauxhall's dependence upon components imported from West Germany was providing real financial difficulties for GM; for a steep rise in the value of the DM against the pound in particular, especially in 1985, increased production costs considerably. Despite sales growth, Vauxhall and GM in Europe made losses. In a move to counter this problem, GM established a wholly separate organization, GM Europe, in 1986 (similar to Ford Europe), relieving Opel of the responsibility for coordination of GM's European sales and production (see Figure 3.7).

At Vauxhall, losses had become almost habitual. In only two years in the period from 1969 to 1986 did it make a profit (1971 and 1978). Restructuring and continued strong sales, albeit down from the peak 1985 share, produced a £31 m profit in 1987, growing to £152 m in 1988. This was achieved at a price: employment fell from 30,000 at the start of the decade to 10,000 by the close. New investment began to flow into the company's plants. Luton (producing the Cavalier, along with Antwerp in Belgium and Russelsheim in West Germany) received £122 m from 1986 to 1988 in preparation for an up-dated version of the car. Ellesmere Port (producing Astras, along with Bochum in West Germany and Antwerp) saw £150 m from 1985 to 1989.

A significant turning point, though, was the announcement in 1990 that GM had selected Ellesmere Port as the location for a new, £150 m engine assembly plant, creating 400 new jobs, after fierce public competition with GM's site at Kaiserslautern in West Germany. In this contest, GM made clear that, as an essential precondition for location in the UK, it required agreement on

# GM-a commitment to Britain for over 60 years.

## A Long UK Tradition

General Motors has been an integral part of British industry since 1925. In that year we acquired Vauxhall. In 1931 we began building Bedford commercial vehicles.

In good times and bad, in peace and in war, we have gone on investing in Britain. Producing in Britain. Exporting for Britain. Providing thousands of jobs.

In our 60 years we have produced 5 million Vauxhalls. At Bedford we have built 3.5 million commercial vehicles.

We also make a wide range of components in the UK. Humble items like filler caps and air filters. High-technology items such as instrument clusters and catalytic converters. Nearly three-quarters of this output is exported.

## Resources, Research and Development

General Motors is one of the world's most successful motor manufacturers. It leads the field in many areas of research, development and the application of new technologies.

GM's British operations have access to those worldwide resources and capabilities. Capabilities that gave the motorist the energy absorbing steering column, the multi-beam headlamp and safety windscreen glass and that now contribute to space exploration.

It is GM's technical excellence in the UK, as elsewhere, that is keeping the Corporation at the leading edge of new product design and the manufacturing systems to make those designs.

## Some UK Milestones.

1925 Vauxhall joins the GM family of companies
1930 'Cadet' launched – first fruits of GM's investment
1931 First Bedford truck produced
1939-45 250,000 Bedford trucks and 5,640 Churchill tanks produced during World War II
1947 Bedford first British manufacturer to make 500,000 trucks
1969 New 700 acre proving ground opened at Millbrook, Bedfordshire
1978 The 3 millionth Bedford commercial vehicle produced
1981 Bedford celebrates 50 years of making British trucks
1982 1,500,000th Bedford exported
1984 Cavalier best-selling car in its class
1985 Astra wins 'Car of the Year'*
        GM's commitment to Britain in the year included:
        ● £395m in exports (up 25% over 1984)
        ● £1,000m of British goods and services
        ● 100,000 people employed, directly and indirectly
        ● £290m in wages and salaries
        ● playing our part in the community (for example by training 600 young people full-time)
* 'Car of the Year' is sponsored by Telegraph Sunday Magazine, Autocar, Autoweek, L'Equipe, Stern and Vi Bilägare.

## Production and Marketing Skills

Quality and value are GM watchwords in the quest to succeed in a highly competitive worldwide marketplace.

It is with these criteria in mind that GM has invested over £1.2 billion in the UK in the past decade.

The Cavalier has a superb reputation for quality. Vauxhall sales figures prove the point. The Astra, in car and van versions, is another success story – in market/acceptance and in helping to maintain employment in the depressed North West at Ellesmere Port.

Bedford has gone on competing. Nearly half its truck output is exported. And all this despite over-capacity in the world commercial vehicle market.

UK component operations, with advanced design and manufacturing as good as any in the world, export over 70% of their output.

GM is proud of the tradition of its British companies. It plans to build on that tradition.

Into the 21st Century.

## General Motors. The name behind a great British family.

VAUXHALL · BEDFORD · GMSPO · AC DELCO · AC SPARK PLUG · DELCO ELECTRONICS · DELCO PRODUCTS · FISHER BODY · SAGINAW · GMAC

FIG 3.6. General Motors and the UK.

changes to working practices at the whole Ellesmere Port plant. These included "single table" bargaining, with all four unions together; team working, with no restrictions on flexibility; new arbitration procedures; and the use of temporary or seasonal employees. Building the new engine plant in the UK was an indication of GM's renewed favour in its bases there. In Western Europe, the company had four engine assembly operations—at

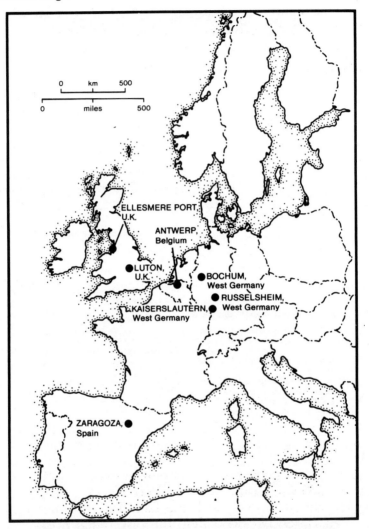

FIG 3.7.   General Motors: major operations in Western Europe.

Bochum, Kaiserslautern and Russelsheim in West Germany, and at Aspern in Vienna[4]. It had closed its last car engine operation plant in the UK, at Ellesmere Port, in 1984, as one part of its earlier strategic withdrawal from the UK. The new plant would contribute to an amelioration of GM's UK trade deficit and leave it better placed to cope with exchange rate fluctuations. It came on top of record profits at Vauxhall in 1989 of £254 m, as the company nudged Rover out of second place in UK sales (behind Ford), and was followed by plans to export cars from the UK to the rest of Western Europe for the first time in almost a decade.

### 3.4.4 Peugeot

Peugeot, the French-based manufacturer, took over the Ryton and Stoke plants near Coventry, and the Linwood works in Scotland, when it acquired the UK operations of the American company Chrysler in 1979. The Linwood plant was closed in 1981 with the loss of 5,000 jobs (to a furious political reaction in Scotland); Stoke suffered from the loss of a crucial export market in kits for assembly elsewhere, and saw a sustained run-down; whilst Ryton saw substantial investment from the mid-1980s as the centre of assembly of two new models in an attempt to improve sales within the UK.

The tricky interplay between international investment decisions and national political environments was clearly exposed in decisions over where to invest in production of a new model, the 309. The group's main manufacturing sites in the early 1980s were in France, Spain and the UK. In 1983, negotiations between Peugeot and the UK government over financial aid for production of the 309 were hastily suspended as dispute over a proposed redundancy programme at Poissy in France erupted with violent intensity, continuing into 1984. The company was anxious not to pursue (publicly at least) investment outside France at a time when cutbacks in France were proving so fiercely unpopular. Later in 1984, though, Peugeot announced an investment programme of £30 m on the new model at Ryton, safeguarding the jobs of the 1,400 employed there. One of the incentives for the company was that the UK government had looked to call in a £28 m loan, made in 1969 when the UK plants were owned by Chrysler (and subsequently taken over, with the factories, by Peugeot), if the plant had closed as was widely forecast. This threat was now withdrawn and instead the government offered a further £2 m in investment support. Most of the parts, though, for the new model would be made at Poissy, and shipped to the UK for assembly.

At this time, the fortunes of Talbot UK, the holding company, depended heavily on the profitability of a long-running contract to supply car kits to Iran from the Stoke plant, which employed 2,000 of the 2,600 there. In 1983, 87,000 such kits were shipped out, but the figure dropped to 58,000 in the following year and, in 1985, production was halted for several months at a time. In the next few years, gradual rundown at Stoke was to be only partially offset by expansion at Ryton.

In 1985, the first 309 rolled off the Ryton assembly line, and the car was introduced to the UK market in 1986. Later that year, Peugeot introduced production of lefthand drive models at Ryton for export to Europe, and in October it was announced that Ryton was also to build a second new model. This, the Peugeot 405, was to compete with the Austin Montego, Ford Sierra and Vauxhall Cavalier in the fleet car range. The UK government contributed £1.5 m out of £20 m total investment costs. Production began in 1987, just as the Stoke plant producing for Iran was finally closed down, leaving only 200 employed there on component production. Workers transferred to Ryton as a second shift was introduced in 1988, increasing output there to 2,500 cars/week.

Peugeot's production of two new models at Ryton was often cited as an indication of the extent of resurgence in the UK vehicle industry in the mid to late 1980s. In introducing the 309, the company pointed to dramatically improved labour productivity—up from 25 cars/person/year in 1979, to 41—as evidence of a changed attitude. But it is important to place these developments in perspective. The greatest single success was in terms of the company's increased share of the UK market, up from 4 per cent in 1984 to 9 per cent in 1988, on the back of new products. In employment terms, the balance was not as favourable as sometimes indicated, partly because of the extent to which components were shipped in from France—and in any case well down from the 4,200 employed by Chrysler at Ryton alone in 1975. In 1984, Ryton employed 1,400 and Stoke 2,600. By 1988, decline at one plant had more than offset growth at the other: Ryton employed 2,500 but Stoke just 200. The closure of Linwood was also often conveniently "forgotten" in such calculations.

The way in which Peugeot had sought investment support from governments is also worthy of note. Not to be outdone by the UK, for example, the Spanish government offered Peugeot a £15 m package to assist the modernization of its plants in Spain (entailing 3,000 job losses there), including that at Villaverde in preparation for production of the 309. The "resurgence" of Ryton, then, was but one small part of a far broader mosaic. By the end of the decade, it appeared that Ryton might again "benefit" from this global dance, as Peugeot suffered a protracted seven-week pay dispute at its two major assembly plants, Sochaux and Mulhouse in north east France, in 1989. This was settled on terms which left rumbling grievances, including a claimed 13 per cent pay disparity below equal work at Renault. Together with record profits at Peugeot-Talbot UK (after a string of losses from 1978 to 1986), this prompted speculation that the parent company, Peugeot, might invest a further £100 m at Ryton to double capacity there to 200,000 cars annually.

### 3.4.5 Nissan

In the course of the 1970s, the Japanese motor industry increasingly found the path of exports blocked by national governments imposing protectionist measures. In the UK, Japanese imports were informally limited by agreement to 11 per cent of the market from 1975 onwards in an attempt to protect the ailing British Leyland. The response was straightforward: to locate production overseas. In this, Nissan led the way, as it sought to expand its share of the world market from 6 per cent at the start of the 1970s to 10 per cent by 1990 under a strategy codenamed "Global Ten". This entailed major expansion of production outside Japan from the start of the 1980s onwards. In the USA, truck manufacture was established at Smyrna, Tennessee; in Mexico, existing plant was expanded; in Spain, Nissan bought a share in Motor Iberica, a commercial vehicle manufacturer; in Italy, it undertook a small joint venture with Alfa Romeo. Of all of these projects, the most significant for the European market was its decision to locate vehicle production within the UK.

Despite the hype and publicity, Nissan's arrival really was one of the most significant inward investments in the UK in the 1980s (see Crowther and Garrahan 1988; Garrahan 1986). It was a "first" in a number of ways: first Japanese car manufacturing plant in Europe, first new UK car plant since the 1960s, and the first ever in north east England. Nissan's choice of the UK owed much to three factors, two of which had already made the UK Nissan's largest European export market: relatively high selling prices, the lack of a strong domestically owned market leader, and an extremely supportive government. The UK government welcomed Nissan not only for the jobs and investment it brought, but also for its introduction of wholly new styles of industrial relations and production organization within the vehicle industry. To many towns and local authorities, the jobs were incentive enough. Some 53 different locations in Britain and Ireland lobbied Nissan before it finally settled on a site near Sunderland. In addition to very high levels of prevailing unemployment, the chosen area also had one other major advantage—no tradition of vehicle manufacture. To great chagrin at the time, none of the new vehicle plants built in the 1950s and 1960s found their way to the north east of England. There was thus no tradition of vehicle industry working practices and so the company could more easily develop its own. (The whole question of Nissan's impact in north east England is discussed more fully in Chapter 4).

The expansion of Nissan's plant at Sunderland, then, came about as one part of a global strategy. It was also (reportedly) the subject of a fierce debate within the company itself. An initial proposal in 1981 envisaged a full-scale £300 m manufacturing plant employing 5,000, beginning production in 1984 and reaching maximum output of 200,000 cars a year by 1986. Nissan president Takashi Ishihara strongly supported this plan. Chairman Katsuji Kawamata and the head of Nissan's union, Ichiro Shioji, both wanted the UK project scaled down so that the company could concentrate instead on expanding capacity in the USA. After three years of debate, they won the day. Smyrna in the US received further investment to build cars as well as trucks, and the UK scheme was slimmed down to a much smaller version. From 1986, an assembly plant employing just 450 was to produce up to 24,000 cars a year from parts exported from Japan.

However, Nissan also indicated that if this first phase was successful it would invest in a further larger plant. In 1986, it confirmed that phase II would commence operation in 1990, have a capacity of 100,000 vehicles annually, employ some 2,100 and require, along with phase one, an investment of some £390 m, of which the UK government contributed £110 m in regional aid. Operations to be established included engine assembly, metal stamping and plastic moulding. In the first phase, cars built at Sunderland counted against the "unofficial" UK quota on Japanese imports; but not in the second stage when local content (defined as EC content) would rise from 60 to 80 per cent, and exports to the EC would commence from the UK base (see also Dicken 1987).

In 1987, the company announced a third expansion of the plant aiming to take output up to 200,000 cars/year (on the scale of the original 1981 proposal) with a further investment of £216 m, including some £25 m in government grants. A second model, replacement for the Micra, was to be added to the Bluebird range, and an additional 1,400 jobs created, taking total employment to 3,500 (well below the 1981 proposal of 5,000). Then, in 1989, after Toyota's decision to follow its Japanese rival into the UK (see below), Nissan indicated that it was considering a fourth phase, taking output up to 400,000 cars annually by the late 1990s, adding a third model range. It also proposed to double capacity in four wheel drive and commercial vehicles in Spain to 200,000.

This expansion in the UK was significant not just as an assault

**In the last 11 years Nissans have been exported by a small island with a highly skilled workforce.**

In Japan, the people who build Nissans have a variety of skills and they're encouraged to use them.

There aren't the strict job demarcation that have done the British motor industry so much harm.

New ideas and ways of working are welcomed.

So people are more involved, more satisfied, more employable, less bored and better paid.

There isn't a wide gap between managers and workers: the general manager of the Nissan factory in Tokyo wears the same work clothes as the men on the line.

And every morning, workers and management get together to see how they can make things better.

The relationship is friendly and constructive. There's also an agreement designed to make disputes unnecessary. Consequently there's never been a strike. No-one has ever been made redundant either.

As a result, the cars these people make are better. To the extent that every one has a 100,000 mile/3 year warranty.

In 1984, the 1,000,000th Nissan made the thirty-day sea crossing from Japan to England.

In fact, they've been the top imported car in Britain for eleven years running.

**NISSAN**
They don't half work.

**In the next 11 years Nissans should be exported by a small island with a highly skilled workforce.**

In England, the people who will build Nissans will have a variety of skills and they'll be encouraged to use them.

There won't be the strict job demarcations that have done the British motor industry so much harm.

New ideas and ways of working will be welcomed.

So people will be more involved, more satisfied, more employable, less bored and better paid.

There won't be a wide gap between managers and workers: the general manager of Nissan's new Sunderland factory will wear the same work clothes as the men on the line.

And every morning, workers and management will get together to see how they can make things better.

The relationship will be friendly and constructive. Already there's an agreement with the AUEW which has been designed to make disputes unnecessary. No-one should ever need to be made redundant either.

As a result, the cars these people will make will be better. To the extent that every one will have a 100,000 mile/3 year warranty.

In the 1990's, over 100,000 Nissans a year should be made in Britain. Many of them will cross the sea to Europe.

In fact, they could very soon become the top imported car in Europe.

**NISSAN**
They don't half work.

FIG 3.8.  Nissan and the UK

upon the European market, but also in terms of the way in which that production was organized. A Nissan advertisement neatly encapsulated its ambitions for the UK base (see Figure 3.8). Four features of the trade union agreement at Sunderland were totally new to the UK car industry (if not to other branches of manufacturing). It incorporated single union status for the AEU; no-strike pendulum arbitration; common conditions; and complete flexibility, with teamleaders and supervisors responsible for shopfloor production. All the major motor industry unions offered such conditions. In this "beauty contest", the immediate concern was for employment. As Joe Cellini, north east divisional organizer of the AEU said of the deal (struck before phase two was confirmed): "Our aim is to make it work constructively and to justify the second phase" (quoted in *Financial Times* 23 April 1985).

The conditions which Nissan sought were explained as follows by personnel manager Peter Wickens: "What we are attempting to do is to eliminate the need for industrial action" (quoted in *Financial Times* 23 April 1985). To this end, it operated a highly selective recruitment procedure, making full use of rigorous screening to appoint the first 22 supervisors from 3,000 applicants. Its departure from previous norms was re-emphasized in 1987 when it hired temporary labour to meet a seasonal peak in production. This was not uncommon elsewhere in Europe, but it was the first time it had happened in the UK motor industry since the 1940s. In many ways, working at Nissan was different (see also Chapter 4).

But Nissan's expansion within the UK was not without difficulties. It was at first fiercely opposed by other motor manufacturers established there, anxious to preserve "their" market. Ford claimed that Nissan would save between £330 and £530 per car due to new working practices and conditions, and force the other manufacturers to lay off workers. Phase two coincided with Nissan's first ever operating loss since it became a public company in 1951 (in 1986/87), one result of an appreciating yen and a squeeze on export profit margins, leading to further questioning of the wisdom of overseas expansion in Japan. Nonetheless, production of the Bluebird gradually built up, from 5,000 in 1986 to 30,000 in 1987 and 55,000 in 1988. In that year, exports to the rest of Europe began in earnest as the plant sought to reach an export target of 100,000 cars a year by the early 1990s. This met with opposition from the French and Italian governments. Both had fiercely resisted Japanese imports: France maintained a rigid 3 per cent limit, and Italy only allowed 2,500 cars annually from Japan together with 14,000 Japanese vehicles from other European countries. France, in particular, maintained that 60 per cent EC content was insufficient to qualify as EC produced, and threatened to limit exports from the UK under its existing quota until an 80 per cent EC content level was reached. Both France and Italy backed down after EC intervention under pressure from the UK Government—demonstrating again its support for Nissan and other Japanese manufacturers investing in the UK. This established a point for Nissan and enabled it to export relatively freely from its UK base across the EC.

Mindful of trade friction between member states of the European Community and of protectionist pressures within the USA, Nissan evolved an increasingly sophisticated international strategy for its car assembly and production operations, now spread through 21 countries (coincidentally, the same number as Ford in 1929). The company's annual report for 1989 confirmed that:

> Today, Nissan is taking globalisation much further through a long-term localisation programme—which involves the creation of bases in key markets to coordinate all regional research and development, procurement, production, marketing and financing in line with local conditions .... Nissan has long been Japan's most globally active company. Localisation is just a logical extension of this.

For the UK, "localization" entailed the creation of a new subsidiary, Nissan European Technology Centre, the European link in the company's global research and development network, which was announced in 1989. Some £26 m was to be invested at Cranfield, creating 250 jobs, and £5 m at Sunderland, entailing 100 extra jobs. As Ian Gibson, Nissan UK's managing director explained, "the target is that we should be able to design a vehicle from scratch in Europe" (quoted in *Financial Times* 30 November 1989) within five years, distinct from those originating in the USA or Japan, but nonetheless still dependent upon Japanese designed engines and transmissions. The new design capability (also responsible for production in Spain) was important for the Sunderland plant, even if the bulk of the investment went elsewhere, for production there was rescheduled in the early 1990s. The Bluebird was replaced by the Primera in 1990, an upper-medium range car which was a deliberate attempt to take the company up-market in Europe. It was to be produced at the rate of 100,000 cars/year. Together with the Micra range car scheduled for 1992, it would take the Sunderland plant's output up to the 200,000 cars/year of phase three.

## 3.4.6 Toyota

Toyota, the largest Japanese motor manufacturer and third largest in the world, lagged well behind Nissan in terms of internationalization of vehicle production. Its early US operations were limited to the 200,000 cars/year joint venture with GM in Fremont, California. Not until 1988 did production begin at its wholly owned plant at Georgetown, Kentucky. Once engaged on the road to international production, though, Toyota pursued it with determination. In the mid to late 1980s, plants were constructed in Canada, Indonesia and Taiwan. Then, in 1989, it announced plans to follow Nissan into UK car assembly, aiming to produce some 200,000 cars there annually. The investment was split between two sites: a car assembly plant at Burnaston in Derbyshire, where a £700 m investment would create 3,000 jobs; and an engine assembly plant at Shotton, where £140 m would be invested creating 500 jobs. Burnaston was to come onstream in two stages, with the first cars produced in 1992, 100,000 cars/year by 1995 and 200,000 cars/year by 1997/98. Engine production at Shotton would also start by 1992.

This decision effectively marked the start of a new, even more competitive phase for the European motor vehicle industry. Concerned about possible restrictions on exports from Japan when free trade was created within the European Community after 1992, Toyota intended to produce inside any potential barriers, following the examples set by Nissan and Honda. Its announcement came as the EC was still wrestling on a uniform policy for Japanese imports, and met with some opposition, especially from France—though not on the scale of that to Nissan's project. This was partly because Toyota was to receive less state aid, in contrast to the generous assistance offered Nissan. From January 1989, all state aid to motor manufacturers exceeding £8 m had to be approved by the EC in advance (although West Germany and Spain disputed this)—and approval could take some considerable time. Given continuing uncertainty over the EC's stance on imports, the UK government negotiated a similar voluntary agreement as with Nissan. Local (i.e., EC) content of the model to be produced—in the 1.6 to 1.8 litre range—should be 60 per cent by 1993, when the car would count as UK-produced and hence freely exportable, rising to 80 per cent by 1995.

Some of the reasons behind Toyota's initial reluctance to invest in production in Western Europe and North America were neatly encapsulated in its 1989 annual report which reviewed the company's experience of internationalization. One caption opposite a

picture of a mildly aggressive looking Western car plant worker
read as follows:

> This was our fear. A worker whose face we could not read—whose heart
> was a mystery to us. When the time came for us to make a wholesale
> structural shift and move our manufacturing overseas, this was our
> greatest fear. We had developed a very finely tuned production system.
> What would happen if we turned it over to him (*sic*)? .... As it
> turned out, there was no problem; these "foreign" workers weren't one
> bit different from us .... . Now we don't think of "foreign" workers
> anymore. That's nonsense. All our people not here in Japan are just
> Toyota, that's all. They're family.

The difficulties which Toyota had anticipated, and worked
actively to overcome, were in transshipping its systems of production and industrial relations, and its corporate culture, to a
different context. In other parts of the globe, though, it had
displayed less reticence. In South East Asia, for instance, a
region anticipated to be the fastest growing car market in the
1990s, Toyota was extensively involved. In Thailand, Indonesia,
Malaysia and the Philippines, it was market leader; it had vehicle
assembly plant in each of these countries (two in the case of
Thailand); and, in 1989, Toyota committed £134 m to expand
component production there and to set up complementary
exchanges between the various centres. Whilst Toyota took time
to expand into Europe and America, then (compared at least to
Nissan) it nonetheless similarly recognized the profit potential of
global production strategies.

### 3.4.7 Summary

The UK motor vehicle industry experienced a dramatic resurgence in fortunes in the mid to late 1980s in terms of both sales
and production after a dismal performance in the early 1980s.
Whilst the single most significant element in this for the 1990s
was the arrival of the Japanese manufacturers, longer established
American multinationals continued to use the UK as a base for
production, employing the full scope of their powers to plan
investment across national frontiers (and, of course, within those
same boundaries) so as to encourage various dramatic changes
in the organization of the production process at their many
sites—exemplified in the campaign waged by Ford for improved
quality and productivity at Dagenham. At the same time, adoption
of new production systems, including a reduction in the level of
stocks and the increased interdependence between operations in
various European states, meant that disruption at one source of

supply could easily ripple into other plants and other countries. This served to intensify the pressure upon companies to maintain harmonious labour relations and also to deepen the impact in terms of future investment decisions of actual or threatened industrial unrest. Ford and GM's differing responses to the UK in the late 1980s neatly emphasized these points, and the international nature of vehicle production—for GM's decision to invest in engine production at Ellesmere Port was in contrast to Ford's revised plan to split investment in engine production between Bridgend and Cologne. The two acts were symbolic of the kinds of balance weighed up by multinational corporations. Ford felt that it had become over-exposed in the UK, whilst GM was reinvesting there after a long period of disinvestment. Ford was guided by the threat of industrial unrest; GM, whilst acutely conscious of this, was also aware of its parallel over-exposure in West Germany. Similarly, Peugeot's re-investment in the UK (in a neat irony, in plants acquired from an American company) reflected both its growing impact in the UK market and problems of labour unrest in its French bases.

It was the Japanese, though, who stole most of the headlines in the 1980s, not just for their massive investment plans but also for their radically different style of production. If nothing else, the opposition to Japanese exports from the UK by other companies and countries served to emphasize the significance of these new producers. That the UK was home to all three major Japanese vehicle companies' first European car assembly plants was due to a combination of factors, including the weakness of the "domestic" producer British Leyland (later Rover) in contrast to Volkswagen in West Germany or Fiat in Italy or Renault and Peugeot in France, and the extremely supportive UK government stance. Effectively, the arrival of Nissan, followed by Toyota and Honda, acted to initiate a transformation in the geography of vehicle productio: in the UK (see Figure 3.9), and in the social organization of production: and the linkage of the two was not coincidental. In their assault on the European market, the Japanese sought to transplant their systems of production and industrial relations styles; in this process they actively avoided old established traditions. For the "domestic" manufacturer Rover, too, the Japanese presence was crucial—especially the Honda link and its contribution in terms of technology to the evolving up-market strategy. Rover, like Ford and GM and other European manufacturers, also borrowed increasingly on Japanese labour management ideas. These were such a central focus in the decade because the detail of reforms to working practices and collective

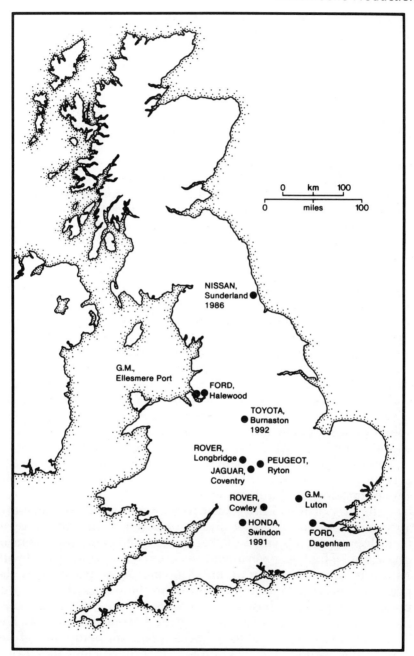

FIG 3.9.   Location of automobile assembly plants in the UK.

bargaining enabled dramatic increases to labour productivity at minimum capital cost. In a whole variety of ways then, the UK vehicle industry in the 1980s—American, Japanese, European and UK-owned—was in a state of considerable turmoil. How that might be clarified in the 1990s is examined in the concluding section to this chapter; but first we focus upon a further vital issue to the geography of the UK car industry—the production and supply of automotive components.

## 3.5 The automotive components industry

A recurring theme in the previous section was the significance to the major vehicle assemblers of component supply; the myriad bits and pieces which go into a motor vehicle, from nuts and bolts through to castings, sheet metal, glass, plastics and mechanical and electronic systems. Whilst a varying proportion of such work could be done internally (GM in the USA relied far more on inhouse sourcing, for instance, than Ford), the purchase of materials and components from outside suppliers was a substantial part of any vehicle assembler's operation. In 1987, Ford Europe spent $3,700 m in West Germany on such goods, $1,600 m in the UK, $700 m in Spain, $500 m in France and $600 m elsewhere. Just as the motor vehicle industry underwent a deep structural transformation in the 1980s with the rise of Japan and the increasing number of Japanese-owned plants in the USA and Western Europe, so too did the relationship between component suppliers and motor manufacturers undergo a period of substantial change.

The significance of component supply was perhaps most clearly evident in negotiations over Nissan's plant in the UK. Here, the whole question of "local content" was vitally important to phase two: the proportion of the vehicle which was assembled from parts and materials produced locally, as opposed to the kits shipped from Japan which formed the backbone of Nissan's operations in phase one. The UK government negotiated a voluntary deal with Nissan in which 60 per cent, building later to 80 per cent, of the price at which the vehicle was sold from the works (the ex-works price) should be purchased locally. This subsequently came to be the model followed in negotiations with Toyota and Honda. The 80 per cent limit was established because at that point most of the major (and technologically complex) manufacturing operations, in particular production of the engine and gearbox (or the "power train") would, in the government's view, have to be undertaken locally. The hope was that in this way the Japanese plants would become more than just "screwdriver" operations assembling cars exported from Japan in a knocked-down form, and instead make a substantial contribution to the domestic economy through their purchases of goods and services.

In itself, though, this very attempt at defining "local content" raised a whole host of problems. In the first instance, "local" effectively meant produced in the European Community, not in the UK. For the UK government to attempt an interpretation in any other way would have been counter to the EC treaties. France and Italy disputed whether even at 80 per cent EC content, the Japanese operations could count as "local" at all, and for some time threatened to block imports of cars produced in the UK. EC regulations were far from precise on this matter. To qualify as European-produced according to this definition, a good only had to have the last substantial act of manufacturing performed on it within the EC.

The UK government's agreement was frequently challenged in other ways, too. The definitional basis of "ex-works price" was described as follows by the Department of Trade and Industry:

> Local content is measured on an ex-works price basis—the price at which the vehicle is sold to the dealer or distributor (but excluding delivery charges). The value of the parts and materials originating from outside the European Community is deducted from this price to give local content. (memorandum to Trade and Industry Committee 1987 p. 304)

As one component supplier argued, though:

> It is easily possible, by including administration, marketing, distribution, depreciation, financing charges and gross margin, as well as assembly, to achieve 80% local value content, yet still import the power unit and transmission, or other technically strategic parts, probably at transfer prices. (Trade and Industry Committee 1987 p. 198)

In summing up its investigation into the UK components industry, the Trade and Industry Committee (1987 p. xiv) concluded that the use of ex-works *cost*, excluding profit, would be a preferable basis for measuring local content.

Whilst these issues were significant in the short-term, they tended to underplay other longer-term implications of restructuring in the automobile industry. In the first place, greater participation between supplier and manufacturer (as embodied in the Japanese production system) went alongside an overall reduction in the number of suppliers. In Europe during the 1980s, most of the major companies developed away from dual-sourcing strategies where the emphasis was on competition between suppliers to keep costs down for the assembler, and into "preferred supplier" programmes where a smaller number of approved component suppliers was drawn into development at an early stage. As Sleigh (1989 p. 21) put it, a "first tier" of automotive components companies was emerging, which was "forging its own special links and relationships with the vehicle manufacturers who generally are willing to have the larger and more competent suppliers as 'partners' ". Ford cut its number of regular suppliers from 2,500 to 900; Rover from 1,200 to 300. In return for strict quality control, these gained a regular flow of business. Equally, growing adoption of just-in-time production systems had an impact in terms of the spatial pattern of production organization. Within the USA, clusters of major suppliers had begun to emerge; in Japan, they were an accepted feature. Regular deliveries meant, in effect, a case for spatial proximity.

A growing proportion of these companies, tied both spatially and organizationally to the assemblers, consisted of Japanese-owned component manufacturers. This process was farthest advanced in the USA, where the Japanese motor companies had been established the longest; but two companies rapidly established operations to supply Nissan at Sunderland in the UK. TI Silencers and Nihon Radiator jointly produced exhausts; Hoover Universal and Ikeda Bussan (a Nissan subsidiary) together produced seats (see also Chapter 4 on Nissan's local impact). Concentration of new facilities around Japanese owned assembly plants was nowhere near as marked as in North America, and tended to be confined to certain product ranges, but there was expansion of Japanese investment in components production within the UK.

This emerging trend was perceived quite clearly within the UK's vehicle manufacturing heartland, the West Midlands, as a threat. Mauled by the knock-on effect of the decline of Rover Group, any tendency towards location near the new vehicle assembly locations was regarded as harmful to the West Midlands economy. The West Midlands Industrial Development Association (1989 pp. 8–9) argued as follows:

> changing patterns mean that the traditional role of the West Midlands is under threat . . . . the region's position is being challenged because of the emergence of the north east and South Wales as alternative centres; the continued growth in component imports as UK manufacturers increase overseas sourcing; increased vehicle import penetration; and the relative decline of Rover (the most important local purchaser) in terms of market share.

The West Midlands was far from alone in facing this formidable list of difficulties. A fundamental problem from the viewpoint of British capital was the weakness of the UK motor components industry against not only Japanese newcomers, but also European rivals. Some 2,000 companies produced components in the UK, but many of these were very small: the top 100 accounted for over 80 per cent of output. Even the larger UK-owned companies lagged well behind their European rivals in terms of sales (see Table 3.10). Only two, Lucas and GKN, figured in the top ten; along with Turner and Newall, Pilkington, and BBA, these were the only companies with any real international standing (Sleigh 1988). Most UK-owned companies were excessively dependent on the relatively small UK market, and had not internationalized production in the manner of their European counterparts. As GKN put it in a memorandum to the Trade and Industry Committee (1987 p. 89): "It is unlikely that those [UK] component manufacturing businesses which do not have plants outside the UK and whose customer base is therefore essentially confined to UK vehicle builders will be sufficiently profitable to survive in the long term".

In these circumstances the threat of the Japanese presence was very real. The large companies (outwardly, at least) welcomed an opportunity to supply new customers: indeed, GKN announced that "frankly, as component manufacturers, if we are successful, we do not care if it is Martians building cars here" (Trade and Industry Committee 1987 p. 94). Whilst Nissan went out of its way to play down suggestions that a wave of Japanese component manufacturers was in prospect, others were less convinced. TI

TABLE 3.10
*European automotive component manufacturers, 1987*

| Company | Automotive sales m dollars (1987) | Principal country of manufacture |
| --- | --- | --- |
| Michelin | 8,070 | France |
| Bosch | 7,611 | West Germany |
| Philips | 3,786 | Netherlands |
| Pirelli | 2,900 | Italy |
| Valeo | 2,063 | France |
| Magneti Marelli | 2,038 | Italy (parent = Fiat) |
| GM Components | 1,997 | France |
| Lucas | 1,989 | UK |
| ZF | 1,942 | West Germany |
| GKN | 1,803 | UK |

Source: Sleigh 1989 p. 29.

explained its policy of engaging in joint ventures with Japanese component makers as follows: "If a substantial Japanese component industry, closely linked to Japanese vehicle assemblers and not also linked with European companies, is allowed to develop [in the UK], it will eventually overpower its local competitors" (Trade and Industry Committee 1987 p. 220).[5] Pilkingtons (makers of glass for windscreens and windows) similarly sought participation with and sales to the Japanese when, in 1989, it sold 20 per cent of its US subsidiary to Nippon Sheet Glass in an attempt to broaden its market into Japanese car manufacturers both in the USA and Japan. Chairman Anthony Pilkington explained the sale in the following fashion:

> this is first and foremost a major strategic move. Our customers are globalising and they want globally consistent supplies. More Japanese companies are moving abroad to manufacture, rather than exporting directly, and their major target is the US. We need to be sure that we are in a position to get their business. (quoted in *Financial Times* 16 March 1989)

In this "globalizing" environment, the UK sometimes gained, sometimes lost. Not just the vehicle assemblers, but also the major component suppliers, had become highly international. In the process, the production of components in the UK had become increasingly foreign-owned. Of the 60 largest companies in 1977, 43 were UK-owned; by 1989, this was down to 28. There were plenty of instances of loss of production capability, particularly in certain crucial areas. As Ford put it to the Trade and Industry Committee (1987 p. 51): "capital equipment areas of major presses and major transfer lines have to be imported". One example of a gain came in 1989 when the West German company Bosch, Europe's dominant component manufacturer, announced its intention to invest £100 m in a new plant at Miskin, near Cardiff. This would be its sole supplier of a new generation of compact alternators, employing 560 by the start of production in 1991. Other sites considered had included Sunderland in the UK, and Spain. Factors in its decision included the strength of the DM, making West Germany an expensive production base; low wages in the UK (partly, but only partly, a function of exchange rate comparisons); and impending growth in vehicle output in the UK. But Bosch was already a major multinational company in its own right, with 31 plants in 15 countries outside West Germany employing about one-third of its total 160,000 workforce.

Put together, such gains and losses epitomized the dilemma facing the UK as a base for automotive component manufacture.

From the standpoint of British capital, most of the component-supplying companies were too small and depended excessively upon the UK vehicle market. Very few had gone international and located production overseas. Those that did, had of course entered the race to supply "globalizing" motor manufacturers and located production and jobs accordingly; whilst those that had not, faced an uncertain future. From both directions, the future of employment in UK-owned component manufacture in the UK was under threat. From the standpoint of the British worker, internationalization of the supply industry only reinforced the vulnerability of the UK to the vagaries of the market. Foreign direct investment by companies such as Bosch provided jobs, but previous experience of both the motor vehicle assembly industry, and other branch plant type operations suggested that this was a particularly fragile basis on which to rest hopes of lasting prosperity. At the same time, the changing pattern of ownership and supply was having an impact upon location, with tentative signs of the north east and South Wales as preferred sites over the West Midlands, where decline was long-standing and easily counterbalanced any growth in employment elsewhere. For both labour and capital, then, in their different ways, the component sector in the 1980s was in a phase of considerable turmoil, and the UK was unashamedly exposed to global corporate strategies.

## 3.6 Concluding comments

In the introduction to this chapter, three key features of the ongoing transformation of the motor vehicle industry inspired by the Japanese challenge were identified: the global decentralization of assembly and component production; spatial reconcentration of production via integrated just-in-time (JIT) complexes; and increased cooperation between rival vehicle assemblers. These were exemplified first with reference to the Western European market, then with respect to the UK, and finally in the context of evolving patterns of automotive component production. It is apparent that the future geography of the global automobile industry is intricately tied up with questions to do with the future pattern of production organization, including the spatial distribution of component supplying companies. What is far from clear is what shape that pattern is likely to take. This should not be surprising for, in the process of transition, the actors—vehicle assemblers, governments and component producers—are themselves feeling their way into a new environment, testing the limits and evaluating the appropriate mixes of the respective strategies of decentralization, reconcentration and cooperation. In interpreting these decisions, opinion is particularly divided over two related issues to do with the extent to which Japanese-style production systems can be and are being adopted in the USA (where Japanese investment is longer established than in Western Europe, although similar questions are beginning to emerge there) and in the UK: Is there an emerging spatial clustering or reconcentration of component suppliers? Are labour management styles freely transferable?

In their analysis of the US automotive components industry, Glasmeir and McCluskey (1987) found little evidence for a reconcentration of production in the Midwest (heartland for US giants Ford and GM) except in research and development activities. By contrast, Mair *et al* (1988) focused on the 250 Japanese component companies which had located in the USA in the 1980s. They argued that these had created integrated production complexes around the transplant investments (the vehicle assemblers), partly because of problems experienced by the latter in obtaining satisfactory quality from local suppliers. Japanese component suppliers, they argued, like the bulk of the assemblers, had located production in rural areas to ease the adoption of JIT. They concluded:

> While it is still unclear how the likely diffusion of JIT into the big three firms [Ford, GM and Chrysler] will affect the geography of the indigenous automobile industry, the JIT complexes have already created a new geography of automobile production in their very backyard. (p. 370)

Yet the activities of these Japanese manufacturers in the USA was interpreted differently by Hill (1989), who argued that:

> Thus far, Japanese transplants are primarily assembly operations rather than integrated, fully-fledged manufacturing complexes along the model of Toyota City. (p. 471)

In his view, the dominant feature was still decentralization—the global sourcing of components. The key growth here was in the low-wage economies of South East Asia:

> Parts produced in Pacific Rim NICs will be sent to assembly transplants in North America and domestic operations in Japan. (p. 473)

Secondly, in the UK at least, a great deal was made of the likely potential impact of Japanese-style industrial relations practices. Turnbull (1987) found that the low stock levels associated with

JIT, plus the heightened interdependence of different plants, was a potentially awkward combination in the context of radical labour management reforms:

> The labour relations consequences of the long-term squeeze on prices combined with JIT deliveries of vital components are only just beginning to surface. They signal serious problems, if not a gross miscalculation, of both the transferability of Japanese techniques and the extent to which British workers can be cowed by the threat or actual experience of job loss and factory closure. (pp. 14–15)

Because the sensitivity of JIT to any form of disruption was extreme, he labelled such industrial relations issues the "limits to Japanization" in the UK. Cautioning that unless this was recognized, there would be an escalation of unrest in the industry, he went on also to argue that the system only worked in Japan because of the nature of trade unionism there. For Starkey and McKinlay (1989), too, the Japanization of Ford's industrial relations procedures in imitation of the new style meant that it was in the midst of an awkward transition period—exemplified only too clearly in the disputes at Ford UK in 1988 and 1990. Such questions were of course at the root of reticence on the part of companies like Toyota to invest in Europe; even their assertion that the problems of assimilation had been overcome could not disguise the seriousness of the issues at stake.

The growth of Japanese production in the UK during the 1980s and into the 1990s meant that these were certain to be pressing issues. For the European Community, the Japanese transplants posed a fundamental challenge, and opened up tremendous differences of opinion between member states which stood in the way of agreement. In 1989, VW, Fiat, Ford and Renault issued calls for there to be continuing controls on the import of Japanese cars into the EC after the creation of a single market and the lifting of national quotas in 1992—possibly for a further five-year transitional period. This argument was tentatively accepted by the EC, although member states still had different opinions over the nature and extent of restrictions and how to treat production from the Japanese transplants in the UK (Nissan intended to export 40 per cent of its 200,000 annual output to the rest of the EC; Toyota 75 per cent of its 200,000 capacity; and Honda 60 per cent of its 100,000). Debate on these issues continued well into 1990 with little sign of agreement.

One key factor behind the strong calls on the part of other companies and some countries in favour of protection was concern over the future structure of the industry once the Japanese transplants reached full capacity. Nissan's impact in the EC in the 1980s was partly masked by the long sales boom and, on the strength of this, many vehicle assemblers also invested in new capacity; but it was apparent that the boom could not last forever. In addition to the 0.5 m units of capacity at the Japanese-owned UK plants, other companies were building factories in Western Europe with an annual potential output of 1 m units. In the USA, the problem was even more acute. Ford warned that by the early 1990s there would be around 6 m units of capacity in excess of demand in the US alone (8.4 m in the world). Its vice-chairman Harold Poling argued that "we will be facing a brutally competitive environment worldwide" (quoted in *Financial Times* 9 January 1990). Toyota chairman Eiji Toyoda picked up the challenge, disclosing that in the late 1990s his group planned to increase vehicle production by a third to 6 m units annually, of which one-half would be built in Japan and one-half overseas. Much concern was focused on the Japanese transplants. In 1989, a Japanese car, the Honda Accord, emerged as the best-selling model in the US for the first time ever, and the traditional manufacturers—Ford and GM—faced the prospect of losing even more ground. In both the USA and Western Europe, the Japanese companies represented not only a new wave of investment with radically different systems of production, but also a serious challenge to the profitability of the previously dominant manufacturers, which might easily lead to a new round of closures and retrenchment.

One way out of this dilemma (in terms of profitability at least) for the major volume producers like Ford and GM was belatedly to recognize the moves being made into high-quality market niches by the Japanese companies Toyota and Nissan, with their Lexus and Infiniti ranges. In Western Europe, in particular, attention centred on the future of the small, independent, luxury car producers. In 1989, this rapidly crystallized when Ford gained effective control of the UK-based company Jaguar, privatized in 1984 and previously protected from foreign takeover by a government-owned "golden share". Ford paid £1,600 m for Jaguar, sealing its control after a hard-fought encounter with its rival, GM. Within a matter of weeks, GM bounced back, securing a controlling 50 per cent stake in the Swedish company Saab-Scania's car operations—this time itself ousting a rival (in this case Fiat) in the closing stages of negotiations. For Ford and GM, these acquisitions were a crucial component of their strategy into the 1990s. They represented an attempt to penetrate the upper-market ranges where, amongst other potential benefits, profit margins were relatively high. For other established luxury-market producers, and for the newly arrived Japanese companies, they clearly posed a new challenge, opening up an intensely competitive prospect in this product range as well as the mass production volume market.

It would be wrong, however, just to focus on the impact of Japanese motor vehicle production—great though it was—in an assessment and evaluation of likely future trends in the industry. For, in addition to the rise of other producer countries like South Korea (see Gwynne, 1989), several other issues were clearly apparent in the early 1990s which were likely to shape the course of the industry in that decade. These included the dramatic process of political reform in Eastern Europe, and possible environmental constraints on the very future of the automobile.

As the 1980s drew to a close, dramatic reappraisal of long-term corporate planning was forced upon car manufacturers by the process of political reform in Eastern Europe. In the short-term, these newly liberalized states offered a vast potential reservoir of low-wage labour: in the medium to longer term they also represented a tremendous, newly accessible and potentially rapidly growing market, easily capable of doubling in size from the 2 m annual sales recorded at the end of the 1980s. Fiat had by far the strongest presence in the Soviet Union and moved rapidly to strengthen this position, signing a major £870 m joint venture agreement in 1989 to produce eventually 300,000 cars annually there. Other companies quickly followed. In the early months of 1990 alone, Suzuki announced plans for an £85 m joint venture in Hungary; and GM for a joint £90 m engine production and vehicle assembly plant in Hungary, and a possible 150,000/year car assembly operation in East Germany. VW, aware of the economic and political significance of German re-unification, openly considered the prospect of a complete £1,700 m modernization of the East German car industry, entailing a new plant capable of building 250,000 cars per year from 1995. This subsequently epitomized the swings and roundabouts of global investment: welcomed in East Germany, it provoked concern in Spain that investment in Eastern Europe might act to divert funds away from modernization at VW's Spanish subsidiary, Seat.

A final important issue—by no means an afterthought in many companies' strategic plans for the 1990s—was the environmental impact of the motor vehicle at a time of growing public awareness of pollution, the greenhouse effect and pressure on non-renewable resources. In the late 1980s, California's South Coast Air Quality Management District estimated that meeting new environmental standards would require more than 6 m of the region's cars and vans—70 per cent of the total—to be electrically powered by 2010. The City Council of Los Angeles promoted an "Electric Vehicle Initiative", under which it hoped to have 10,000 such vehicles operating in the region by 1995, in order to assess the viability of the technology. In 1990, GM announced that it had developed an electric-powered car, the Impact, with an acceleration performance comparable to internal combustion engines and a range suitable for urban driving. In a context of mounting pressures on pollution control and energy conservation, such vehicles appeared increasingly attractive. The Impact, for instance, required one-third of the energy of a conventional car and emitted none of the pollutants such as oxides of nitrogen and carbon monoxide which were at the heart of photochemical smog, nor the greenhouse gases such as carbon dioxide. Yet the announcement was greeted with considerable caution. Not only were the full benefits dependent upon the kind of technology used to recharge batteries; there was also a sense in which much had been promised before, but not delivered. General Motors first announced its intention to build 100,000 battery-powered cars a year within four years in 1980; Ford announced that it had developed the technology to make mass production of electric vehicles commercially feasible within five to ten years as far back as 1966. Both projects failed to come to fruition.

It is perhaps wholly appropriate to end the chapter on this note—one new market opportunity in Eastern Europe, one potential barrier to sales in the form of environmental legislation—as the industry shaped up for the 1990s and beyond. One thing was certain: the arrival of the Japanese as a major world producer of automobiles had transformed the structure of the industry. How it responded in the 1990s was to be another story.

## Notes

1. The growth of production in Spain in the late 1970s and early 1980s was by any standards spectacular. Spain first produced more cars than the UK at the start of the 1980s; by 1988 an output of 1.5 m cars was more than double that in 1974, making the country the world's sixth largest car producer. In addition to longstanding plants owned by the French companies Peugeot and Renault, and by the Spanish company Seat, Ford began production at Valencia from 1976 and GM at Zaragoza in 1982. Both US companies sought to reap the benefits of cheap labour and free access to the EC after Spain's accession in 1986. This wave of investment contrasted markedly with the new wave of Japanese investment in the late 1980s which was concentrated in the UK.

2.  The political storm over the sale of Rover to British Aerospace centred initially on an enquiry by the National Audit Office. This revealed that for its £150 m BAe obtained:

    -   a concern whose 1987 profit of £28 m, on a price-earnings ratio of 5:1 (as suggested by the Secretary of State) suggested a minimum value of £140 m; plus
    -   tax benefits of £33 m to £40 m; plus
    -   surplus sites worth £34 m at the time of the sale; plus
    -   holdings in nine other companies, of which two had already realized £126 m

    The enquiry concluded in no uncertain terms that "the sale price of £150 m fell significantly short of the real value of the company" (NAO 1989 p. 12).

    Its already damaging impact was heightened by the publication of a leaked confidential memorandum from the NAO to the House of Commons Public Accounts Committee which revealed that the Government also granted an additional £38 m in concessions to BAe when it appeared, at the last minute, to be backing out of the deal. The memo also recorded that other companies expressing an interest in Rover included Ford, Volkswagen and Toyota; and indicated forecast profits at Rover of around £100 m annually in the early 1990s. A further aspect of the sale was emphasized by the Oxford-based Motor Industry Research Project—the extent to which BAe would benefit from disposal of Rover's surplus land and property assets:

    > BAe looks set to become a major property developer over the next few years ... . If Rover go ahead with the policy of closure in the early 1990s, the company will have an enormously valuable piece of real estate to develop. (MIRP 1990 p. 71)

    Subsequently, Leon Brittan, European Community Competition Commissioner, demanded that BAe repay £44.4 m of illegal state subsidies to the UK government.

3.  Rover's new strategy was described by its chairman Graham Day as follows:

    > We're looking to have a determined, product-led repositioning in the market place, a bit away from head-on competition with those companies that mass-produce cars. We are looking to promote distinctive products. We are looking for product differentiation, particularly as the market increasingly segments. We are trying to set ourselves apart from mainstream competition. We're probably a medium-volume producer. We're smaller than Daimler-Benz, we're about the size of BMW, maybe about the size of Volvo, much bigger than Saab, but we're not a Ford, a Fiat, a Peugeot or a Volkswagen. We now produce about half a million units. That is the level at which I believe we can sustain and renew our business and indeed contribute to our shareholder. (quoted in *Financial Times* 18 August 1989)

## The Global Region

4. This site was a legacy of GM's search for new locations in the late 1970s. Whilst Zaragoza in north-east Spain was chosen as a site for vehicle assembly, Aspern in Vienna became a new engine assembly base. A not inconsiderable element in this decision was the level of state subsidy offered, for together the Viennese and Austrian governments covered one-third of GM's investment costs (in return for the 2,400 jobs). This was subsequently described as "the largest industrial subsidy in Austrian history" (Sinclair and Walker 1982 p. 438)

5. One (low-technology) product area where Japanese companies gained effective control was in the production of radiators, after Nippondenso bought out the UK's last remaining large independent car radiator manufacturer, IMI Radiators, in 1989.

# Part II

# Restructuring in an Old Industrial Region: North East England

# Introduction

In the second part of this book, the emphasis switches to the changing geography of production at a smaller scale than the global patterns mapped out in Part I. In particular, Part II focuses upon some of the key components of change within one old industrial region, north east England, in an attempt to draw out some of the main implications of and preconditions for international restructuring. It draws on examples from the three sectors considered in Part I—coal, steel and motor vehicles—which have been selected to demonstrate the interdependence of regional, national and global change.

Recent developments in the north east of England are not reducible to these industries alone (far from it), but coal, steel and motor vehicles have been significant to the region both in absolute terms and in the broader sense of leading the character of change from one, older, economic base to a newer, different one, the main features of which are tentatively becoming more and more concrete. Similarly, the sweeping international transformations discussed in Part I have touched far more than just one region, often in many very different ways. Yet within the north east, there is a clear expression of massive decline in coal and steel, which is shared by many other old industrial regions in Western Europe and North America. This is coupled with the first signs of growth in a "new", largely Japanese-owned, automotive sector which encapsulates the global emergence of Japan and the challenge its automobile manufacturers pose to the West. These three sectors are therefore revealing in their own terms as well as for the ways in which they overlap and intersect within one region. The north east is significant for its uniqueness—the particular combination and the precise working-out of time and place—and for its broader role within the global system of capitalist production. Part I identified the broad outlines; Part II aims to paint a finer-grained picture and, in so doing, expand our understanding of the overall canvas.

This part of the book is organized as follows. Chapter 4 introduces the broad context of the changing geography of production in north east England. It describes the decline of "old" industries such as coal and steel, focusing on sweeping cutbacks in deep-mining alongside the increased role of opencasting; on closures and reorganization at British Steel's South Teesside works; and on the rupturing of previously long-established links between coal and steel within the region. This is contrasted with the rise of the "new", epitomized in development of the Nissan plant at Sunderland, to ask what differences and similarities there are between "old" and "new" sectors. Chapter 5 goes on to question how such changes were possible: what preconditions existed for radical decline in the existing industrial base and the implantation of new forms of manufacturing. It locates the answer in the context of high unemployment and the weakening of labour, symbolized in defeat for the anti-closure campaign at Consett steel works in 1980 and the year-long miners' strike in 1984/85. This chapter then turns to the question of what production reorganization actually means, focusing upon experiences of flexibility in the "old" industries of coal and, especially, steel. It investigates the extent to which "new" production practices and methods have been mirrored elsewhere in the region, particularly in the wave of small businesses established in response to state policies for the "re-industrialization" of coal and steel closure areas. It also explores some of the implications of a growing service sector within the region, and ends with some further questions about the future which act as a springboard to the concluding chapter.

# 4

# The Decline of the Old and the Rise of the New: Coal, Steel and Motor Vehicles in North East England

## 4.1 Introduction: the changing geography of production in north east England

This chapter—essentially a bridge between the two parts of the book—starts with a very brief introduction to the changing geography of production in the north east region of England: not a comprehensive account, but a glimpse into the key features which make it of significance to industrial capitalism (see also Figure 4.1). In such a brief exposition, it is obviously impossible to do full justice to all the subtleties. Instead it provides regional context for more detailed discussion of particular evidence. Then, in the remainder of the chapter, the key features of the decline in coal and steel, and the growth of the Nissan complex at Sunderland, are introduced and assessed.

In the early post-1945 period, the region's economy was relatively prosperous and near full employment was not exceptional, largely built on the strength of the emphasis placed on coal by the UK's single-fuel policy. After 1958, this began to change, and by 1963 the region faced what appeared at the time to be a major crisis of unemployment, as coal-mining redundancies coincided with a cyclical downturn in the national economy. In response, the government appointed Lord Hailsham as first (and last) Minister for the North East. His regeneration programme (HMSO 1963) envisaged selective public investment in the region's infrastructure, with a new road network and enhanced development of the postwar new towns. For a time at least in the 1960s, these measures, along with a strengthened regional policy, appeared to

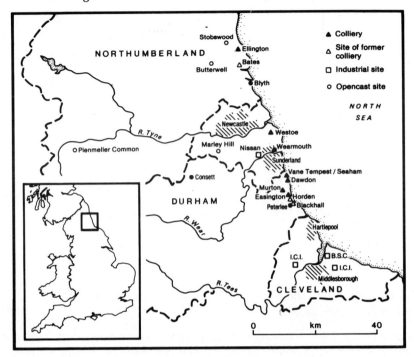

FIG 4.1.  North east England.

be working, as there were substantial increases in manufacturing output. In this period, the region was particularly attractive to certain forms of investment, in existing heavy industry such as steel and chemicals on Teesside, and in new factories established in response to the reconstitution of labour supply following run-down in coal and increased encouragement for women to work for a wage. In the main, though, these factories tended to be branch plant operations with limited skill requirements, which in recession proved to be the first to suffer. From the 1970s onwards, the story of the north east economy was essentially one of steadily rising unemployment and factory closures as the region—aptly characterized as a global outpost of multinational capital, but suffering also from the effects of state policies—saw decline in both the new employers of the 1960s and the staple industries, the latter increasingly underpinned by state-supported investment in new, capital-intensive production methods.

In the 1980s, the north east became one of the UK's most intractable "depressed" regions. One in every three manufacturing jobs disappeared from 1977 to 1985, and three-quarters of these were

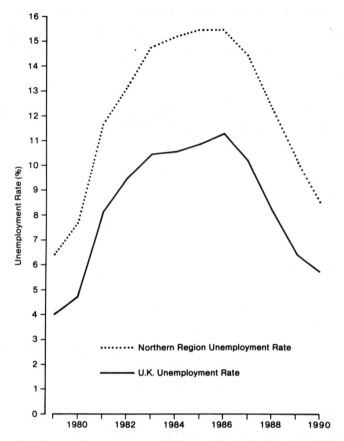

FIG 4.2.   Unemployment rates, UK and Northern Region, 1979–90.
(Source: NOMIS. Note time - series is consistent with unemployment
coverage in 1990.)

from the traditional industries. As the number of long-term
unemployed grew, household incomes fell to the lowest of any UK
region, and the single biggest regional element of public spending
became social security and unemployment benefit—a new and,
to the individual at least, even more inadequate form of state
intervention in the region's economy. At the end of the 1980s,
it was apparent that the Northern Region was still characterized
by a greater concentration of jobs in production industries than
the UK as a whole, despite higher than average rates of job loss
over the previous decade—partly because employment in the
service sector had grown at a lower rate than the UK average
(see Table 4.1). The only major area of service growth was in
banking, insurance and finance, a marked contrast to the picture

181

TABLE 4.1
*Employment change: Northern Region and UK, 1979–89*

| | Employment, m | | % of total | | Change 1979–89 | |
| | 1979 | 1989 | 1979 | 1989 | m | % pa |
|---|---|---|---|---|---|---|
| *Northern Region* | | | | | | |
| Production | | | | | | |
| industries | 0.48 | 0.33 | 39 | 29 | −0.15 | −3.5 |
| Services | 0.67 | 0.72 | 55 | 64 | 0.05 | 0.7 |
| Total | 1.2K | 1.12 | 100 | 100 | −0.12 | −0.8 |
| *UK* | | | | | | |
| Production | | | | | | |
| industries | 7.78 | 5.63 | 34 | 25 | −2.15 | −2.8 |
| Services | 13.37 | 15.63 | 59 | 69 | 2.26 | 1.7 |
| Total | 22.72 | 22.56 | 100 | 100 | −0.16 | −0.1 |

Note: figures are estimates for December
Production industries = SIC 1–4; services = SIC 6–9; total = SIC 0–9
Source: *Employment Gazette* (various dates).

in the traditional production industries—such as energy, metal manufacture, chemicals and engineering—of almost unremitting decline (see Table 4.2). National economic recovery towards the end of the decade had only a limited impact, as the total number of employees in employment in the Northern Region picked up only slowly from the low-point of 1.06 m in 1983, to reach 1.12 m by 1989, still well below the 1979 total of 1.24 m (see Figure 4.3).

In the spiral of decline, the traditional industries were in the forefront, if by no means exceptional. In steel, closures at Hartlepool in the 1970s and Consett in 1980 were only part of a growing roll-call of casualties—although Consett was the subject of a fierce and highly symbolic anti-closure campaign (see Chapter 5). The 44,000 jobs lost from British Coal and British Steel in the course of the 1980s were equivalent to one-third of the total absolute fall in production industry employment in the Northern Region (see Table 4.3). Although this partly overstates the impact of these two industries in that absolute figures also include gains in other sectors, coal's demise was remarkable both for its very protracted nature (see Figure 4.4) and the widespread extent of its influence across the region. This held true not only in the broad dispersal of pit closures (see Figure 4.5), but also, and in the long term perhaps even more significantly, in the extent

TABLE 4.2
Employment change in the Northern Region, 1979–89

| 1980 SIC Description | (1000s) 1979 | 1989 | % change pa 1979–89 |
|---|---|---|---|
| 0 Agriculture, forestry, fishing | 15 | 12 | −2.0 |
| 1 Energy and water supply | 75 | 37 | −5.1 |
| 2 Metal manufacturing and chemicals | 102 | 60 | −4.1 |
| 3 Metal goods, engineering and vehicles | 179 | 116 | −3.5 |
| 4 Other manufacturing | 123 | 114 | −0.7 |
| 5 Construction | 82 | 69 | −1.6 |
| 61–63, 66–67 Wholesale distribution, hotels and catering | 106 | 105 | – |
| 64–65 Retail distribution | 127 | 113 | −1.1 |
| 7 Transport and communication | 64 | 52 | −1.9 |
| 8 Banking, insurance and finance | 59 | 84 | 4.2 |
| 91–92 Public administration and defence | 96 | 98 | 0.2 |
| 93–99 Education, health and other services | 216 | 264 | 2.2 |
| Total | 1,244 | 1,124 | |

Source: *Employment Gazette* (various dates).

Table 4.3
Employment by British Coal and British Steel in the north east of England,
1979 and 1989

| | Employment, 1000s 1979 | 1989 | Change, 1979–89 1000s | % pa |
|---|---|---|---|---|
| British Coal | 34 | 11 | 23 | 6.8 |
| British Steel | 28 | 7 | 21 | 7.5 |
| Total | 62 | 18 | 44 | 7.1 |

Source: British Coal *Annual Reports*; British Steel author's estimates.

to which state planning had deliberately kept out alternative jobs in the period from 1945 to the early 1960s at a time of potential labour shortages. In other words, because of the national political priorities attached to maximizing coal output, other male employing industries had deliberately been discouraged from locating in the north east and diversifying the regional economy.

**183**

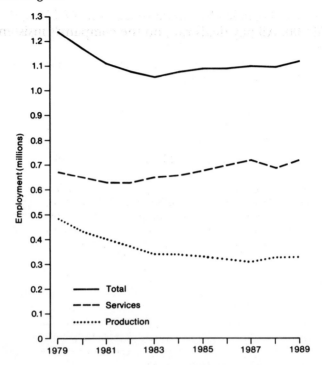

FIG 4.3. Employment change in the Northern Region, 1979–89. (Source: *Employment Gazette.*)

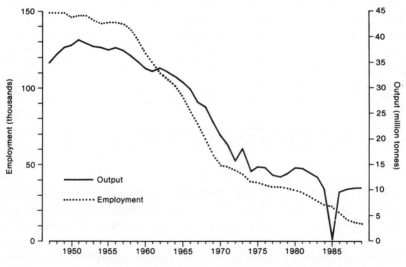

FIG 4.4. Employment and output in the north east coalfield, 1947–90.

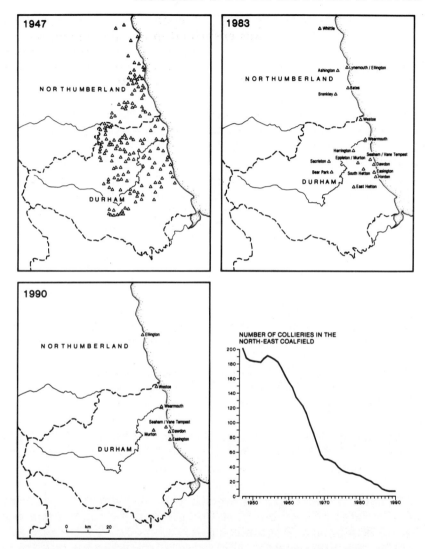

FIG 4.5.   Pit closures in north east England, 1947–90 (each symbol
represents an active colliery at that date).

In the early postwar years, the Ministry of Town and Country
Planning commissioned an outline plan for the north east (see
Pepler and MacFarlane 1949). On coal-mining, it argued as
follows:

> With coal the most precious and urgently needed of industrial raw
> materials, to introduce into mining areas [at this time, practically
> all of the industrial north east] male employing industries based in

185

up-to-date factories and able to offer pleasant work at good wages, would inevitably attract men away from the mines with disastrous consequences for coal production [therefore] no appreciable volume of alternative male employment should be introduced into stable long-life mining districts.

As the former managing director of Peterlee New Town later described, this philosophy was certainly put into practice:

The newly established National Coal Board were concerned to maintain their labour force and unreceptive, if not hostile, to the development of any new industry which might attract men away from the pits. They had welcomed the designation of the new town as a means of stabilising their labour force and offering them better living conditions, and had no objection to the creation of jobs for women (which by stabilising families would also stabilise the male labour force) but the idea of a large-scale male-employing industrial estate at Peterlee was unacceptable. (Philipson 1988 p. 126)

Such arguments formed the basis of local economic development policy. Even when local authorities such as Durham County Council began to develop plans for the creation of new jobs from the early 1950s onwards, they were frustrated first by the NCB's refusal to provide information and then by its power to veto new development such as industrial estates on the grounds that they might sterilize coal reserves (that is, prevent the NCB from mining underneath new buildings for fear of subsidence). As late as the 1960s, when the pace of colliery closures accelerated alarmingly, the NCB refused to reveal details of production plans which could assist long-term local economic planning for fear, in the divisional director's words in 1965, "that manpower in the coal mines might run down too fast if miners lost confidence in the industry". The impacts of the NCB's policy in this period were to become clear later. By discouraging other employers, it guaranteed itself a stable labour force; but in so doing it laid the foundations for future economic and social collapse.

One revealing aspect of the region's limited industrial diversification was that until Nissan arrived, it had never had a car assembly plant, unlike other peripheral regions of the UK such as the north west or Scotland—although Ford looked closely at several sites in the north east in the late 1960s. This is what made Nissan's plant such a significant entrant into the region's industrial structure and culture; and again, it was sponsored by the state, with the UK government heavily subsidizing Nissan's total investment costs. In being so different—the first Japanese car manufacturing plant in Europe, with production methods and organization heralded even before it arrived—the implantation of Nissan represented an important opportunity to analyze the character of change in the 1980s. This is essentially the task in the remainder of this chapter: to examine the pattern of decline in coal and steel, and explore the new dimensions of production associated with the Nissan complex.

## 4.2 Pillars of the old industrial base: coal and steel

The 1973 ten-year development strategy for the British Steel Corporation had envisaged a dramatic expansion in steelmaking on South Teesside (see Chapter 2). It proposed massive investment in a new complex which, together with expansion of the existing site, would result in a steel works with an annual capacity of 12 m tonnes by the 1980s.[1] As the forecast growth in demand for steel failed to materialize, these proposals became increasingly uncertain and a halt was effectively called to the programme in 1978, throwing into question the investment then underway. The modernization and expansion projects approaching completion were finished, but there were to be no further starts on steelmaking capacity. Priority was given to stage two, construction of new iron-making capacity, but a new plate mill (stage three) was specifically deferred. Stage two was in fact completed when a new blast furnace, the Redcar no. 1, started up in September 1979. Additionally, the steel converters had been upgraded to increase their annual capacity to 4.65 m tonnes.

This truncated expansion of the steel works had wide-ranging implications. In 1978, the complex relied upon the old Clay Lane blast furnaces for the supply of hot iron as all the other blast furnaces on Teesside (associated with obsolete open hearth steel capacity) had been closed. The maximum annual output of the Clay Lane furnaces, however, was of the order of 2.1 m tonnes—sufficient for the steel plant as originally scheduled but by no means sufficient for the uprated plant. Consequently, when the Redcar blast furnace came into production in 1979, the Clay Lane furnaces were closed as their future capability appeared highly limited—they were unable to replace the Redcar no. 1 furnace without substantially reducing the output of the steel works.

This was a crucial decision for it meant that, from 1979, the entire South Teesside complex was totally dependent upon one blast furnace for the supply of iron. Since the steel making process required at least 70 per cent hot iron, the ramifications of this dependence upon one giant, technologically sophisticated but highly delicate item of capital investment were far-reaching. South

Teesside's reliance upon one blast furnace was both unusual and uniquely handicapping. The original intention had been to build three similarly massive blast furnaces; indeed the steelwork for a second such plant was purchased but never assembled. Yet most, if not all, steelworks producing steel by the basic oxygen route were supplied with hot iron by a series of blast furnaces. This was necessary since all blast furnaces required periodic renewal of the refractory brick lining which protected their steel shell from the temperatures within. With more than one blast furnace, this could be accomplished in rotation, so that there was always capacity available to meet the demands for hot iron. With only one blast furnace, steel production effectively had to cease when this was cooled for relining.

The uncertainty engendered by this situation was particularly acute in 1982 at a time when BSC was seeking actively to close capacity and was reviewing the future of all its major works. Whilst the Ravenscraig complex came to be seen as most under threat, concern was also growing on South Teesside since a renewal of the Redcar blast furnace's lining was imminently necessary, yet no plans had been announced. A specially convened local Steel Conference met in January 1983 to discuss the issue (see Cleveland County Council 1983). By this date, the future of Ravenscraig had been temporarily resolved in a fashion which implicated all five remaining integrated sites. They were each given a five-year guarantee of continuing steelmaking, but no such assurances were made on the future of rolling mills or on capacity utilization levels.

Faced with this position, Cleveland County Council commissioned a further special report to investigate the options open to BSC on South Teesside (see Hudson and Sadler 1984), and the company's intentions came gradually to light. It aimed to complete the reline during a five month period in the summer of 1986, keeping the rolling mills occupied with a stock of semi-finished steel created before the reline commenced, and with supplies from the BSC works at Scunthorpe. Small quantities of steel would still be produced by converting two small furnaces previously used to produce ferro-manganese to the production of iron, and export orders which were not of strategic significance would temporarily be discontinued.

The reline was successfully completed more or less in line with this strategy. However, the debate which it had fostered, and the knowledge that a similar situation would inevitably arise again in the future (barring the unlikely possibility of an additional blast furnace being constructed), brought to light a more deep-seated consequence of premature termination of the 1973 expansion programme. This was the chronic lack of investment in South Teesside's rolling mill capacity, coupled with a sweeping series of mill closures——one result of the focus upon primary iron and steel production and the uncertainty caused by the periodic necessity to renew the one blast furnace's refractory lining. This represented the greatest threat to the South Teesside works in the long term: for more and more it meant that the complex was geared towards the production of relatively unsophisticated semi-finished steel.

The two main mills remaining on the site had markedly different prospects. The beam mill operated in a major growth area, the construction industry, and was able to produce to specifications and dimensions not readily achieved elsewhere. The coil plate mill by contrast delivered a standard product in considerable over-supply within the European Community. It was also operating in the same product area—strip (essentially narrow-gauge plate)—as the three mills at Llanwern, Port Talbot and Ravenscraig which had been publicly threatened with closure in 1982. Very little new investment had gone in to the Teesside mills, certainly by comparison with other sites such as Port Talbot. In effect, the South Teesside site had already begun to play a particular role within BSC, producing relatively unprofitable bulk steel for rolling elsewhere in the UK or for export direct. In 1984, the Cargo Fleet rolling mills on Teesside were closed and production transferred to a newly modernized mill at Scunthorpe. During 1985, a long-term contract was signed under which BSC Teesside was to supply Tuscaloosa Steel of the USA with 0.25 m tonnes of semi-finished steel annually. The logic behind such moves was clear. With a periodic need to reline the blast furnace and cease production, or at best slow down supplies to a marginal level, new rolling mill investment was best concentrated elsewhere, whilst South Teesside was left to focus upon the production of crude steel.

The combined impact of these developments on Teesside was dramatic. From 1971 to 1978, employment in steel fell from 29,000 to 23,000 as the Redcar scheme paved the way for the closure of older plant. After 1978, the pace of decline quickened dramatically. In total, three batteries of coke ovens, three blast furnaces, three electric arc furnaces and seven rolling mills were closed as BSC employment fell to 18,000 by 1981 and 7,000 by 1984.

The ramifications of BSC's changed policy for the South Teesside works extended far deeper though than an emerging concentration upon bulk steel production. For just as national political priorities helped to chart the course of BSC's withdrawal from an over-ambitious expansion programme, so too did politics come to play an important role in mediating the relationship between one nationalized industry, BSC, and another, the National Coal Board, within the north east (for a detailed account, see Beynon, Hudson and Sadler 1986, 1991).

The 1973 ten-year development strategy in steel was mirrored by the similarly long-term and expansionist Plan for Coal of 1974. Under this, the south-east Durham pits in particular were to be redeveloped to supply coking coal for the proposed expansion at BSC South Teesside. Some £40 m was to be invested in the Horden, Blackhall and Easington coastal complex of collieries and in Kent, to supply ranks 501 and 204 coals respectively, suitable for blending with rank 301b coals from the west of County Durham to a quality acceptable for the Redcar blast furnace.[2] Tests conducted in 1978 proved the suitability of this blend for BSC requirements, and the Redcar coke ovens commissioned during 1978 and 1979 incorporated technology appropriate to the use of such a mixture.

This investment was made in the Durham coastal collieries and opencast output from the west of Durham was expanded partially to meet BSC's requirements. As late as 1978, BSC continued to assure the NCB, which in turn assured the NUM, that it would need these coals. But, in October 1979, under a new government, BSC announced that nationally it would import about 25 per cent of its coking coal requirements in the following year (see Chapter 2). On Teesside, this involved a dramatic about-turn—using, for the first time, to import coal, a harbour designed originally to import iron ore, as BSC turned its back on locally available coal supplies. In County Durham, a series of investments in particular collieries and seams was placed into question overnight. With no warning and no long-term contract (the agreement between BSC and the NCB was similar to that between the CEGB and the NCB, an understanding between two public corporations with no binding force), the NCB faced a catastrophic loss of a major market.[3] By September 1980, coking coal stocks at Durham collieries had risen to 1.8 m tonnes. In the newly created situation of over-supply, pit closures followed swiftly and ruthlessly in this part of the coalfield, from Blackhall in 1981 to Horden in 1986.

Despite subsequent repeated attempts to justify BSC's switch in purchasing policy in terms of coal quality, it is clear that the over-riding priority was one of price (see Beynon, Hudson and Sadler 1986 pp. 33–40). BSC was taking advantage of temporary global over-supply regardless of long-term consequences and previous understandings. In the process, the international coal market made a deeply visible impact upon the economy of this part of north east England, encouraged by a particular political conception of the appropriate role of nationalized corporations. The power of short-term market forces was imposed and a local economy opened to the full weight of international competition.

Not that the NCB appeared to care. Concerned only to meet government-set financial targets, it rapidly became only too keen to close capacity, particularly in a peripheral coalfield such as the north east, and for a time even seemed to be agreeing with BSC in the argument that the quality of coal provided locally for Redcar was not satisfactory, despite adequate evidence to the contrary from the late 1970s (see Beynon, Hudson and Sadler 1986). In reality, of course, the NCB's main target was to trim capacity with as little opposition and as rapidly as possible, even if that meant ceding existing markets with barely a whimper. In this process, it ignored longstanding consultation procedures with the mining unions, especially in the wake of the 1984/85 dispute, and re-allocated coal reserves to different collieries practically at will. The closure of Horden colliery, for instance, took place in 1986 after mining unions forced the case to become the first taken to a newly established and rapidly discredited independent review procedure (see Chapter 5). It came about not only in response to the loss of the Redcar market, but also—and in the long term, crucially—because of the loss of substantial reserves of coal which had been ceded to neighbouring Easington Colliery. This left Horden—once proclaimed, along with Easington and Blackhall (the latter closed in 1981), a long life colliery with access to 200 m tonnes of undersea reserves—with very little coal left to mine (Beynon, Hudson and Sadler 1991). In effect, it was actively planned out of existence.

In the west of the region, where the coal seams were nearer to the surface, a different but no less troubling picture emerged. Expansion of opencast mining had begun, supported at first by the NUM on the grounds that it was required for Redcar. But even with the Redcar market lost, British Coal continued to push for increased opencast output, claiming profits earned this way helped to balance the books. In the face of new circumstances and a growing list of colliery closures, the Durham Area NUM joined a range of environmental groups which were strongly committed to opposing opencast mining.

British Coal sought extensively to increase its opencast output in a bid to produce low-cost coal, albeit at an environmental price. The national arguments over opencasting (see Chapter 1) were particularly acute in a region where deep-mining was, in severe decline, yet which also held a large proportion of national opencast reserves. Five major public enquiries were held into appeals by British Coal against planning refusals by Durham County Council in 1986 and 1987 alone, over reserves amounting to some 2 m tonnes. In 1987, permission was granted by Environment Secretary Nicholas Ridley (after a public inquiry) for opencasting to take place on a 1,100 acre site at Plenmeller Common in Northumberland, with total output estimated at nearly 2 m tonnes of coal. Shortly afterwards, British Coal announced plans to mine a further 11 m tonnes at Stobswood near Morpeth in Northumberland from 1990, to replace its 2,000 acre site at Butterwell. Whilst these were representative of the larger sites, a continuing stream of smaller projects was undertaken. Output from Durham ran at around 1 m tonnes annually, and from Northumberland 2 m tonnes each year—roughly 20 per cent of total national opencast production. As environmental campaigner Des Napier put it,

> A third of all the total opencast reserves in the country are in the north east, about 200 m tonnes, so we are the biggest target for both the Coal Board and the private sector. (quoted in *Newcastle Journal* 12 May 1986)

Opencast coal production also exposed several fractures, if not deep rifts, in the debate over employment versus the environment. At several public inquiries, British Coal was supported by smaller local authorities (below the County level) anxious to see some jobs created despite the overall impact on coal-mining employment and the extent to which opencast contractors moved a team of skilled labour from one site to the other, limiting local employment creation; and also by the TGWU, which represented opencast workers. At the Plenmeller inquiry, Haltwhistle Town Council supported British Coal, and its chairman, Ian McMinn, welcomed the promise of 120 jobs at the site as follows:

> If only 20% of the jobs come here it would have a significant impact on the employment situation in the town. If the figure was 70 per cent, it would become the town's third or fourth largest employer. (quoted in *Newcastle Journal* 26 June 1986)

In other instances, whilst the environmentally destructive impact of opencasting was recognized and provoked concern, the lure of jobs still proved too strong. For instance, in 1986, Derwentside District Council granted permission to private contractors R and

A Young to extract 47,500 tonnes of coal from a site near Consett (bringing 20 jobs) despite objections from two newly established businesses that the dust generated would disturb their production processes.

The harmful impact of opencasting on the region's image was a recurring theme. Durham County Councillor Bob Pendlebury commented as follows on British Coal's proposals to develop more sites:

> Their attitude seems to be that if it involves wiping out pleasant areas of County Durham then so be it. We can forget all about an increase in tourism and tourist-related jobs. Who is going to come to County Durham if at every turn of the road, all you see are huge piles of waste? After all the dereliction of deep mining we are going to have to go through it all again—not for thousands of jobs like before, but for just a handful. (quoted in *Newcastle Journal* 14 May 1986)

In 1989, a public inquiry was convened to hear British Coal's appeal against a decision by Durham County Council and Gateshead Borough Council not to allow the opencasting of 2.8 m tonnes of coal from a six hundred acre site at Marley Hill over an eight year period. The arguments rehearsed at this inquiry exemplified many of the controversies and issues associated with this form of coal extraction. British Coal's regional opencast director John Stevenson put the case for the site in the following terms:

> This proposal will allow us to stand still. We are an extractive industry and sites are exhausting rapidly all the time. The north east produces 3.4 m tonnes a year and if you take that to its logical conclusion we ought to be putting 3.4 m tonnes a year back. (quoted in *Newcastle Journal* 22 November 1989)

Opposing the application on environmental grounds, chief planning officer for Gateshead Borough Council Terry Simons argued that it would affect the improving image of the north east:

> It would appear inevitable that this opencast proposal would have a negative impact on the economic prospects of Tyneside. It would not only confirm visitors' preconceptions that the region was very industrial and depressed, but also that it was losing some of its great natural beauty. (quoted in *Newcastle Journal* 13 December 1989)

Similarly opposed was neighbouring Derwentside District Council, on the grounds that its economic development programme would suffer in consequence of the adverse environmental impact. John Pearson, the Council's industrial development officer:

> While opencast mining is acceptable at some locations, development of prominent sites such as Marley Hill detracts from the district's environment and image. It would prejudice both the attraction of new jobs and the local development plans of existing businesses. (quoted in *Newcastle Journal* 20 December 1989)

These questions were taken further by the Council for the Protection of Rural England (CPRE). One of its witnesses, Pitch Wilson, indicated that, within a five-kilometre radius of Marley Hill, 32 opencast sites had been worked since 1945. This had significantly altered the local countryside:

> The Marley Hill site should not be considered in isolation, it is another piece in a jigsaw designed by British Coal's Opencast Executive which has destroyed an entire landscape. (quoted in *Newcastle Journal* 8 February 1990)

The CPRE case also rested on the excess production created by a continuation of opencast mining, in the context of deep mine closures and a falling demand from the electricity generating industry. Malcolm Brocklesby, a further witness for the CPRE, expounded as follows:

> Either opencast or deep-mined production or a mixture of the two will have to be reduced by 10 m tonnes a year by 1992–93. The great majority of opencast production is now irrefutably in direct competition with the deep mines. Unless opencast is reduced by the full 10 m tonnes a year there will be further costly closures of deep mines because of the reductions in sales to the electricity industry. (quoted in *Newcastle Journal* 7 February 1990)

Most of these arguments were dismissed by British Coal with countervailing assertions (opencast coal was needed by the electricity industry, the environmental impact was unlikely to deter investment) which had been used at other inquiries. Yet British Coal (and private operators) had also devised ingenious ways of placating opposition. At the Plenmeller inquiry, for instance, opponents were told that a 25 metres tall, 55 metres long concrete bunker would look like a church. The one and a half mile long conveyor carrying coal to the bunker would not be intrusive, but would look like a wall. At Marley Hill, the only group supporting British Coal was the Tanfield Railway, a local light railway. This had been promised a special extension around the site to take visitors on specified days. British Coal's John Stevenson explained this as follows:

> It's government policy that industry should open its doors to tourists. Factories like Komatsu are encouraging people to go in and see their

earthmovers. This will be an opportunity for people to see earthmovers in action. (quoted in *Newcastle Journal* 22 November 1989)

More importantly perhaps, British Coal was backed by a government anxious to expand opencast production; several public inquiry decisions which went against British Coal were overturned by the Secretary of State. In the process, the geography of coal production in the north east region was being re-cast in a very different mould.

The other component of this changing geography was continuing decline in the deep-mined industry as the number of pits in the region halved after the 1984/85 strike to seven by 1989, employing a bare 10,000 men—a far cry from the industry's past (see Figures 4.4 and 4.5). Even these remaining deep mines—at Ellington in Northumberland; Westoe and Wearmouth in Tyne and Wear; and Easington, Murton, Dawdon and Vane Tempest in County Durham—were vulnerable to the sourcing strategies of the electricity generating industry, for they largely supplied the Thames power stations which were most accessible to deep-water imports of low-priced foreign coal. Alternative markets at the Yorkshire power stations were blocked off by the growth of the Selby coalfield and the only major coal-fired power station within the region at Blyth in Northumberland was also susceptible to imports, being on the coast.

In 1990, the closure of Dawdon (then employing over 1,000 men) by 1991, and the loss of 400 further jobs at Wearmouth Colliery, were confirmed. Reflecting on the implications, British Coal's regional director Michael Haynes commented that

> obviously some of the collieries have a limited life by virtue of the reserves that they hold. It's no secret that Dawdon has a limited life and will close comparatively shortly.

He went on in a more optimistic vein:

> Of the rest, we have some long life pits which are producing at a very reasonable cost of production. We are producing the lowest cost deep mined coal in the country. In addition, we've got things going for us in as much as our coal is of excellent quality. Our coal is 1.2 per cent sulphur and we have some coals which are as low as 0.8 per cent. Chlorine, which is a problem in some of the Midlands coal, is also low here. We've got the coal the market wants. (quoted in *Newcastle Journal* 3 May 1990)

Whether north east deep-mined coal could be produced at a price competitive with imported coal was, however, a more important question; and in leaving this unanswered, assurances about a "long-life" for the coalfield had a hollow ring. This was all the more so when placed alongside earlier pronouncements by the National Coal Board. Bill Etherington, vice-president of the North East NUM, reflected that

> In the 1960s we were told that Dawdon had a life of one hundred years. I saw plans marked with over one hundred faces. We were told it would be working well into the next century. (quoted in *Newcastle Journal* 20 April 1990)

Now, it seemed, north east deep-mines had an acute problem of reserves, with major investment necessary to access new undersea measures dependent (according to British Coal) upon agreement on flexible shift patterns to reduce the impact of travelling time underground. As Prior and McCloskey (1988 p. 5) succinctly put it, the future for the north east deep-mines after electricity privatization appeared "clear-cut and grim", with only two, Ellington and Westoe, expected to survive.

In many ways, the decline of coal and steel epitomized the collapse of the north east's traditional industrial base in the face of global competition. The Teesside steel industry and its integrated colliery complexes had once, in the nineteenth century, been a production base of considerable international significance; the north east coalfield a source of cheap energy for much of British manufacturing. Perhaps the keenest indicators of the region's new role in the UK economy were proposals to develop a new coal-import terminal on the banks of the Tees, capable of handling 5 m tonnes annually (half the output of the north east coalfield); and a 1725 MW gas-turbine electricity generating plant at Wilton on Teesside, to supply power to ICI's complex there and to several of the newly privatized area distribution companies. Within the north east, it seemed, coal was to continue to pale into insignificance by comparison with new components of the region's economy—such as the Nissan car plant at Sunderland.

### 4.3 The new arrival: Nissan in the north east of England

Nissan's interest in building a car plant in the UK prompted mixed reactions: competition amongst a host of places which campaigned vigorously for the promised new jobs, and criticism from those places where the broader impact of Nissan's investment appeared more likely to threaten employment. In the West Midlands, in particular, the project was condemned as a "Trojan Horse" which would in time undermine the viability of Rover (then British Leyland) as an independent volume car producer. A series of statements made it apparent that the UK government welcomed, Nissan not just for its jobs and investment, but also for the new technology and production methods which the plant seemed likely to bring.[4] At the same time, the government tacitly encouraged potential locations for the project to participate in a contest,[5] ensuring that the company's preferences for location came first over debate about the broader impacts of the proposal upon the economy.

Once Nissan's choice of site had been made public (amidst widespread celebration and rejoicing in parts of the north east: see Figure 4.6), the full terms and conditions which it intended to spell out at its new factory gradually became apparent. Announcing the selection of Washington near Sunderland, company vice president Kaichi Kanao indicated Nissan's concern to install just one trade union and to negotiate a wide-ranging labour flexibility agreement. He placed clear emphasis on Nissan's desire to implant Japanese-style industrial relations procedures and made it clear that further development of the plant to a second stage would depend on success in this regard:

> I am confident that we will have the type of labour management and industrial relations that we have in Japan when we settle here. In the course of 1987 we will determine whether we will look into the second stage. Whether we have good working relationships with the unions will be a big factor in determining whether we go on to the second stage. (quoted in *Newcastle Journal* 31 March 1984)

Within north east England, the trade union movement broadly welcomed Nissan's arrival, and had already indicated its openness to negotiation. Northern TUC chairman Tom Burlison commented before the choice of site was announced:

> When Nissan first came to the north east three years ago we said we would bend over backwards to help and our attitude remains the same. We want Nissan and we will do whatever we can to bring about the kind of union agreement they seek. (quoted in *Newcastle Journal* 28 February 1984)

The amenability of north east trade unions to new forms of agreement in the motor industry was arguably a major factor in Nissan's ultimate choice of location. Later that year, newly appointed personnel director Peter Wickens made clear the kind of deal he was seeking:

> We would hope to create a package under which people would have faith that problems can be resolved through the negotiating procedures, and would not feel the need to go on strike. People will have to be prepared to adapt to new and changing technology. We do not want

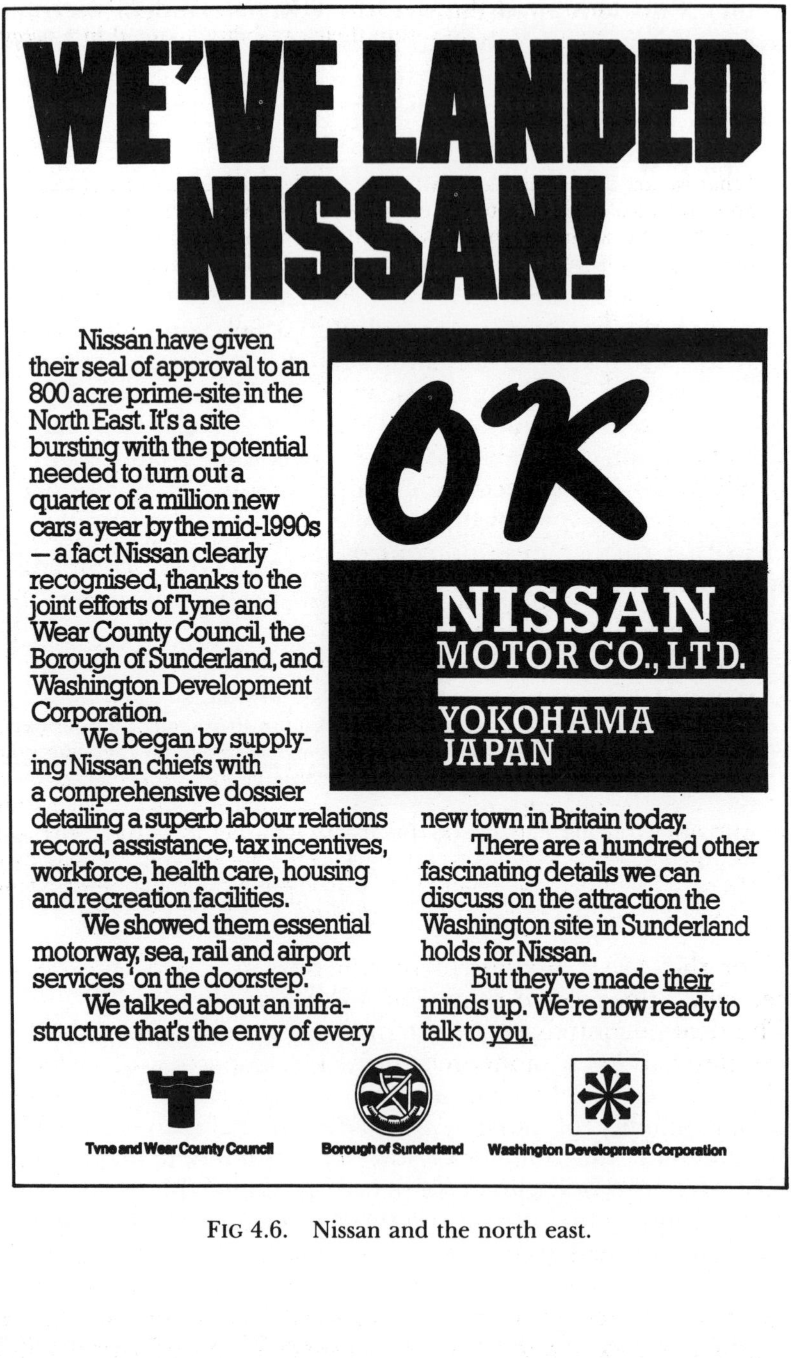

# WE'VE LANDED NISSAN!

Nissan have given their seal of approval to an 800 acre prime-site in the North East. It's a site bursting with the potential needed to turn out a quarter of a million new cars a year by the mid-1990s — a fact Nissan clearly recognised, thanks to the joint efforts of Tyne and Wear County Council, the Borough of Sunderland, and Washington Development Corporation.

We began by supplying Nissan chiefs with a comprehensive dossier detailing a superb labour relations record, assistance, tax incentives, workforce, health care, housing and recreation facilities.

We showed them essential motorway, sea, rail and airport services 'on the doorstep'.

We talked about an infra-structure that's the envy of every new town in Britain today.

There are a hundred other fascinating details we can discuss on the attraction the Washington site in Sunderland holds for Nissan.

But they've made their minds up. We're now ready to talk to you.

**OK**

**NISSAN**
**MOTOR CO., LTD.**
**YOKOHAMA JAPAN**

Tyne and Wear County Council

Borough of Sunderland

Washington Development Corporation

FIG 4.6.   Nissan and the north east.

rigid demarcations, and they will have to be flexible about the type of jobs they are prepared to do within their capability. (quoted in *Newcastle Journal* 8 August 1984)

As negotiations proceeded he added:

> What we are after are people who are totally flexible in working practices and attitudes. We want to have no demarcations and as few job titles as possible. We want employees who put quality before anything else. Our one target is to produce the best quality car possible and we expect our people to have genuine motivation and to identify with the aims and objectives of the company. (quoted in *Newcastle Journal* 16 March 1985)

The two biggest motor industry unions, the TGWU and the AEU, along with the GMBU, were all prepared to offer a single union package, but in April 1985 the company, in its own words, "appointed" the AEU as its trade union. The final deal had a number of features new to the UK motor industry, and met with considerable criticism, largely from the AEU's unsuccessful rivals. Joe Mills, northern regional secretary of the TGWU, complained of being "forced to parade before prospective employers like beauty queens" (quoted in *Sunday Times* 28 April 1985). He subsequently expanded on these views as follows:

> Many trade union officials in the north east are facing tremendous pressure from within their organisations because they are allowing companies who are moving into the region to treat unions like supermarket products. Because of high unemployment and in desperation to co-operate with inward investment, some unions are ignoring their traditional role to organise workers and are standing back and allowing companies to choose which union they want, similar to choosing washing powder from a supermarket. (quoted in *Newcastle Journal* 26 November 1986)

But for the AEU, anxious to recruit new members, the Nissan agreement appeared to represent a lucrative proposal.

The deal encompassed four main areas: none new to the UK, since they had been pioneered in the electronics industry by the EETPU, but certainly, as a package, new to the motor industry. It provided only for recognition of the AEU for every member of staff up to and including the grade of senior engineer. Whilst Nissan would encourage union membership, it would not be compulsory and the main negotiating forum would be a company council elected from all employees, not necessarily trade union members. Although not strictly a no-strike agreement, it precluded industrial action until a complex negotiating procedure was exhausted. The only possibility of industrial action was if either party chose not to go to the final stage of the process, independent pendulum arbitration. Complete flexibility was enshrined in the agreement, both in the present and in any future changes to production technology, with a very limited number of job classifications. Finally, all employees would be subject to common conditions such as hours of work, holidays and overtime.

One of Nissan's greatest concerns from the earliest stage was to fashion a workforce that was prepared to adapt to its rigorous demands. This was achieved through a complex recruitment and screening process, which was made all the more legitimate and competitive by the sheer volume of employment applications received from the job-starved north east. The first appointments after the managerial team were 22 "supervisors", selected in 1985 from over 3,000 applications. Each successful candidate was interviewed several times, put through a series of practical and written tests, and medically examined. They were sent as a group to Japan for a two-month period of intensive training in the Nissan plant at Oppama. On their return, they participated in the process of interviewing and recruiting 40 "team-leaders" from 1,000 applicants; these, in turn, were sent to Japan and participated (along with their supervisors) in recruiting the two grades of manual employee, manufacturer and technician. Each team-leader was responsible for some 15 employees. The whole approach was carefully designed to build considerable team loyalty, as described by one manager, Clive Griffiths:

> The man (*sic*) who does the interviewing is recruiting his own team. He tells the people he sees that they will not just be working for Nissan UK, but for him. He then passes them on to his manager and I decide if they are right for my team. (quoted in *Financial Times* 29 August 1986)

Competition for employment at Nissan was intense. The first 240 manufacturing jobs prompted 11,000 applications; the introduction of a night shift a further 5,500. When temporary labour was recruited in 1987 (itself a novel feature in the UK car industry), 1,300 applied for just 47 jobs—encouraged perhaps by the indication that after five months, the "best" employees would be kept on permanently. Workers recruited in this fashion were typically young, fit and agile. In 1987, the average age of the 690-strong workforce was just 27. Of these, only one-quarter had come straight from unemployment: the majority had had a job elsewhere immediately before moving to Nissan. Initial wages for the supervisors (in 1985) were set above UK standards for the equivalent rank of foreman, at £12,500, but other grades were relatively low-paid by comparison with other car factories within the UK. Team leaders initially received £7,750 and manual grades £6,700. All pay deals ran, on the company's insistence, for two years.

As the workforce was being assembled and trained in the UK and production in stage I began, comparisons were inevitably drawn with Nissan's operations in Japan—especially the Oppama plant where the first supervisors and teamleaders were sent for induction. Here, Western observers were struck by the company's detailed control over the production process, exerted in a variety of ways. As the *Financial Times* (18 September 1985) put it:

> The principal tools for fashioning human behaviour at Nissan are far more complex and meticulously designed than is imagined by most western companies that attempt to draw lessons from Japanese manufacturing techniques. The operation of quality circles, use of so-called bonus payments, temporary workers and outside contract labour, selection of employees and attention to training have all been carefully geared to generate build reliability and favourable production costs. At Oppama, however, it is often difficult to pinpoint where positive features of human organisation blur into coercion and the deliberate promotion of privileged elites.

The core Nissan workforce of 8,000 at Oppama was regularly augmented by some 500 temporary workers, earning in effect one-third less than permanent employees, excluded from pension rights and job guarantees, and distinguished by different markings on their overalls. For the salaried employees, participation in production organization was encouraged by compulsory membership of small quality circles, which were pressured to come up with suggestions for cost-saving improvements to the production process in (mainly unpaid) overtime. Self discipline and peer group pressure were reinforced by imposed discipline over, for example, absenteeism. Trade union representation was confined to the All Nissan Motor Workers' Union, heavily criticized by some for its subservience to management. From producing its first car in 1962, Oppama had never had a strike. Away from work, the company also exerted influence through its provision of low-cost accommodation (compared at least to Japan's generally high-priced housing). Across the country, Nissan owned 16,500 one-room units in dormitory blocks for its non-married workers along with housing for married couples; it also provided loans for the purchase of a home. Effectively, the company's control pervaded home and work.

The seemingly peaceful industrial relations system at Nissan, and in Japan more generally, was only installed after a very long managerial campaign against independent trade unionism.

In the early postwar years, left-wing influence in trades union and political affairs had been repressed with strong American backing. At Nissan, a bitter four-month long dispute was fought in 1953, which ended with management victorious. In the mid-1960s, Nissan merged with Prince Motor, and the newly installed Nissan company union led, even then, by Ichiro Shioji, used a range of tactics to undermine the Prince Motor Union and incorporate their members into one union. Prince Motor Union had been Communist-led and belonged to the National Metal Workers, a comparatively left-wing influence within the national union structure. In other words, the company union campaigned as much, if not more, against other trade unions which were potentially disruptive to the overall system as with the company itself.

The Japanese production system relied upon far more, though, than subservient trade unions. A further feature was the complex network of interlocked contracting and subcontracting companies. In a 30-mile radius around Oppama, for instance, there were some 150 subcontractors supplying Nissan. Whether this aspect of production organization could be transplanted to the UK was another point at issue.

Within Japan, companies such as Nissan depended heavily upon subcontractors for guaranteed regular deliveries of high quality components. Around 70 per cent of Nissan's manufacturing costs in Japan consisted of purchases from its suppliers (compared to 40 per cent for General Motors in the USA, for instance). Dependence also extended to cooperation in the development of new parts and models. In a sense, the contractors acted as a buffer for the parent, externalizing some of the risks and costs associated with new product development. Nissan's managing director, Takashi Matsuura, commented on the relationship with these subcontractors as follows:

> It's in our interest that they thrive. We transfer total quality control and management systems for industrial engineering to these companies. We can give them a rough sketch or ideas of components and they come up with the product: develop, design and bring forward the prototype. (quoted in *Financial Times* 29 February 1988)

In the UK, Nissan looked to establish similar long-term supply contracts with component suppliers. There were three, largely interrelated, questions in this regard: whether the existing European companies could meet standards of quality and reliability, and integrate with Nissan's production system; whether Japanese or European companies would supply Nissan; and whether suppliers would tend to concentrate around the Sunderland assembly plant.

The standards that Nissan demanded were higher than the previous norms for the European components industry, leading to some speculation that they had been set deliberately high to clear the way for an influx of Japanese component manufacturers. Nissan moved hastily to dispel suggestions that it had been "appalled" at the quality on offer from European companies, although clearly some uncertainty remained. One leading UK supplier, Lucas Industries, commented that:

> They are using higher quality components throughout their cars than we are used to. It is a challenge to suppliers like us to meet those standards. But any suggestion they are beyond our capabilities we strongly reject. (quoted in *Financial Times* 22 May 1985)

UK purchasing manager Ian Gibson also emphasized Nissan's determination to build in quality from the outset:

> We have spoken to people who are proud of their track record, with perhaps only half a per cent rejection from the customer. That's simply not acceptable to us. We expect zero reject from suppliers. If a supplier gives us rejects, he (*sic*) ought not to be a supplier. If he cannot make sure every single component is right, he is wasting our time as well as his own. (quoted in *Newcastle Journal* 16 October 1985)

Not only was component quality a key issue, but also the extent to which companies were competent to participate with Nissan in product design. The choice in this regard was laid out very clearly by Nissan's Takashi Matsuura:

> The good thing about Japanese parts manufacturers is that they can design on their own. Only the top-class parts makers overseas can achieve that level of service. Other parts makers can't deliver.

He went on:

> The Japanese are successful in transplanting efficient Japanese manufacturing overseas. Now we must transplant the parts technology. So we ask our suppliers to go abroad. Alternatively, we can change our specifications so our parts can more easily be made by domestic suppliers. (quoted in *Financial Times* 29 February 1988)

This became of ever greater significance as Nissan moved from the assembly operation of phase I to full manufacturing in phase II. The first Bluebird produced in 1986 contained parts supplied from 27 UK companies, accounting for 20 per cent of the car's content. Within a year, this list of suppliers had increased to 58;

but only six of these were from the north east. Clearly there had been a limited immediate impact upon the region's economy. This was recognized by purchasing manager Ian Gibson, who referred to "administrative difficulties" posed by "having the bulk of the UK motor industry over two hundred miles away in the West Midlands" (quoted in *Newcastle Journal* 29 January 1987), and, in 1988, Nissan introduced a team of skilled engineers to improve relationships with suppliers. This was, of course, a double-edged sword: in the initial stages Nissan had played down the possibility of wholesale restructuring and relocation within the UK vehicle component industry, anxious to allay suspicions in regions like the West Midlands; and in any case it chose not to locate there quite deliberately so that it could more easily introduce radical changes. By phase II though, a desire to integrate suppliers into the production system was reinforcing pressure on quality and reliability to encourage location in and around the Sunderland plant. Nissan's Toshiaki Tsuchiya indicated that "we would like component suppliers to locate near us", whilst personnel manager Peter Wickens affirmed that "we do not require subcontractors to locate in the north east, but it may become advantageous to locate in the area" (quoted in *Newcastle Journal* 15 July 1987).

Indeed, when the investment was first announced in 1984, Nissan had taken steps to secure the possibility of developing a spatially concentrated production complex around the Sunderland plant (see Crowther and Garrahan 1988). In addition to its own site of 297 acres, Nissan also had an option to buy a further 436 acres within three years at 1984 prices. This it took up in 1987, and began selling off parcels of land to suppliers; the first being Ikeda Hoover, which took about 25 acres. It was rapidly followed by a joint venture between Nissan and Yamato Kogyo, known as Nissan Yamato Engineering, formed to supply small body pressings. Announcing the project, Ian Gibson made it clear that Nissan had favoured this option after considering existing suppliers within Europe:

> Although many European manufacturers produce these types of part, we decided that by involving an acknowledged expert in this specialised field we could provide a better quality product. (quoted in *Newcastle Journal* 18 July 1987)

By 1990, Nissan was able to announce that it was purchasing components from 177 different European-based companies, of which 120 were in Britain and 20 were located in the north east. Only five of its suppliers were Japanese-owned, whilst a further eight were joint ventures between European and Japanese companies. It had brought forward the date for reaching 80 per cent local (i.e., EC) content of the new Primera and Micra replacement models to the scheduled launch date of the latter, 1992–93 (initially it had agreed with the UK government to reach 60 per cent local content of this model on its launch, building only later to 80 per cent). By that time, it would be spending £600 m on European produced components and the Sunderland workforce was expected to have risen from 2,500 to 3,500. These efforts should, of course, be interpreted in the context of Nissan's continuing concern to establish its European production as separate from any European Community import quota; but there were several significant areas where Nissan had no plans to purchase European components, in particular gearboxes and engine components.

Whilst the choice between European and Japanese component companies gradually took shape, the broader impact of the Nissan project was emerging in other forms too. Promotional agencies within the north east latched on to Nissan's decision as a sign that other Japanese companies, in a whole range of fields (not necessarily automotive-related) were likely to follow. It was all a far cry from the experience of the first Japanese company to locate in the region, NSK, which had been positively discouraged by trade union leaders and MPs back in 1974. Instead, now, as the North of England Development Council's Steve Brydon commented, "Nissan have put us in the forefront as far as other Japanese companies are concerned, from a marketing point of view" (quoted in *Newcastle Journal* 9 September 1986). His sentiments were shared by Jim Gardner, who had led the negotiations with Nissan from within the region:

> We have sown the seeds for what will be a major public relations exercise as more and more people move to the north east. As the word gets round so the region will be revitalised. I regard the arrival of Nissan as the most significant industrial landmark in the history of the north east in the last twenty years. And I remain convinced it will be the single biggest factor in the regeneration of the region. (quoted in *Newcastle Journal* 8 September 1986)

However accurate, such messianic prophecies held a key to understanding the impact of the Nissan project. For much depended upon a series of expressions of intent and assumptions of effect——perhaps inevitably, given the absolute novelty of fully fledged Japanese car manufacturing within Western Europe. Whether many of the promises were capable of delivery could only be ascertained over a relatively long time scale. Yet in the whole process, Nissan maintained a very tight control. Nissan was always very much in charge as it sought to transplant both production and production methods overseas, taking each step both gradually and carefully. Its meticulous consideration of potential locations served to defuse opposition to the proposal in principle within the UK. Its offer of single-union status to several unions deflected trade union criticism. Its declaration that phase II would depend on the successful operation of phase I was a powerful inducement in the search for quality and high productivity. At every stage, Nissan's strategy evolved in a responsive and sophisticated fashion.

This is not to argue that there were no problems along the way. One such problem concerned the trades union agreement. Nissan opted for a single-union deal with the AEU because it felt that craft workers were less likely to join a general union than general workers were to join a craft union. It chose not to adopt a non-union stance because it did not want the distraction of fighting off trade union attempts to gain recognition (see Wickens 1988). In this sense then it envisaged a positive, if tightly defined, role for the AEU, as expressed by Peter Wickens back in 1985:

> Whichever union ends up representing Nissan workers, it will not mean to say that Nissan will want to have the union in its pocket. We are looking for a strong trade union that can properly represent the interests of employees when it is necessary to do so, and will also have the well-being of the company at heart. (quoted in *Newcastle Journal* 16 January 1985)

Yet in April 1988, local trade union returns showed that only 7 per cent of the workforce had bothered to join the AEU. Even the claims by Nissan that representation was up to 30 per cent, "in some areas of the plant" by 1989 raised questions over the continuing viability and role of union representation at Nissan.

In some respects, of course, this was a reflection of Nissan's success at building identification with the company. The Sunderland works strove long and hard to better productivity and quality at Nissan's Japanese plants. As Clive Griffiths, body shop manager, put it:

> We have to beat the Japanese. Many of us have been to Japan and seen how things work there. We are deliberately looking for quicker and easier ways of doing the job, that can be taken back to Japan. (quoted in *Financial Times* 29 August 1986)

This reflected considerable effort on the part of the workforce, since in terms of technology (one of the UK government's original great hopes) Sunderland was, initially at least, disappointing.

There were only 22 robots installed in phase I, mainly because in Peter Wickens' words:

> Robots cost a lot of money. For phase I the emphasis is largely on people. (quoted in *Newcastle Journal* 8 September 1986)

The process of implanting Japanese production methods, then, was long, involved and complex, and entailed continuing interaction with the region's existing industrial traditions and practices. Nissan recognized this and demonstrated a grasp of diplomacy in its own commemorative advertisement on the commencement of production in 1986. This made valiant attempts to integrate Japanese organization with north east culture, in a fitting epitaph to the initial stage:

> There has been no attempt whatsoever to transfer the archetypal Japanese working environment, with its early morning physical exercise and sometimes almost obsessive company loyalty, to Sunderland. What the Japanese have done in fact is to re-export to the north east something that was forged on Tyneside a generation or more ago—the Geordie's pride in his job and teamwork. (Nissan advertising supplement published in *The Observer* 14 September 1986)

## 4.4 Concluding comments

By the close of the 1980s a substantial shift had taken place in the north east regional economy. Deep coal-mining in particular was in practically terminal decline, whilst the steel industry had shrunk to a fraction of its former size and, in any case, had much less linkage with the local economy than it once did. Collapse in the region's traditional economic base had been heavily supported—to some extent even orchestrated—by the UK state. Despite attempts at opposition, the power of international market forces was imposed through the vehicle of the state-owned corporation. Through the same means, the state also connived in the reconstruction of conceptions about the nature of employment. Flexibility and adaptability became the key words in the search for work in the recession-conscious 1980s. Long-established practices underwent radical change in the face of a concentrated managerial offensive.

At the same time, a growing consensus was emerging—at least amongst those whose task it was to sell the region to potential investors and central government—over the shape and significance of the new economy rising out of the ashes of the old. Chairman of the Northern Development Company Ron Dearing, for instance, was clear that

> What has happened is the recreation of a new industrial society. In that sense we can sell the North not as the old industrial economy but as the new one. (quoted in *Newcastle Journal* 23 January 1990)

As Les Henson, chief executive of County Durham Development Company recognized, the competition was getting increasingly tight:

> It sometimes seems as though every part of the UK outside the south east has its own development agency. Everybody claims to offer much the same benefits. As new enterprise zones are created and the Urban Development Corporations begin to flex their financial muscles, the competition to attract inward investment is intensifying. (quoted in *Newcastle Journal* 24 November 1989)

Locally at least, however, it was argued that the north east had one unbeatable attribute: the "Nissan factor". Consider this comment in the *Newcastle Journal's* special eight-page advertising feature celebrating "The Great North":

> it is the "Nissan factor" that has been the catalyst for an upturn in Northern manufacturing fortunes. Ever since the Japanese giant was persuaded that Wearside was the ideal site for its European operation, there has been a steady build up of some of the most well known names from the world's most buoyant economic climate, south east Asia. (*Newcastle Journal* 26 January 1990)

The interaction between new employers and the region's existing industrial base was far more complex than often assumed, even if companies like Nissan were well aware of the subtle processes taking place. Whilst Nissan was not typical in every respect of new investment in the north east, it was so significant because in many ways it was held up as a stereotype—or, perhaps more accurately, a prototype—for others to follow. The number of Japanese companies in the north east, for instance, grew rapidly in the course of the 1980s, but none received as much attendant publicity or developed so fully the features of Japanese-style production organization. In terms of crude numbers of jobs, the overall impact of the Nissan project was not that great (in the short to medium term, at least), certainly when weighed against the scale of decline in other industries such as coal and steel. But in terms of what Nissan was held to stand for, it was far and away the most significant new industrial presence in the north east in the 1980s. To local authorities and central government, the sheer public relations value of Nissan's investment in the north east was enormous.

Two further points are important here. The first is that Nissan's investment in north east England was heavily subsidized by the UK state, and at every turn the UK government strongly promoted Nissan's corporate goals—even if it meant arguing with other members of the European Community over import controls, for instance. To the UK government Nissan was an instance of the successful regeneration of the north east, a shining example of the enterprise economy. By contrast, the region's existing staple employers such as coal and steel were deemed to be uneconomic, old fashioned and unnecessary, and allowed—even encouraged—to wither in the face of global competition.

The reason for this contrast in government attitudes was apparent from an examination of the true differences between old and new employers. The UK government initially welcomed Nissan apparently for its technology and production methods; but it was evident by the late 1980s that the most significant feature in the style of production system being installed at Sunderland (whether or not it was specifically Japanese in origin) was control of the labour process. The essence of the famed Japanese production method involved close managerial control both inside the factory and, as far as possible, out of it down the supplying chain. Hence Nissan's great concern and care to screen its workforce so as to minimize potentially disruptive elements and to develop a "team spirit" in the manner of company loyalty. Labour, then, not technology, was the key to the Nissan project.

Yet in many ways the old industries such as coal and steel which had underpinned the north east economy represented much that was abhorrent to the UK government (and, by implication if not association, Japanese companies) in terms of industrial practices and traditions. How was it that such radically different change—in the sense of qualitative shift resulting from quantitative alteration in the degree of control over labour—had taken place? This is a question addressed in the following chapter.

## Notes

1. The proposed development under this scheme had five stages. The first, the development of iron ore unloading facilities at a sea terminal, was completed in 1973. The second stage consisted of a completely new iron works covering the production of raw materials such as coke, and a huge new blast furnace to replace the existing blast furnaces at Clay Lane, along with additional capacity at the existing steel works. The third stage was to be a plate mill to replace older plate mills at Hartlepool and Consett. The fourth and fifth stages involved further iron-making capacity along with a new steel plant and rolling mills.

2.  The widely ranging qualities of different coals—in terms, for instance of sulphur, chlorine and ash content, volatility, caking properties and hardness—were reflected in a scale of coal rank. Broadly speaking coals spanned a spectrum from high quality anthracites to coking coals (such as ranks 204 and 301) and steam coals (such as rank 501) to low quality lignites. A steam coal was not necessarily suited for coking, nor a coking coal for steam-raising. The "Redcar blend" was specifically tailored to the requirements of a large blast furnace, in particular the creation of a coke bed which would not deform too rapidly in the process of making iron.

3.  In many ways this mirrored the situation facing the NCB in the same area in 1967 when, after several years spent reorganizing production so as to supply an anticipated new coal-fired power station at Hartlepool, an Advanced Gas-cooled nuclear Reactor was ordered instead. It is estimated that this was responsible for the loss of 5,000 coal-mining jobs.

4.  John Wakeham, junior Industry Minister, referred, for instance, to the "dynamic benefits" of Nissan's investment: "the introduction of new technology, production and management methods." (*Hansard* 23 March 1982 col 912)

5.  Described as follows in evidence to the Public Accounts Committee (1984: p. 23): "It is very difficult for the government to tell a company such as Nissan where it should go and that would seem to be the only alternative to allowing the various localities to put their case."

# 5

# Laying the Foundations for a "New" Economy in North East England: The Forced Acceptance of Flexible Employment

### 5.1 Introduction

Given that one of the fundamental emphases in the evolving new industrial base of the north east was control over labour, this chapter addresses the question of what made such change feasible: what created the conditions which enabled companies like Nissan so radically to alter the dominant conception of appropriate employment patterns. Part of the answer, of course, lies in the simple assertion that with so many unemployed, people were willing to work for a wage at almost any price. But there was far more to it than that, for the north east represented one of the heartlands of industrial trade unionism, and to change attitudes so substantially entailed a fundamental shift in the balance of power between employers and trade unions. In this process the UK state intervened heavily, almost exclusively on the side of the employers—especially, in sectors like coal and steel, where it was effectively the employer—to encourage the reconstruction of the region's economy in a different mould, with a new sectoral and gender constitution to its workforce. That shifting terrain of conflict is the focus here.

This chapter, then, plots some key moments of organized labour's downfall in the region, and some significant elements of government policies for new job creation which laid the foundations for the emergence of a new kind of economy in the 1990s. It begins with steel and the unsuccessful campaign to prevent closure of the Consett works in 1980; and goes on to consider the even more symbolic defeat of the national miners' strike in 1984/85. It then introduces the changes in employment practices which have been initiated in coal and, especially, steel in the wake of such losses. Finally it analyzes policies adopted by British Steel and British Coal to introduce new jobs into the north east (and elsewhere) and considers the kind of low-wage, insecure economy, with a highly changed gender composition of the workforce, emerging in parts of the region.

## 5.2 Stages in the downfall of organized labour in the north east

With the benefit of hindsight, many changes—such as the decline of the north east's traditional industrial base—seem more or less inevitable. Such a perspective is of course misleading; for whilst there were undoubtedly powerful underlying trends at work, this emphasis obscures the fact that the process of contraction was not preordained, but rather resulted from a series of conscious and deliberate decisions, largely (especially in coal and steel) but not wholly taken by successive governments. Resurrecting history in this latter sense then reminds us that the desirability of the collapse of employment in sectors such as coal and steel was by no means unanimously accepted. Quite the reverse: in large parts of the UK it met with considerable challenge, which on occasion spilled over into outright opposition. Sometimes (as in the case of Consett) this was on the basis of attachment in one community to one place of work. At other times (notably the UK miners' strike of 1984/85) it drew on the strength of a much more generalized disavowal of government policy and expressed a desire for criteria other than profit to decide the rationale of particular communities. By and large, such opposition was unsuccessful in Britain in the 1980s (and that this was so generally true is another measure of the strength of the UK state in that decade). But in crushing those alternatives, the government of the day not only imposed its will and authority in terms of industrial policy; it also cleared a space for radical labour market changes too. This is jumping ahead slightly though, for the task of this section is to deal first with two of the north east's most symbolic anti-closure campaigns in the 1980s: the campaign to save Consett steel works, and the miners' strike in defence of the region's coal industry.

## 5.2.1 "Save Consett Steel" 1980

In many ways steel is an appropriate starting point for an analysis of this kind, for the main union, the ISTC, had historically been highly accommodating ai d anxious to avoid industrial confrontation. In the course of the 1970s it passively accepted wholesale job loss, preferring to take at face value BSC's assurances that alternative jobs would be made available to ex-steelworkers (see Upham 1980). After 1979, though, it became apparent that steel was to bear the brunt of savage restructuring, and the unions hardened their stance. After a brief and unsuccessful campaign to prevent closure of the Corby works in 1979, the ISTC voted for a more aggressive approach on capacity reduction, just as it became the focus of a protracted industrial dispute over wages in the first three months of 1980. At the same time, its resolve was tested by BSC's proposal to close Consett works—never adopted as a national issue by the trade unions despite partially coinciding with a wages strike—which was contested in a fashion that only confirmed the steel unions' reputation for moderation and pliability.

BSC's announcement that it intended to close Consett was made in December 1979. Despite many years of uncertainty at this inland, isolated plant, the announcement was a considerable shock to the town. A plate mill had been shut down two months previously (with the loss of 300 jobs) and it had been hoped that with this loss-making plant gone, the works had a brighter future. Consett was a classic one-industry town and the 4,000 jobs under threat overshadowed local employment prospects.

A campaign developed to save the works, the course of which was to prove highly significant for the north east labour movement.[1] A small rally against closure in February 1980 was followed by much larger ones of some 3,000 people in March and 2,500 in June, and a demonstration by some 600 Consett people in London in July. A trade union commissioned document, *No Case for Closure*, was presented to BSC in July, and a further protest march of some 2,000 people took place two days later. BSC argued, though, that the trade union case presented no new evidence and, in September, a meeting of 2,000 workers voted to accept closure and begin negotiations on severance terms; days later the last cast of steel was poured at Consett (for details of the events of the campaign, see Hudson and Sadler 1983).

BSC's initial case for closure rested upon a criterion of "profitability" at works level. Consett's MP David Watkins took a deputation to meet BSC in October 1979:

> we were told that Consett is not safe unless it is profitable and that BSC can guarantee absolutely nothing. We were told that we must talk about profitability and not about numbers employed. (*Hansard* 7 November 1979 col 466)

In presenting such an argument, BSC could point to the poor operating record of the plant over the previous five years, with the cumulative loss amounting to £54 m. Unfortunately for BSC (given this position), from September to December 1979 the Consett works made a small profit, a change due mainly to closure of the plate mill. However, BSC's apparent concern with profitability only masked the real issue, a need to cut capacity in response to a reduced external financing limit imposed on it by the government. This was later recognized by David Watkins in an interview about the meeting with BSC Chairman, Charles Villiers:

> There is no denying we were quite deliberately misled. We were told at that meeting the Consett works must be made profitable if it is to survive. That profitability was already in the process of being achieved, yet it was only a few weeks later that the closure of the whole works was announced. (quoted in *Consett Guardian* 13 March 1980)

And as Villiers himself later said of Consett: "They did just get a profit but we had too much capacity elsewhere" (quoted in *Newcastle Journal* 19 May 1982).

The trade union case, though, followed a line of argument that Consett as a works was profitable and could remain so in the future. In so doing, the unions, by accident or design, overlooked the fact that BSC wanted to close Consett because of corporate over-capacity, and therefore did not consider the reasons why BSC wanted to close capacity. In reply, BSC did not need to contest Consett's improved productivity but simply cited once again the need to cut output potential.

This concern with the profitability of Consett's steelworks—in many ways a dialogue of the deaf—took a further twist in the final episode, simultaneously tragedy and farce, of the campaign to save it. On 2 September, it was reported that a consortium headed by John O'Keefe (managing director of Chard Hennessy, a Gateshead engineering firm) wanted to take over the Consett steel works. The consortium was reportedly named the Northern Industrial Group, borrowing the name, accidentally or deliberately, of an earlier grouping of capitalist interests in the north east. Exploratory talks were held with Department of Industry officials in London, although considerable mystery surrounded the identity of the consortium members.

Seemingly no approach was made to BSC, however, who announced that unless a firm offer was made by 12 September, the furnaces at Consett would be allowed to die down. Four days after the last batch of steel was produced, the first details of the consortium and its plans became public (in the *Newcastle Journal* 16 September 1980). It allegedly consisted of ten (un-named) British businessmen who planned to buy Consett works for £3 m (BSC was asking £100 m), operate it with a workforce of 2,700 and Western Europe's highest productivity rate of 320 tonnes/employee/year, and produce a forecast first year profit of £20 m.

Whatever credibility the consortium had did not last long. The names of its members were revealed after a fortnight of speculation in an announcement which served their interest in the plant. Only two of the companies, Cronite Alloys and British Benzol Carbonising (with a combined turnover of £20 m) had shown any serious interest. O'Keefe's own company, Chard Hennessy, was revealed to have made pre-tax profits of less than £3,000 in 1977 and 1978 and its subsidiary, Potts and Sons, losses of over £50,000. More revealing still perhaps, given his prospective role as Chairman of the Northern Industrial Group consortium was O'Keefe's revelation that

> I'm not really good at running companies. That sounds stupid, but I tend to get involved in the start of things and leave them to run themselves. If they don't do very well I close them. (quoted in *Sunday Times* 28 September 1980)

This final bizarre act of the campaign, then, deflected attention away from the impact of government policies, placed Consett into competition with other works, and isolated it from support either within the north east or from workers at other plants within BSC. By reinforcing and replicating the claim for decisions to be made only within the context of one plant, the campaign failed to consider the broader issues in a fashion which would have invited support from other sources than just steel workers at Consett—whose own determination was in any case severely tested.

The failure at Consett was highlighted two years later (admittedly in a different political climate, with a general election pending) with a successful campaign to prevent closure of the Ravenscraig steel works in Scotland. With a broadly based Scottish lobby mobilized in its defence, the government was forced to concede on purely political grounds that the works should remain open (see Sadler 1984).[2] But the Consett campaign was deeply significant within the north east. Even though it faced formidable opposition, the campaign's evident failure to appeal to, let alone receive support from, elsewhere left it very isolated in every way. If the labour movement could not find common cause over such a major plant, it was unlikely to do so over a score or more of other, smaller ones—nor did it do so, as a multitude of increasingly anachronistic and brief campaigns were fought and lost. Such was the situation, then, on the eve of the UK miners' strike in 1984.

### 5.2.2 The miners' strike in the north east: 1984/85 and its aftermath

The UK miners' strike of 1984/85 was an historic dispute reflected in a vast and growing literature (see, for instance, Adeney and Lloyd 1986; Beynon 1985; Samuel *et al*, 1986; Seddon 1986). It had all the elements of highest drama, including vivid leading characters; it was also deeply significant to the course of UK politics in the 1980s, especially when the miners' failure to extract any concessions from an intransigent government was contrasted with events following the earlier dispute in 1974. This section charts the events of 1984/85 within the north east, and analyzes their subsequent impact.

One of the most hotly contested issues in the year-long strike was the question of the ballot. National Union of Mineworkers (NUM) members nationally had been operating an overtime ban since 1983, when announcement of a further round of closures early in March 1984 provoked the Yorkshire and Scottish areas to proclaim an indefinite strike and seek the support of other areas for a rolling programme of action. In north east England one pit, Herrington, was scheduled for closure under the NCB's plans and two (Horden and Bates) were to shed 700 jobs each. The initial response was highly confused. On 9 March, after a vote split 7 against 7 was swayed by the president's casting vote, Durham miners' executive committee agreed to support Yorkshire and Scotland and proceed to strike action, if necessary without a national ballot. Rapidly, all except three of Durham's thirteen pits (Dawdon, Seaham and Vane Tempest)[3] agreed at lodge meetings to abide by this recommendation; but in Northumberland only two of the five pits (Bates and Whittle) were in favour of a strike, and there the area executive initiated a local ballot. This was rapidly overtaken by events. Within five days all pits in Durham had stopped working in the face of picketing from other Durham collieries, and two days later the last pit in Northumberland to continue working, Brenkley, was picketed out. As the Northumberland miners' president put it:

> The outcome of the [area] ballot is purely academic. There will be no return to work until there is a national ballot. We promised the men a ballot and it is being held. But even if there is a vote not to strike, the coalfield will be at a standstill. Picketing would see to that. (quoted in *Newcastle Journal* 15 March 1984)

Many of the Durham lodges, as well as most of those in Northumberland, respected the strike call but still sought a national ballot. The extent of support was definitely mixed. Whilst all the region's pits were idle, a ballot of 5,700 Durham mechanics resulted in a 64 per cent majority against action; of 3,500 clerical workers, 95 per cent were against; and of 800 enginemen, 85 per cent were against. In Northumberland, the ballot of all NUM members initiated by the executive showed 52 per cent in favour of action, almost but not quite reaching the majority of 55 per cent required by the local area rules. Announcing this result, Northumberland NUM general secretary Sam Scott proclaimed:

> The strike goes on. The area executive unanimously agrees that because of the volatile situation which exists throughout the country each branch will continue to picket their pit. (quoted in *Newcastle Journal* 17 March 1984)

In the event, there was no national ballot, just a national delegate conference; but once the north east coalfield was out, it stayed out, in compliance with the delegate conference's decisions. In July, the NCB laid on free buses in an attempt to start a back-to-work movement, but not one miner took up the offer. In August, though, the first signs of a break began to appear, as a very few miners returned to work accompanied by heavy policing and picketing, most especially at Easington (see Beynon 1984b). In September, the Bishop of Durham declared in his enthronement sermon that "the miners must not be defeated"; but even as he spoke, the seeds of future conflict were being sown, as three Durham mechanics became the first NUM members to be expelled for breaking the strike.

In September, the deputies' union NACODS voted 82 per cent in favour of strike action after the NCB threatened not to pay NACODS members who refused to cross NUM picket lines. Faced with the possible closure of all collieries—even those where NUM members were working normally—the NCB agreed to NACODS' demands that discussion proceed on a new, independent stage to the colliery review procedure, and the strike threat receded. From November onwards the return to work began to accelerate, as no sign of any negotiated settlement appeared, amidst a concentrated NCB publicity campaign. By late February 1985, more than half the north east coalfield was estimated to be back at work, and early in March the Durham and Northumberland areas voted in favour of the national return to work without a settlement which effectively ended the strike.

Even without a ballot, then, the north east coalfield was—until the closing stages—one of the strongpoints of the dispute nationally for the NUM, reflecting a remarkable degree of solidarity in the face of considerable hardship and a concerted assault by the NCB and the government. One of the arguments underlying the whole dispute nationally was the devastating impact of colliery closures in coal-mining districts, and their cost both to the individual and the broader community. Within north east England these costs were particularly acutely felt, and in part responsible for the strength of support for the strike. An attempt at quantifying these costs of closure was commissioned by one of the local authorities most directly affected, Easington District Council (see Hudson, Peck and Sadler 1985).

Easington, in the east of Durham (see Figure 5.1) was historically heavily dependent on coal (for reasons outlined in the introduction to Chapter 4). In 1971, coal-mining employment accounted for half the district's jobs (18,000 out of 36,000) and two-thirds of all male employment. By 1981, after gradual decline, coal still accounted for more than one-half of male employment and two-fifths of total employment (12,000 out of 32,000 jobs). There had been only limited gains in manufacturing industry despite the presence of Peterlee New Town, and the service sector had also begun to decline from the mid-1970s onwards. The Local District Plan of 1982 envisaged that at the very worst, coal-mining employment would not fall under 7,000 before 1991. By early 1984, on the verge of the strike, it was down to 9,000, pushing the male unemployment rate to over 20 per cent. The research into the costs of decline was therefore constrained to investigate the effects of an additional 2,000 mining job losses within the district at some time before 1991.

Hudson, Peck and Sadler (1985) estimated that the direct costs of these 2,000 job losses to government by 1991, in terms of redundancy payments, unemployment benefit, lost taxes and increased social security spending was of the order of £65 m to £88 m, depending on the timing of redundancies. It also investigated the indirect impact of coal's decline. This was measurable

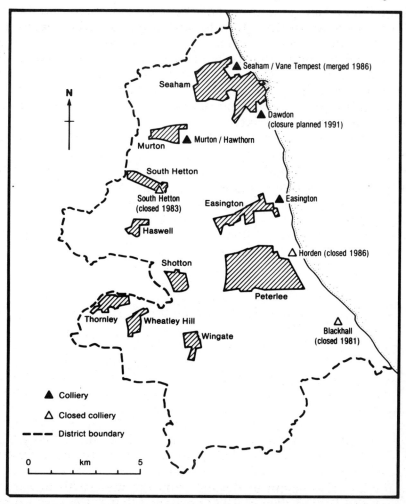

FIG 5.1.   Easington District, County Durham.

both in terms of the linkage effect on companies supplying goods and services to the NCB, and the downward multiplier effect of lost purchasing power on the local economy. A survey of companies supplying the NCB revealed that very few of these were located within the coalfield district (a further revealing comment on the area's limited diversification), but the loss of spending power was likely to be heavily concentrated locally. In total, the indirect impact amounted to a further 1,000 to 2,400 job losses, costing government from £13 m to £33 m by 1991. Overall therefore it was estimated that the cost of 2,000 coal mining job losses amounted to somewhere in the range of £78 m to £121 m. Additionally, the report considered non-quantifiable costs to the community. One young school-leaver commented that there would be "no change, just more unemployed people" whilst another felt that

> In a few years time, Easington won't exist. People will have moved away to try and find a job elsewhere. I don't think anyone will even know Easington existed if all the coal mines were closed down.

After the strike's conclusion, the artificial nature of the planning constraints imposed on these cost estimates was clearly apparent, for coal-mining employment in Easington District fell below 7,000 as early as December 1986 (Hudson and Sadler 1987c), which meant that the costs being incurred were at the top end of the original estimate, and likely to be even higher as the seemingly inexorable decline continued.[4] Similar attempts at quantifying the quantifiable costs of closure, and elaborating the non-quantifiable costs, were widely attempted in the 1984/85 dispute. They were significant politically as a means of broadening the debate to emphasize the future of whole coal-mining areas. They were important too as part of the continuing drive to attempt to force the NCB to take account of such concerns even after 1984/85; especially through the Independent Review Body (IRB) procedure installed after long and difficult negotiations between the NCB and NACODS.

The story of the IRB was inextricably bound up with that of two north east pits which were the first to come before it: Horden in Durham, and Bates in Northumberland. At the strike's end, both were designated by the Area Director, David Archibald, as "manpower reservoirs". As such they were to be used as bases from which to transfer miners not wishing to leave the industry (despite the generous redundancy terms on offer) to pits where miners did wish to leave; and if all the miners had left Horden and Bates, then they would close. To the NUM this appeared a way of dodging all established consultation procedures, confirmed when the NCB soon announced the closure of both collieries even though many miners remained there. In September 1985, their cases were taken—unsuccessfully—to the then final-stage of the colliery review procedure.

This was not the end of the matter, though, for early in 1986 Horden and Bates were the first cases to come before the Independent Review Body—its terms of reference having finally been agreed after fifteen months of negotiation. In his ruling after the Horden inquiry, Mr Stuart Shields QC dealt first with the question of rundown of the pit immediately after the end of the strike. He was in no doubt that this had prejudiced the hearing and was in breach of procedure, but was not convinced that the NCB's actions materially affected his conclusions. These were that, whilst "serious consequences" would result to the local economy if Horden was closed,

> to consider the general economic position of the area, the cost to central and local government, are in my view matters for Parliament. Where the social consequences of a decline in coal mining in a region would be particularly acute, it is for the government to decide what action to take.

The NCB therefore had no statutory obligation to take "social consequences" into account, and its proposal to close Horden was upheld.

Several weeks later, however, the report on the Bates inquiry argued along very different lines. In his ruling, Mr Bowsher QC noted that throughout the negotiations establishing the review body NACODS had made it clear that

> the social consequences of closure of a pit were matters which it wished to be taken into account in the New Modified Colliery Review Procedure. The NCB never agreed to this. But so far as I can ascertain from the evidence before me, it was never explicitly stated that social consequences would be disregarded.

The unions' case was that Bates could be made economically viable within two years, and the possibility of this was accepted by Mr Bowsher. Accordingly, he recommended that in the light of the social consequences of immediate closure, Bates be given a period of two years to prove its potential, and if this was fulfilled, it should remain in operation thereafter.

This judgement, standing directly against the NCB's forcefully expressed wishes, was a real bombshell.[5] But almost immediately, the NCB demonstrated its determination to cut capacity and exercise the "right to manage" it had won in the strike, with an announcement that despite the IRB ruling, Bates would still close. Local and national opinion was outraged, and the NCB was roundly condemned within the north east; but the closure went ahead. It had become only too apparent that the IRB, upon which NACODS had pinned so much hope, was a rather hollow institution.

Indeed the NCB's view of the IRB was laid out very clearly in evidence to the Energy Committee (1986: p. 26). Chairman Ian MacGregor commented that the Bates ruling of the IRB

> went far beyond the terms of reference under which that organisation was constituted. There was nothing in the review procedure that had anything to do with political or social considerations. The decision had a very large bias on political and social matters, and it agreed with us on the economic aspects.

And as he later emphasized, the IRB "added frustrating steps to the process of shutting a pit" without "giving away our right to run the business" (MacGregor 1986: pp. 282, 296). In such circumstances, it was difficult to fault the judgment of Arthur Scargill, president of the NUM, that "the establishment of the Independent Review Body was a sop to buy off the deputies union, NACODS" when it was thought NACODS would join the NUM in the strike; or to criticize Peter McNestry, general secretary of NACODS, who argued that "we have learnt that the present Board do not know the meaning of truth and honour" (evidence to Energy Committee 1986: pp. 79, 86).

With the IRB fully revealed as the toothless tiger that it was, the NUM and NACODS were totally powerless to prevent a sweeping round of pit closures; especially, in the case of the NUM, as it faced massive problems of its own to do not just with falling numbers, but also the establishment of an alternative union. Whilst this movement was strongest in Nottinghamshire, it also had significance in the north east, where the first expulsions from the NUM had taken place during the 1984/85 strike. Rebel unions were rapidly established at Westoe and Wearmouth, which evolved into the Durham Colliery Trades and Allied Workers Association. In 1985, this organization voted to join the newly established Union of Democratic Mineworkers (UDM), claiming 1,500 members in the Durham coalfield.[6]

Protracted and bitter debate ensued, with the NUM in the north east especially keen not to recognize the UDM, and disputing its claimed membership. The very existence of the UDM was significant, though, especially in the context of proposed changes to working conditions (see Taylor 1988). Far more than the NUM, the UDM was willing to negotiate on longer shifts and flexible working patterns. Already weakened by its evident inability to prevent closures, the NUM was put under increasing pressure to acquiesce in new employment patterns and working conditions at the pits which remained open; with the added threat that without such agreement, more pits would close and investment be increasingly concentrated in those pits and areas where such conditions were accepted. From almost every direction, it seemed, the NUM was under threat.

Thus the miners' strike was significant in a range of ways: symbol of the assertion of management's claimed "right to manage", and creator of a split within the trade union movement with substantial long-term implications. If not mortally wounded, the NUM was certainly severely hampered in its movements. In such circumstances, rebuilding of the region's political and economic base continued apace.


## 5.3 New conditions of employment in coal and steel

Management at both British Coal and British Steel moved rapidly to assert their newly found authority and impose radical changes in the process of production. In steel, these shifts began at the start of the decade; in coal, slightly later, but with the same principles in mind. This section reviews managerial strategies and experiences of flexibility in these sectors, beginning with steel.[7]

At BSC Teesside, far-reaching changes began to happen after the defeat of the three-month long national strike in 1980. Many workers were clear that the ISTC had been selected as a soft target for the newly elected Conservative Government's anti-union strategies. Tony Cook, a member of the ISTC's national executive committee at the time, argued later that "the steel unions were targeted—absolutely no doubt about it". He went on to describe the aftermath:

> We lost men, we had closures, and the eyes across the negotiating table had steel shutters. They were enjoying it.

In the minds of many, these changes were associated with the management style of the chairman Ian MacGregor. According to Tony Poynter, ISTC branch official:

> MacGregor was a completely different kind of guy. He met the stewards and management early on Teesside, and said there'd be no more pay rises without productivity increases. He was very abrasive. "People have got to go", he said. Every year, they were coming back for more redundancies, more changes in working practices—things that had never been put to the unions in this area before.

Much of the new climate was associated with the spectre of redundancy and closure, even of the whole complex. Such a prospect was a major impediment to the trade unions, for management utilized it to assert what they saw as their right to manage. In many parts of the works, this created an atmosphere of fear and uncertainty. Alan Deans, an ISTC official, gave one example:

> Management are going absolutely berserk on time-keeping. If you have
> two shifts off or you're late twice, you'll get a written warning. If it
> happens a third time inside thirteen weeks, you're out of a job. That's
> what I call whipping the workforce into line.

Whilst such concerns were by no means minor (especially
in what remained, despite technological advances, a physically
strenuous industry), they were symbolic of broader changes—the
re-assertion of managerial control and the increased exploitation
of those workers remaining on the BSC payroll. In this process,
management was keen to foster a sense of competition between
individual production sites; a collective fear of greater success at
other BSC plants in whipping the workforce into line. Ron Agar,
AEU convenor, said:

> The four BSC divisions now are running businesses separate from each
> other. We're competing against each other. If Ravenscraig were to close,
> that would be to our benefit, because on certain items customers would
> come to us. The same goes for Llanwern. As a trade unionist I never
> wish to see these works close. But from a purely selfish point of view it
> would help us—and you'd get the same reaction from my counterpart
> at Ravenscraig. That's how MacGregor got it organised. Every business
> must be self-financing.

One central element of this new approach lay in the devolution
of responsibility for labour costs (but not, significantly, for capital
investment). After sixteen negotiating sessions, local agreement
was reached in March 1981 for 3,800 redundancies on Teesside
under a scheme in which the remaining workforce would receive
quarterly 3 per cent lump sum bonuses provided these job losses
were carried through on time. This was subsequently extended
at Teesside and at other BSC works to include a range of
other efficiency improvements, and local rises came to form
the major source of wage increases. From 1981 to 1984, there
was no national pay rise at BSC. A deal agreed in January 1985
provided only for a 4.25 per cent increase on basic rates for fifteen
months, and in May of that year Teesside pioneered a further
extension of BSC's decentralized bargaining. Local negotiators
concluded agreement on a new-style bonus scheme linked not
only to productivity, but also—for the first time—to works profit.
Under this, employees would receive lump sums each quarter
rising to a maximum 9 per cent of basic pay if quarterly works
profit reached £5.75 m.

The introduction and subsequent strengthening of locally negotiated wage increases was important in putting stress upon local
labour productivity as the means to local works viability (even
though many of the elements in the bonus calculation, including

steel plant yield or works profit, depended partly or wholly upon central decisions to do with production, marketing and capital investment). The emphasis upon labour costs was indicative of management's newly found strength. A further factor in this was a drive on labour force flexibility—both in numerical and functional terms. The clearest expression of this was at the BSC Hartlepool works, on the north bank of the Tees.

After a long rundown in the 1970s, this site comprised a plate mill and two other mills capable of rolling pipes up to 20 and 44 inches in diameter. In February 1983, BSC closed the 44-inch pipemill and in May, announced its intention to close the plate mill. Subsequently, however, an alternative plan emerged, which included retaining the plate mill with a much reduced workforce of 250 and recruiting 220 workers for the 44-inch pipe mill on short-term contracts lasting until February 1984. The nature of these contracts proved to be particularly innovative. The letter of appointment made it clear that "collective agreements between the Corporation and any of the recognized trades unions are not applicable to your short term employment", with the sole exception of a memorandum agreed in May specifically for short-term workers at this mill. This made only too apparent the conditions under which waged employment was being offered. To quote:

2.1 Employees will be required to work any system, days or shifts according to the needs of the business.
3.1 *Maximum* flexibility and mobility shall apply.
4.7 Employees will not be entitled to a redundancy payment, unemployment and income security benefit or any other severance pay.
5.2 There will be no minimum holiday entitlement.
5.4 It is accepted that priority will be given to operational requirements and that holidays will normally be paid as cash on the completion of the employment contract.

Just to make the message absolutely clear the memorandum also included a seven-side, 66 point schedule of working practices which included the following:

12 Craftsmen will maintain the cleanliness of their work areas and own amenity facilities (e.g. meal cabin).
13 Craftsmen will be expected to operate production equipment and machinery as the need arises.
24 Semi/non-skilled grades will perform any work as directed.
59 All grades will undertake cleaning duties as instructed.
63 It is in the interests of all employees to complete any pipe contract at least cost, on time and to the customer's specifications. This criterion necessitates the employment of the minimum number of people working together as a team and operating sensible flexible

> working practices which contribute to maximizing the production operation.

When further production contracts were signed, local union officials met BSC seeking certain changes, but BSC refused to recognize continuity of employment across two or more contracts, claiming that each new order represented a break in service. Thus BSC had secured, via its earlier threatened and actual closures, transition from a workforce employed under standard agreements and procedures to one employed on a rolling series of temporary contracts under radically different working conditions.

In other parts of the giant complex, BSC followed a variation on this theme. The use of subcontracted labour grew enormously in the UK steel industry during the 1980s (see, for instance, Fevre 1987). Teesside works director, Mr Ward, explained the rationale behind this as follows:

> The spine of our operation is iron and steel production. We had to look at other activities, work out their fixed and variable costs, and sub-contract accordingly.

A whole range of such activities was contracted out to other companies, including, for example, catering, cleaning, transport, relining furnaces and computer support.

By far the most contentious area concerned the use of subcontracted labour in maintenance work. In a process industry such as steel, it was often difficult to draw a line between production and maintenance tasks. The wrecking and bricking (or relining) of steel converters, for example, was a "maintenance" operation performed regularly, and one essential to continued steel production. Yet concern over the extent to which BSC had cut back on its own labour force for essential maintenance was expressed by Bill Purvis, AEU district organizer:

> BSC say they can't carry a full maintenance crew on a permanent basis, but maintenance really has been cut beneath the bone. If anything serious crops up they just can't handle it.

Another view came from Mr Davey, the ISTC's senior organizer on Teesside:

> Let's face it, we can't say to BSC, "you can't have that contractor". We're really just the policemen of agreements. What we are concerned about is contractors taking regular jobs of BSC employees on the production side. We have resisted that most strongly.

Whilst these different emphases partly reflected varying membership bases, there was no doubt that for "policemen", the steel unions had relatively limited powers. This was apparent not just in the scope of subcontracted operations but also in the conditions under which the sub-contractors employed labour. For the expansion of sub-contracting was an integral part of the corporation's drive to reduce its central or core workforce, shed some of the burden of employment costs such as pensions, retirement and sickness benefits, and at the same time tacitly accept, if not encourage, a re-definition of working practices.

On Teesside, the conditions under which the growth of subcontracting took place were supposed to be regulated by a "Contractors Agreement" signed between BSC and the steel unions in 1981. Under this, contractors paid no less than the minimum rate; but much evidence suggested that this was observed only in passing. A growing concern in the area was the use of labour by subcontractors from the informal economy. The ISTC's senior organizer, Mr Davey said:

> There's no doubt that contractors do employ people off the dole. Some of them recruit a dozen or so people in a pub, and offer money in the back pocket.

Whilst Ron Agar, AEU convenor, was even stronger in his views, and fully conscious of the implications:

> A lot of the men who come in to work for contractors are claiming DHSS benefits. I have proof of this, and I'm in close contact with management about it. BSC claim not to know. Certainly they wouldn't condone it. But they've used the economy of this country to help the profitability of the steel industry. They've used the black economy, indirectly—although they wouldn't admit it. There's no way that a contractor coming in for one day would sign off—he'd lose all his benefit. And in a week he could earn more than a skilled craftsman. That's a sore point.

It was also a point not lost upon others. BSC spokesman Mr Adamson responded that "at present no one who is on the dole is on this site" (*Middlesbrough Evening Gazette* 17 June 1986). A letter was despatched to all contractors warning them not to employ such labour. But others were showing interest, including a special team of Department of Employment investigators. After a four-week enquiry this announced, in the front-page headline of the local newspaper, a "dole swoop on 100 at BSC". The article continued:

> More than 100 people face prosecution for false benefit claims after an anti-fraud swoop on men working at British Steel. Some of the men

netted by the Department of Employment investigators were allegedly being paid up to £180 a week working for sub-contractors. But they were also receiving as much as £60 a week in unemployment or supplementary benefit. (*Middlesbrough Evening Gazette* 28 August 1986)

Such a high profile enquiry (its findings were formally announced by a Government minister) was significant in a number of ways; not least in the message it sent out to the rest of Teesside's unemployed about the burgeoning surveillance activities of the state, and the apparent vindication of many of the steel unions' claims. But the deeper reasons behind the growing informal economy remained shadowed from the public view. A large part of the potential for abuse lay in the fact that subcontracted labour was casual work; and the transition from stable to casual employment in the steel industry had been actively and positively encouraged by BSC. Part of the reason for this lay in the use of outside labour to encourage changes within the remaining core workforce. Ron Agar, AEU convenor, said:

> On the one hand you do away with direct labour, on the other you bring in the indirect labour. It's not seen on the balance sheet, but it's a matter of balancing the books. We could muster three or four hundred craftsmen within twenty four hours on Teesside. The contractor hires and fires these men at a minute's notice. They pose a threat to us every day of our working lives. We don't know whether we've a secure future. It's an uphill battle all the way. It seems we can never get security of employment, because of the contractors.

The elision between contractor and contracted was significant. In the minds of many core employees, the subcontracted labour force became the challenge, not the system under which subcontracting had grown. This too was by no means unwelcome to BSC, and was actively promoted by the contracting companies. In the process, a fragmentation within the labour force was developed and strengthened.

An early subcontracting agreement concerned the transfer of catering services from BSC to Gardner-Merchant. One of the few women branch officials in the ISTC, June Milburn, described the consequences:

> Our girls today don't like to fight. They don't want to argue. You get the area manager telling our girls what to do and they'll do it, because they're frightened to lose their jobs. When we were with British Steel, the men backed us. They don't today, they say we're contractors. I believe they would come out if it came to a real fight, but only some of the men back us now. We're on our own, more or less, and the girls are frightened of that. The managers play on the fact that the girls are frightened. They're splitting us up into little families.

At the same time the content of the job had become more demanding:

> You can't do the job properly, you can't finish a job you set off to do. The standards of service have gone right down. The managers know the standards are well below par, they're putting us under pressure to up the standards, but we can't do it. We've not got the time. There's not enough staff to cope.

And the rewards were uncertain:

> We haven't got half the fringe benefits we used to have. We were supposed to stay on the same terms as British Steel, but that got waylaid after the first two years. And the pension scheme we've got now is no way up to British Steel's standards.

Meanwhile active trade unionists like June found themselves increasingly discriminated against:

> We were all interviewed for our jobs by Gardner Merchant. Some of us had been there ten or twenty years. It was a case of "if your face fits". Mine nearly didn't. They offered me a shift job and said if I didn't take it, I was out. It took me two years to get off shift work. The night-shift was no good for my union work, and they knew it.

Such active discouragement of trade union activity was a further clear manifestation of the re-assertion of managerial power. This is what many of these changes in steel on Teesside were about. Competition between and within works to stay in employment was buttressed by the fear of unemployment in a jobs crisis area and the knowledge that some workers were on short-term contracts or ignoring skill boundaries, probably for an outside contractor. The reward to individual core employees for increased labour productivity and, whilst not necessarily directly associated, greater profitability, was only too tangible in the form of lump sum bonuses. The price, in terms of individual job control and quality of work environment, was one that many workers were prepared to pay because they saw, and were offered, no alternative.

It was the imposition of similar changes which workers at British Coal had resisted for so long, on the grounds not just of job control but also the very practical and real concern of safety, especially significant in such a hazardous industry. The national debate over flexibility in coal-mining—meaning longer shifts and greater use of sub-contracted labour, as well as new production techniques—was particularly acute in the north east's coastal pits where British Coal argued that new investment could only be justified if there was agreement on flexible working.

Numerous flashpoints occurred where British Coal management sought to introduce new working arrangements, often succeeding in negotiating local deals which fell outside the national NUM's guidelines, due partly to the continuing presence of the UDM. The most contested innovation, though, was the introduction of coal production not for five days in the week (allowing weekend rest time and scope for maintenance) but on a six or seven day basis, improving machine utilization at a stroke whilst going against long-established practice within the industry.

In 1989, for instance, workers at Wearmouth Colliery were told by their manager that in the light of mounting losses, the pit would need to move to seven day coal production at those faces which were suffering from geological deterioration in the course of each weekend. Arguing that this would be in clear breach of national agreements, north-east regional president of the NUM, David Guy, argued that

> Miners are tired of being threatened with an axe hanging over their heads. British Coal is clearly using intimidation to encourage our members to break the five-day working agreement. (quoted in *Newcastle Journal* 18 August 1989)

Workers at Wearmouth voted in favour of an overtime ban if British Coal management pressed on with its plan. Wearmouth NUM spokesman Alan Mardghum explained the threat to miners' safety perceived in seven day coal production:

> There is a chance that the action will hit coal output, but we told management that as far as we are concerned, safety is of paramount importance and is more important than the pit, profits and production. Seven days a week production could only be sustained for a short time before tiredness sets in. All we were asking of management was that they work within the standing agreements as we want to produce coal in a safe environment. (quoted in *Newcastle Journal* 25 August 1989)

When British Coal did go ahead with its plans, the threatened overtime ban was implemented, lasting for several weeks before both sides met to seek a resolution to the dispute.

This was just one incident among many as across the coalfield, British Coal introduced piece-meal changes to the process of winning coal from the ground. These were by no means as spectacular or far-reaching in their impact as earlier developments in steel production on Teesside, but nonetheless they demonstrated that new working practices were not confined to new industries. This was not the only way, though, that coal and steel were associated with the transition to a new economy. They were also heavily implicated in the creation of jobs to replace those lost via closures; and the character of this employment was an integral component of the emerging regional economy.

## 5.4 Defining the terms and conditions of re-industrialization: British Steel (Industry) and British Coal Enterprise

A further feature of the new social and political climate in the north east was the type of policy response formulated in the quest for new jobs directly to replace those lost in industries such as coal and steel. Typically this focused upon selected aspects of the new "enterprise economy"—the creation of a new generation of small businesses in an attempt to rejuvenate the industrial base, and retraining redundant workers with new skills. Both British Steel and British Coal participated in this process by establishing their own job-creation subsidiaries, charged with promoting just such a task. These agencies were by no means the only ones addressing unemployment in the north east; but they were highly significant to British Steel and to British Coal as a gesture of concern and an attempt at compensating for the scale of decline, in the process easing opposition to closures; and more generally as an indication of the kind of economy being reconstituted in the region.

BSC(I) was established in 1975 with active trade union support; NCB(E) (later BCE) was established in 1984 in the midst of the miners' strike, accompanied by trades union accusations that it was too little, too late, and plainly a tactical ploy. By the end of the 1980s, BSC(I) claimed to have assisted in the creation of 70,000 new jobs nationally and BCE some 50,000. BSC(I)'s objectives were described as follows by its chief executive Roger Thackery in 1987:

> We have never tried to persuade former steel workers to set up in business—in some cases we have dissuaded them from it. Anyone employed for twenty or thirty years in a large company is not going to have the skills which make an entrepreneur. What we are engaged in is diversifying the economic base of local communities which had relied on one industry. (quoted in *Financial Times* 2 June 1987)

Such goals encompassed a clear view of industry's changing demands for labour:

> Basic to the BSC(I) initiative is the understanding that patterns of work and job opportunities are already beginning to change radically. School leavers and young adults will have to develop a more flexible attitude to work and how to gain a livelihood. Changes to long-held beliefs about the

nature of work will not be easy to achieve but the future of employment
and an important part of the UK's industrial future will depend on their
taking place. (BSC *Steel News* March 1987)

Flexibility then was the key to BSC(I)'s view of future employment
change in the UK, and its activities, like those of BCE, were geared
to that end.

BCE closely modelled itself on BSC(I) (see Sloman 1986). It
developed a three-pronged strategy: support for investment in
the form of loans; provision of managed workshop space; and
re-training. Its budget was set initially at £5 m but rose rapidly
to £10 m, then in 1985 to £20 m, in 1986 to £40 m and in 1989
to £60 m. Support to new investment projects was in the form of
loans, usually relatively small. By 1990, it claimed to have funded
almost 3,000 projects of which over 90 per cent involved loans
of less than £50,000 and over 70 per cent loans of less than
£15,000. Repayments on these loans were recycled to other
proposals. It also participated in the development of 79 managed
workshops, intended as seedbeds for very small businesses. Such
support for new companies of whatever size was not confined to
ex-miners, but was aimed generally at employment creation in a
coalfield area, subject to a limit of £5,000 per job or 25 per cent
of the total investment, whichever was the lower. BCE also
had responsibility for British Coal's re-training of ex-miners
under its Job and Career Change Scheme (JACCS). In total,
the 50,000 jobs claimed to have been created up to 1990 by
BCE were broken down into: 25,000 in new businesses; 17,000
via provision of re-training under JACCS; and 8,000 through the
managed workshop programme. In addition, BCE estimated that
commitments in those projects already supported would lead to a
further 12,000 job opportunities in due course.

Like BSC(I), BCE was the target of fierce debate about the likely
effectiveness of its activities, the extent to which it was sufficiently
funded, and even whether it was an appropriate form of response.
Announcing the proposed formation of NCB(E) in August 1984,
NCB director Merrik Spanton held out no great hopes for a
radical reversal in the unemployment crisis in the coalfields: "we
know that the money we shall put in will not of itself generate
a great number of jobs" (quoted in *Newcastle Journal* 4 August
1984). Rapidly, though, the NCB placed increasing emphasis on
its job-creation subsidiary and by June 1986 was claiming that
it could replace all jobs lost from coal mining within a period
of five or six years. By 1989, its Chairman, Merrik Spanton,
was slightly more cautious, but still held to the same optimistic

theme, that the funds available "may prove to be sufficient to enable BCE to assist in the creation of 100,000 new long-term job opportunities." In 1990, BCE's target was the creation of 100,000 new jobs by 1993/94, although its chief executive Tony Hewitt cautioned that:

> the reconstruction of the coal industry has resulted in more people leaving than could have been foreseen five years ago—so there's a need to aim at targets beyond the original 100,000.

Such statements, though, were subject to increasingly critical review; and indeed the very basis on which BCE's success could be measured was itself problematic. The extent to which BCE support was *instrumental* in creating these jobs, and the use of other financial assistance in particular projects so that jobs might be "double-counted" by, for instance, BCE and BSC(I), meant that it was often difficult to disentangle the precise impact of BCE's operations from more general employment trends, despite BCE's own figures and estimates of its success. The Energy Committee's investigation into the coal industry also looked at BCE, and concluded that its funding was woefully inadequate: "the number of jobs created is very small in relation to the number of jobs lost in mining areas in recent years, and some areas have benefited only to a pitifully small extent" (Energy Committee 1987 para. 137). In 1989, Stephen Fothergill, director of the local-authority sponsored Coalfield Communities Campaign, argued as follows:

> The job creation claims are well from the mark. Our research has shown that the jobs created by BCE are a tenth of those claimed. Many of the jobs claimed as created are simply displacing other jobs. (quoted in *Newcastle Journal* 9 November 1989)

In this debate then BCE increasingly resembled BSC(I), for the attempt at compensating for job losses, whilst useful to British Coal and British Steel in easing opposition to closures, also drew further criticism of the apparent inadequacy of such measures when weighed against the scale of decline.

In spite of this, and regardless of the uncertainty of the number of actual jobs created, it remained the case that the *kind* of employment being encouraged was deeply significant, especially given the close associations between BSC(I), BCE and another major vehicle of 1980s reindustrialization policy, the local enterprise agency network. In 1984, BSC(I) had handed over responsibility for job creation to local enterprise agencies in its eighteen locations, known thereafter as "Opportunity Areas" (see Figure 5.2). Much of BCE's activity was also in the form of assistance to

Fig 5.2.   BSC (Industry) Opportunity Areas.

enterprise agencies. These were (sometimes uneasy) coalitions of local businesses, local government and major corporations, with small budgets, aimed at offering advice to potential new companies and encouraging the relocation of existing businesses. The first one was founded in Pilkington in 1978; under the aegis of Business in the Community (itself founded in 1979) and with strong government support, their numbers grew to well over two hundred. As David Grayson, a director of Business in the Community, put it:

> enterprise agencies became the macho symbol of the 1980s. Every town had to have one. (quoted in *Financial Times* 8 March 1988)

The influence of enterprise agencies in areas like the north east was widespread. A network of thirteen covered the whole coalfield. In some areas, such as Derwentside, they were sponsored by both BCE and BSC(I). In many instances they were both suspicious of outside investigation and highly reactive to criticism (see, for instance, Hudson and Sadler 1989: pp. 112–15). It was also in places like Derwentside, where coal and steel closures had such devastating impact, and the local enterprise agency was given such a high profile, that the full nature of the new economy being created was readily apparent.

Many new jobs in Derwentside were low paid, highly exploitative, insecure, and in sectors such as textiles and clothing, often taken by women. Some of the gravest problems concerned the incidence of failed companies. In 1985, premises on one industrial estate greeted the fourth company to start trading there in two years. The first, Fab Fashions, had gone into liquidation in December 1983. Another, Fair Fashions, was set up almost immediately but closed a year later, and a company called Quatriz Ltd opened. This closed in August 1985 and 45 workers, mainly women, lost their jobs. As Derek Cattell of the National Union of Tailors and Garment Workers explained:

> Our people got no notice at all of the closure until the day it happened. They are owed wages in lieu of notice, outstanding pay and outstanding wages. No liquidator has been appointed and until that has been done none of our members can get any entitlement. (quoted in *Newcastle Journal* 21 August 1985)

As the workers successfully went to an industrial tribunal to win compensation, the fourth company on the site in four years began trading, with its managing director (mindful of past events) stressing he had "no dealings with the previous tenants" of the factory (*Newcastle Journal* 13 November 1985).

This was not an isolated incident. Quatriz Ltd was only one of four Derwentside clothing firms taken to industrial tribunals by the National Union of Tailors and Garment Workers in 1985. Another of these was Tab Court Ltd, a clothing firm opened in December 1984 after a different business at the same factory, Tantobie Textiles, had gone into liquidation. Tantobie Textiles was subsequently taken to a tribunal and the workforce awarded 90 days' pay in lieu of notice. Tab Court's managing director, Mr Whittaker, had been involved in Tantobie Textiles, and when Tab Court closed, the same problems ensued. The 46 women workers were also forced to go to an industrial tribunal, and were awarded 30 days' pay in lieu of notice. The average gross wage of the workers had been £73 a week (*Newcastle Journal* 10 December 1985). Their predicament contrasted strongly with that of accountant Mr Burnard, a founder director of both Tab Court and Quatriz. At a public auction selling off machinery from the two companies, he commented that

> as far as I am concerned, we have got our fingers burned and we don't want to come back. It is a business and we are in it to make money. We wouldn't finance this type of thing again.

He added that:

> since last Monday, I have formed at least fifteen companies. (quoted in *Newcastle Journal* 1 November 1985)

Such problems were by no means confined to the textile industry. Within Derwentside, the old economy—dependent upon coal, steel and a few major foreign-owned branch plants—was steadily replaced in the 1980s with a low wage, small firm-centred manufacturing base, and a growing service sector.[8] One of the key attractions which the area presented to prospective new employers was a huge pool of potential labour. One of the largest new companies, for instance, was Blue Ridge Care, established in the early 1980s and by 1990 employing 175 people. Its managing director David Langston indicated the significance of labour availability to his choice of Consett as production base:

> This location has a hard-grafting work ethic. Our labour turnover and absenteeism are close to nil. They've grown a bit from the early days, but they're still low. The goal is not to take advantage of an unemployment blackspot, but Consett is a very good place to operate.

In many of the new companies, several generations of (highly anachronistic) industrial relations practices were superseded by

236

a new industrial culture. In this, insecurity of employment was a clear distinguishing feature. For instance, Blue Ridge Care—one of the District's "success stories"—laid off 44 workers in 1990 after unsuccessfully attempting a move to continuous four-shift operation, which had entailed some new recruitment. The reasons for this subsequent switch and the basis of the redundancies were described as follows by David Langston:

> For the first six months of continuous production we had no increase in output. In terms of productivity it didn't provide us with what it was supposed to. The laying-off was done on the basis of seniority and disciplinary letters in the file. What you're doing there is getting rid of the newest ones and the least productive ones, and that always works. Now that we've gone back from seven-day to five-day production, we haven't lost any output at all.

In solving its productivity problem, the company also neatly reshaped its workforce, further reinforcing the insecurity of local employment patterns and demonstrating—not least to its own workforce—that employers had some considerable power in the local labour market.

Yet (and at first sight paradoxically) one of the consequences of a gradual increase in employment in the District in the 1980s was to expose new companies' previous dependence upon mass unemployment to instil particularly disciplined regimes among their workforces. As the labour market showed the first signs of declining unemployment, in other words (and not for one moment discounting the significance of continuing high absolute levels), companies began to come against the limits of their earlier strategies. For instance, another of the major new companies, Grorud (established in 1981, and by 1990 employing 300) had expanded steadily throughout the decade. Its financial director David D'Arcy commented as follows in 1990:

> Two years ago I could have said we had no turnover of labour. We had an utterly reliable workforce. The same cannot be said of the people that have been recruited in recent times. The turnover of labour is only amongst those people who've just been recruited. The people who've been here a long time have given us no problem at all. The people we find inefficient are those who've started recently. Because the people who wanted to work in this area have got a job. Those left unemployed are hanging on as long as possible and are not genuinely interested in hard work. The labour's out there, I don't have any doubts about that. There's only one factor: we're reaching the bottom of the barrel in the labour market.

Behind this assessment lies the point that companies like Grorud, which were once used to considerable freedom in the local labour market, had begun to experience the first incipient signs of a change in terms of what employees asked and might reasonably have expected from an employer in terms of quality of work. This underlined the extent to which new practices and attitudes were easy to introduce at a time of mass unemployment at the start of the 1980s, and revealed the first tentative re-emergence of bargaining power on the part of labour.

To some, developments in the 1980s heralded the beginning of a new era. Neil Gregory, chairman of the District Council's economic development committee, commented that "Derwentside now has a stronger and more diverse economy than it has had for many years" (quoted in *Newcastle Journal* 29 August 1989). For others, though, it was increasingly difficult to relate such prognoses to the reality of life within the area. One resident, Patrick McNulty, wrote as follows:

> I sometimes wonder if there are two Derwentsides. One which I and others like me live in, and one which the people from the Derwentside Development Scheme [*sic*] inhabit. These people are constantly making statements about the "boom" now taking place in Derwentside. I do look for signs of this "boom" but I'm afraid it continues to elude me. All I see are small business units springing up employing between five and twenty employees, most of whom are on one year adult schemes, ET, or two year youth schemes, YTS. Anyone fortunate enough to have a permanent position is usually low-waged and non-unionised. . . . While I agree that the people in the job creation agencies must not become pessimistic I do, however, believe that they should be frank and objective and not mislead the people. If the Government is led to believe that Derwentside is now "booming" and "prosperous" then it will see no need for the massive assistance which is urgently needed to save this area from total and complete demise. (*Durham Advertiser* 14 September 1989)

This notion of "two Derwentsides", entailing recognition of new forms of social division, was an important one, which is considered again in the concluding section.

## 5.5 Concluding comments

It is clear then that in a whole variety of ways, the UK state was heavily implicated in the reconstitution of the north-east regional economy and, in particular, its labour market. Decline of the traditional industrial base was orchestrated via the public sector corporations in coal and steel, whilst trade unions were taken on and defeated in a highly visible and symbolic fashion. In the wake of such changes "flexibility" in its many different guises was enforced, in particular among the remaining steelworkers but also increasingly in the coal mines (and of course via the expansion of open-cast coal production). This was far from a liberating phenomenon but rather one which both presupposed and made possible far greater managerial control over the labour force. The tenor of government policy was further expressed in the re-industrialization policies of British Coal Enterprise and British Steel (Industry), through their emphasis on the creation of a "new" generation (effectively in many cases the first) of small businesses. This rested upon a highly tenuous footing which depended in large part upon exploiting the insecurity in the local economy created by coal and steel closures, so as to impose draconian work regimes. Even for the new owners of small businesses, the price—in terms of hours of work and financial risk—was often a very high one indeed. It was on this kind of state-inspired blueprint, then, that new companies such as Nissan were able to impose such radically different ideas about production and work organization.

The growing emphasis on the service sector within the region only acted to reinforce these trends, for activities such as retailing and tourism were characterized above all else by low-paid, insecure and often part-time employment. This was exemplified by the massive Metro Centre at Gatehead, a huge complex of shopping malls and leisure facilities. To give just one example: in 1989 the House of Fraser group (which had stores in Metro Centre and Newcastle city centre) sent out letters to its 350 employees requiring them to work on bank holidays. Ron Brown, Newcastle organizer for the shopworkers' union USDAW, responded that

> New contracts have been issued without any warning to staff. We recognise that shops open on bank holidays, but staff should have the right to refuse work. The company is basically threatening people with dismissal if they refuse to work. Yet many of the workers are part-time or working mothers who like to spend holidays with their families and should have the right to continue to do so. (quoted in *Newcastle Journal* 8 November 1989)

On such an analysis, it is difficult to equate the reality of life for many in the north east with the wealth of pronouncements from promotional agencies and government alike about the region's new economic dynamism, which characterized the late 1980s. In many ways, the state of the whole regional economy and the real impact of a selected few investments had become highly contentious issues. It was apparent that a concerted campaign was underway to "sell" the region's positive attributes. This embraced newly created organizations such as the Northern Development Company and a host of other bodies such as the Urban Development Corporations in Tyne and Wear and on Teesside. On more than one occasion there was open friction between these and alternative commentaries, fuelled by central government insistence that to focus on the region's continuing social and economic problems in any way was counter-productive in the search for new investment (see Sadler 1990b). Behind the promotional gloss, though, there was evidence that all was not quite what it seemed.

It was evident that the extent of the proclaimed economic upturn, and the impact of its leading edges, were limited. The number of Japanese companies in the region rose from one in 1978 to fifteen by 1989, accounting for some 5,000 jobs; but over the same period, 35 US-owned manufacturing plants had closed with the loss of 15,000 jobs (Smith and Stone 1989). Overall, manufacturing employment in the region barely remained constant, and the extent of total employment growth from 1983 to 1988 represented only one-quarter of the number of jobs lost from 1979 to 1983; much of this growth was in part-time employment. Unemployment appeared to be falling, but on closer inspection about 75 per cent of the decline in registered unemployment by 50,000 from 1986 to 1988 was due to the expansion of government training schemes and stricter eligibility criteria for the payment of state benefits (see Robinson and Gillespie 1989). On this basis then there was an ongoing transformation taking place in the north east regional economy but, crucially, it still rested upon continued state support and insecurity for many to continue the process of structural change.

## Notes

1.  To say this is not to understate the significance of BSC's sophisticated public relations and negotiating machinery. For instance, BSC only gradually implemented its proposal, allowing uncertainty, indecision and the promise of generous redundancy payments to sway many minds. As John Lee, secretary to the (locally based and largely trade union organized) "Save Consett Campaign" put it in June after six months of virtual silence.

    > We have had no positive information from BSC since the closure was announced in December, and we think this has been a deliberate tactic on their part. We think they planned not to give us any information in order to demoralise and frustrate our members to

the point where they would be prepared to accept any decision. (quoted in *Consett Guardian* 12 June 1980)

2.  The extent to which the decision not to close Ravenscraig was a *political* one, and the way in which the anti-closure campaign forced it openly to be seen as a political issue, was emphasized as follows:

    > In the light of what we were told about prospects for demand and despite the Secretary of State's argument that there was "great difficulty in being able to make any confident forecast" we take the view that his decision to retain five sites was essentially a *political* rather than *economic* decision. (Industry and Trade Committee 1983 para. 12, emphasis added)

3.  At Murton, the miners voted against strike action but the mechanics in favour; with the miners respecting the mechanics' picket line, this amounted to a striking pit. The reason why there were thirteen pits in the Durham coalfield but fourteen votes on the executive was that Blackhall Colliery, closed in 1981 but with 40 members engaged on pumping duties to protect neighbouring pits, still had a vote.

4.  An additional dimension to the District's problems, poor health, was also subsequently revealed (see Townsend *et al* 1988). Easington District had the highest proportion in the entire Northern Region of wards suffering from a combined measure of poor health (including early death, disability, sickness and under-weight births)—over 50 per cent.

5.  A similar ruling was made later in 1986 by Mr Diamond QC over the future of Cadeby colliery in Yorkshire:

    > economic and social considerations do seem to me to be relevant when considering the pace of withdrawal from coal mining in a particular area, and the rate and timing of pit closures. The NCB in my view has an obligation, at any rate where several collieries are concerned or where coal mining is the only economic activity in a certain area, not to close a colliery save on reasonable notice. This is not a legal obligation, it is a moral one.

    He concluded that the NCB's closure proposal was "unreasonable", in that it did not consider "what detriment would be caused to the local community".

6.  In the process, history effectively repeated itself; for after the 1926 General Strike a separate union was formed in the Nottinghamshire coalfield, led by George Spencer, former head of the Nottinghamshire Miners' Association. This was mirrored in the north east by small groups of men who broke the strike and, in January 1927, formed the Northumberland and Durham Miners' Non-Political Trades Union. Although this effectively lost any real influence later that year, the "Spencer" union in Nottinghamshire survived until 1937.

241

7. It draws upon interviews conducted with trade union leaders, branch officials and management from British Steel's South Teesside works in 1985 and 1986.

8. This account draws on interviews conducted with new businesses in Derwentside in 1990.

# 6
# The Constancy of Change

## 6.1 Introduction

This concluding chapter seeks to weave together the remaining
loose threads of the argument presented above, and to speculate
upon several issues which are likely to be significant in influen-
cing, if not quite determining, likely future trends. To this end it
addresses three interrelated groups of questions. In section 6.2,
the main features of global change in coal, steel and automobile
production are reviewed, along with the key points of UK state
policies to those sectors in the context of north east England.
Then section 6.3 considers two particular (partly interrelated)
factors which are likely to have a considerable impact on the UK's
economic future, and indeed in the global sense more generally.
These are the role of European Community policies and the
process of political reform in Eastern Europe. Finally, in section
6.4, the interconnections between these different components of
the global economy are addressed in the light of the debates
introduced in Chapter 1, and some of the main implications are
analyzed.

## 6.2 A backward glance: review and summary

Part I of this book introduced and examined in detail the
geographical patterns of global restructuring in three different
sectors—coal-mining, iron and steel production, and motor vehicle assembly—in the context of one national state, the UK. Within
each chapter the focus was upon key international processes,
before developing further on the manifestations of such change
in the UK. In Part II, the focus shifted to a different context, the
precise appearance of restructuring in these sectors and this state
within one region, north east England. Throughout, the emphasis
was upon the interconnections between these different planes of
analysis—and this is considered further in section 6.4. Before

proceeding to this though, it is useful to take a brief backward glance and review the evidence so far.

One of the key features of the coal-mining industry was the gradual emergence of new sources of supply in response to developments in alternative energy resources, especially oil, in the 1970s. Whilst multinational corporations were major actors in this process (and remain highly influential in the overall coal supply chain), the efforts of various NIC states to open up coal reserves in order to earn foreign currency became increasingly significant. Together, the factors encouraging the growth of alternative supplies set in train a re-shaping of the global geography of coal production and trade. This is far from complete. The volume of coal traded internationally remains small by comparison with total world consumption. As longer-worked reserves become exhausted, though, the importance of these massive newly exploited deposits can only become greater, especially as limited oil and gas reserves become depleted. The extent and availability of coal on a worldwide basis will become a vital issue of global strategy.

A slightly different set of changes has taken place in the iron and steel industry. Since the 1970s, there has been an even more marked shift in production capacity with decline in the advanced countries—especially in Western Europe and North America, but also and most recently in Japan—contrasting sharply with expansion in a few NICs. One of the most important reasons for this geographical shift was the different kind of economic development in NIC and advanced country economies, the latter moving increasingly into less steel-intensive service sector activities. In the steel industry, the influence of national state policies is even greater than in coal, many NIC producers being largely state-owned (and not a few elsewhere in the globe), International trade in steel is also heavily regulated by a series of inter-governmental agreements.

In the automobile industry, a further different set of trends—or (perhaps more appropriately) emphases within the same processes—was at work. The most dramatic of these was the growth of Japanese automobile producers to challenge the world supremacy of American companies such as Ford and GM. This also epitomized the emergence of Japan on the world economic and political stage in the 1980s. In that decade, Japanese companies expanded in a big way into production bases first within North America, then Western Europe, as part of their increasingly global production strategies. Within this sector, given its nature as an assembly-type process, the impact of and responses to the rise of Japan rested upon a series of decisions to do with the global organization and location of production. These ranged on a spectrum from decentralization, to take advantage of lower wage costs or circumvent trade barriers, to reconcentration around new production complexes. Varying combinations of these options were both possible and practised, along with a third strategic response, cooperation in specific product areas and markets with other (on most criteria competing) companies.

At the same time, Part I acknowledged that these sectoral divisions are both artificial constructions and, at times, analytical constraints. The manufacturing process rests not on a series of discrete stages but a highly integrated chain. This is exemplified in the progression from coal to iron and steel and motor vehicles; but it is also evident in the linkages between each of these sectors and other elements of the global economy. Upon decisions to do with coal production and consumption, for instance, rest a series of other issues to do with the technology required to convert that fuel into energy, such as the construction of electricity generation capacity. Iron and steel production depends upon a range of raw materials, not just coking coal but iron ore, scrap and alloy metals, which are in turn produced and traded internationally. Equally, steel production elides gradually into manufacturing. It is no coincidence that many steel companies are indistinguishable from engineering companies. The production of steel as a commodity is inextricably bound up with its use in one form or another. Steel is used for instance in the motor vehicle industry, although assembly of a motor car rests upon sourcing decisions to do with a whole range of other parts. In this fashion then, motor vehicle production is as much about automotive components, with linkages throughout the production chain into plastics, electronics, ceramics and other raw materials and industries, as it is about the assembly of those components. The wheel of production (to coin a phrase) comes round full circle.

Within the UK in the 1980s, such developments had a dramatic impact, both devastating and in some instances, potentially rejuvenating. It is impossible to understand the process of global restructuring and the part played by the UK without detailed reference to the policies of the UK state. In coal and steel, decline was not just a result of the operation of the capitalist law of value across space. It was actively orchestrated and planned by the state through the vehicle of the public corporation, one way of mediating the law of value. In coal, the role of the state embraced its control not just of production via British Coal, but also a large part of consumption through the public-sector electricity generator, the CEGB; and a whole range of other demand issues such as support for competing fuels, in particular nuclear power. In motor vehicles, the state-owned producer British Leyland (later Rover Group) was also forced to contract, in marked contrast to the positive welcome extended to the Japanese automobile companies as they expanded into Western Europe. Privatization of British Steel and Rover, and increasingly (via opencasting) in the coal-mining industry, could not undermine the significance of state policies for these sectors, but rather revealed more fully some of the paradoxes of state intervention.

Finally, Part II turned to the question of production reorganization within north east England. This focused on the same three sectors not because they were somehow the sum total of change in the region—they were not—but rather because they were deeply significant to its economy. In turn, the reasons for that importance to the region were crucial to an understanding of the global system of which the north east was but one small part. During the 1980s, the decline of an old industrial base built largely on coal and steel enmeshed with the proclaimed emergence of a new economy, epitomized in the Nissan plant at Sunderland and its growing production complex. The reasons for this shift and the role played by the UK state in terms of the forced acceptance of labour market flexibility were also considered. These questions about the interconnections between the north east and the rest of the UK and the world are a particular case of a more general set of issues, which are considered in the final section. First, however, it is instructive to consider some possible key future developments in the global economy.

## 6.3 Where next? The global economy in the 1990s and its implications for the UK and north east England

As the global economy entered the 1990s it was evident that a range of often conflicting issues would confront corporate planning, national governments and regions such as north east England. Many of these were longstanding; some were increasingly difficult to resolve; and a few were newly emergent but likely to become increasingly significant as the decade progressed. In so far as it is possible to forecast the future with any great precision, this section concentrates upon two particular such aspects which were likely to have marked consequences in the UK. These are the role of European Community policies and the process of political reform in Eastern Europe.[1]

Even in just the three sectors considered in this volume, it was clear that the 1980s witnessed a growing importance for European Community policies, partly in the context of the impending proposed creation of a free internal market within and between the twelve member states by 1992 (see, for instance, Cecchini 1988). In the coal industry, EC policies had historically focused on the twin dilemmas of security of supply and restrictions on state financial aid to production. In practice the latter was allowed under EC regulations because of the former in an attempt to encourage domestic coal consumption rather than the use of imported oil. As a House of Lords select committee remarked in 1983:

> There has been protracted debate in the Community about coal. There have been many proposals for action. But, although it is thirty years since the ECSC Treaty came into operation, Community coal policy is still pretty modest in scope and coal policy is largely a matter for member states. (European Communities Committee 1983: p. xxi).

From 1985 though EC policy envisaged a gradual phasing out of state aid to coal producers, given a new environment in which there was seemingly greater diversity of energy supply. Then in 1988 the EC turned its attention instead to the barriers on trade in energy within the Community, and the following year the Energy Commissioner proposed a series of changes easing the internal movement of energy, on the grounds that this would save 5 billion ECU by 2000, reducing generating costs by 16 per cent. Such proposals met with a mixed political response, for they meant a searching examination of continuing subsidies to coal producers in West Germany, France, Spain and the UK—but were clearly indicative of the new policy environment.

In terms of regulating automobile production and trade, too, the EC played an increasing role in the context of 1992. Imports of cars from Japan were limited by national government policies in five member states—rigidly so in France and Italy, but also in Portugal, Spain and (despite its encouragement to Japanese investment) the UK. This was incompatible with the proposed free internal market so that the EC had to develop a common policy on the treatment of Japanese vehicles, which also embraced production from the "transplant" operations within the UK which was or might be exported to other EC states. During 1989 and 1990, lengthy negotiations took place, with most other EC car producers (including the US giants) lobbying heavily in favour of incorporating UK-produced Japanese cars in a quota of Japanese imports to the EC as a whole after 1992. Jacques Calvet, president of Peugeot, argued for instance that:

> The UK will have to decide in favour of its national interests or for
> Europe. If it chooses Europe, and I very much hope it will, that means
> that the Nissan, Toyota and Honda plants in the UK will enter into the
> overall limit of Japanese cars, and that will mean a reduction of imports
> from Japan. (quoted in *Financial Times* 3 February 1990)

Later in 1990 the EC at least agreed a common negotiating
position, that Japanese vehicle producers would be able to turn
out as many cars as they wanted from factories inside the EC,
but for a transitional period of probably five years after 1992,
the more they produced in Europe the less they could export
from Japan.

This policy stance was countered by an alternative view, which
argued that Japanese cars produced in the EC should in no way
count as any part of the balance of Japanese production. This
was expressed, for instance, by Nissan president Yutaka Kume:

> We are doing our utmost to increase local content levels in our plants.
> Is it fair to regard these cars produced in Europe as the same as cars
> exported from Japan? (quoted in *Financial Times* 21 June 1990)

Clearly, local content remained a crucial issue, and also a thorny
definitional point. There was little agreement but it was apparent
that the EC was on questionable ground. Trade restraints were
generally outlawed under the provisions of the General Agreement on Tariffs and Trade (GATT), and the EC had already
lost one round of the legal battle when GATT upheld a Japanese
complaint about the extension of EC anti-dumping rules to so-
called "screwdriver" plants which assembled Japanese-produced
components at factories within the EC. Moreover the extent and
speed at which Japanese vehicle companies had moved to increase
local content made it difficult to count such transplant investments
as anything other than EC-produced; particularly as it appeared
that the companies concerned relied on fewer Japanese-owned
locally based component suppliers than in their equivalent plants
in the USA.

In iron and steel, by contrast, the challenge of 1992 was not so
much one of developing a common policy as of downgrading the
scope of the existing EC policy. For as demonstrated in Chapter
2, this sector saw the greatest extent of EC regulatory intervention
of any manufacturing industry in the early to mid-1980s. This was
an indication both of the severity of the crisis in steel production
and of the limits to national state policies. As relatively profitable
conditions re-emerged for steel producers (at least in the short
term) the EC's major concern was to withdraw further from
intervention in this sector. As the *General Objectives Steel 1995*

remarked, the framework of the Treaty of Paris (which created the ECSC in 1951) contributed towards the creation of a single steel market. It went on

> The Treaty of Paris is still in force, but the deregulatory thrust of the Single European Act will probably inject a liberalising influence into the Treaty, which was conceived in a much more interventionist spirit. (CEC 1990 iv/1)

The general tenor of the 1992 proposals was a distinctive one, entailing a particular conception of the EC's role as a guarantor of internal free trade and limited undue competition from external trade. In this sense there was clearly a major role for the EC which resonated strongly with most of the member states[2]. By and large a *deregulatory* conception of the EC prevailed at the start of the 1990s, as its institutions sought to equate the rhetoric with the reality of an internal market. The Community as a whole faced important issues in this context to do with the balance of power between member states and the EC. This was evident not only in occasional reservations from some members on the grounds of "national sovereignty" but also in a resonance with the contrasting capacities of national states (as opposed to a tentative supra-national state organization) and international corporate strategies. Such themes found a focus too in friction between the EC's own institutions, in particular over the respective roles of the (appointed) Commission and the (elected) Parliament.

Such developments within the European Community had also to be evaluated in the context of dramatic changes which occurred in Eastern Europe and the Soviet Union. The process of political reform and the opening up of previously restricted markets at the end of the 1980s could possibly provide an important stimulus to the global economy during the 1990s, with widespread implications not just in Western Europe but across the globe. The declining influence of the Soviet Union strengthened the EC's role within Europe, and the newly emergent fledgling democracies in the east rapidly expressed a desire eventually to join the EC. This also led the six members of the European Free Trade Association (EFTA) to re-assess their relationship to the EC, and several considered moves towards closer integration. For the EC these developments posed some problems, especially in the context of the 1992 internal market programme. For the objective of this was to *deepen* the existing supra-national institutions, strengthening the power of European cooperation, whereas further enlargement would lead to a *widening* of political

249

cooperation across a larger space. Nonetheless, the EC was keen to encourage reform in Eastern Europe and continued to develop new political and economic contacts.

In some basic industrial sectors, such as coal or iron and steel, the biggest impact of openness in and to the former Soviet bloc looked to be in the form of increased exports from these countries, as they sought to earn foreign currency and Western governments freed their previously restricted markets in order further to encourage reform. The six countries of Eastern Europe alone, excluding the Soviet Union, produced more than 60 m tonnes of steel annually. Francis Mer, chairman of the French steel company Usinor, remarked on this threat as follows:

> These underdeveloped countries pose a real threat to our industry. There is a definite risk that these countries, in their attempt to earn foreign currency, will flood western markets, unloading vast quantities of steel. (quoted in *Financial Times* 18 June 1990)

The other side of this equation was that many of these countries could also provide a lucrative production base for a range of industries, enabling multinational capital to profit from their relatively low-waged economies and to open up new markets. This was particularly the case in motor vehicle production, as was highlighted in Chapter 3. There was no doubt that the longer the process of reform continued, the greater the prospect of many investment proposals becoming reality. Volkswagen's involvement in East Germany was followed by many other companies. General Motors planned in 1990 to increase vehicle assembly capacity in Europe by 25 per cent to more than 2 m a year by the mid-1990s, including the establishment of assembly plants in East Germany and Hungary, and a gearbox plant in Czechoslovakia. Some of the most advanced plans were those of Fiat, in response to its dependence upon the Italian market and lack of production bases elsewhere in Western Europe. It quickly developed on well-established links to create a long-term strategy involving wholly integrated operations in Yugoslavia, Poland and the Soviet Union, eventually aiming to produce cars at quality levels which could be sold in Western markets under Fiat nameplates. The most spectacular project was in the Soviet Union where Fiat looked to expand upon its involvement in a 300,000 annual capacity plant at Yelabuga to create a massive complex. Fiat's executive vice-president Francesco Gallo explained the rationale for this shift as follows:

In Western Europe there is already strong competition in a fairly saturated market. With a growing Japanese presence it will become more and more crowded with not so much growth in the market. You make a great effort just to gain a decimal point of market penetration. The big market of the future is eastern Europe. (quoted in *Financial Times* 9 July 1990).

By contrast, the Japanese automobile manufacturers were much more cautious, sending delegations to investigate conditions in Eastern Europe but by and large—apart from one early project announced by Suzuki in Hungary—falling short of concrete investment proposals. This hesitancy mirrored in many ways the careful, gradual way in which these companies expanded into production bases in North America and Western Europe, recognizing the wholly different circumstances which prevailed in these countries and the need to tailor Japanese style systems of production organization. Japanese reticence was epitomized by Toshihiko Morita of the giant Sumitomo Corporation:

In most cases political reform outstrips economic reform. It will take two or three years before we can be sure about making big investments in those countries. Small-sized investments could come earlier. (quoted in *Financial Times* 5 December 1989)

Whichever view prevailed would of course depend on the stability of the new political order, but it is nonetheless instructive to reflect on the potential long-term implications—not just in Eastern Europe, but more broadly. For as Volkswagen's new strategy demonstrated, the pursuit of investment in Eastern Europe was now in competition with other low-waged European countries such as Spain and the UK, posing important questions for these states.

Together then these two developments—reform in Eastern Europe and a growing role for the European Community—showed (if proof was necessary) that nothing was ever static in the global economy. Quite the reverse: it did not rest, but rather was in a constant state of flux, with different actors seeking to create and benefit from changing conditions within a series of constraints, with varying goals and ambitions. The new potential of the EC as an institution was significant not just for its supra-national character but as a possible centre of world power to rival the USA and Japan; subject of course to the tensions between its member states, which were likely to become greater as a united Germany achieved greater economic power. The new opportunities for profit in Eastern Europe and the Soviet Union were partly created as a result of political processes, and included low-wage conditions for the exploitation of labour. These countries were potentially highly lucrative to investment, offering capital a new spatial fix in its never-ending quest for advantage. In the process, of course, the role of particular places within the international capitalist system would undergo another reshuffle as the complex balance between capital, labour and state policies was worked out constantly anew. For the decisive social relation was that between capital and labour, and the most significant aspect of this was the constant unfolding of history. Classes were continually being (re)created and (re)constituted in time and space via the progress of capitalism itself. What all this meant for regions such as north east England, of course, was a matter of contingent circumstance and the precise working out of different strategies; but it was difficult realistically to be optimistic about the region's prospects in the global scramble for investment and employment, especially in the new economic environment of the 1990s.

### 6.4 Global, national, regional: intersecting paths of analysis

In the Introduction the idea that a newly dominant form of production had emerged in the global economy was outlined and assessed. Whilst this focus on production reorganization was helpful in terms of understanding the geographic constitution of the world economy it was suggested that the evidence could not support many of the sweeping generalizations being made. In particular the proclaimed switch from Fordist to flexible production was achieved at the expense of an undue disregard for the national state context and an oversimplification of the international and national integration of regional economies. In one sense, the evidence presented here could be interpreted simply as an example of the "not in this sector/not in this region" type of argument. To an extent, of course, this is true, but the interpretation of changes in steel and automobile production has addressed industries which are among the proclaimed high-points of the new system of production organization, and even here the evidence in favour was very far from conclusive. In this final section, therefore, I want to expand upon the issues raised by addressing three largely interrelated questions. These are the significance of the intersections between nation-states and global capital; the vital importance of labour to production; and the integration of regions within a global system.

Even in motor vehicle production—a sector where multinational corporations are heavily dominant—the movement of global capital flows is regulated within the context of nation-states. As US global hegemony waned, the rising power of the Japanese economy was encapsulated in the success of its automobile assemblers—and in the deals which they struck with the UK government in their assault on the West European marketplace. The rise of these companies was due partly to a particularly Japanese style of production organization; not flexible specialization but a highly organized version of mass production which rested upon a precisely defined role for the Japanese state. The interplay between this system and established practices elsewhere was one of the most revealing processes of the 1980s. In the UK, the significance of "Japanization" was matched only by one other phenomenon, de-industrialization (perhaps one more could be added, tertiarization, encompassing the growth of the service sector). For in the 1980s, the UK state presided over the decimation of much manufacturing capacity (including that operated by American and other foreign-owned multinational corporations), partly creating the country's chronic trade deficit. In this context, the welcome afforded to Japanese companies such as Nissan, Toyota and Honda was doubly significant, in its own terms and in contrast to policies for the rest of manufacturing industry.

Part of the reason for this lies in the Japanese conception of the role of organized labour, which resonated strongly with the Conservative Government's assault upon trades union influence in the UK. The Japanese system rested upon a tightly defined role for labour within production, enshrined in the form of enterprise-based unionism, and in a particular approach to the labour process. In this sense then a focus on production organization in terms of relations between companies had the unfortunate consequence of blurring the vision of what was happening in terms of the balance of power within individual companies regardless of their role within the productive system (although there was no doubt that this was changing in ways which reinforced and drew strength from the Japanese conception of the labour process). For, crucially, flexibility in the workplace rested upon management control over its workforce. In this light it is no surprise that Nissan was so actively courted by the UK state. Nor did Nissan let it down. In the rigorous recruitment and screening procedures, meticulous attention to detail in the design of production systems and rigid control over the workforce, Nissan epitomized all that the UK government saw as good about Japanese—as opposed to existing UK-based, if still largely foreign-owned—manufacturing. The importance of workplace control to new production strategies was evident also in the response of established UK car producers to the arrival of the Japanese. Ford and GM's emphasis upon changes to working practices, and Rover's adoption of 24-hour vehicle assembly, were just the tip of the iceberg in the vast array of detailed changes to work organization which took place in the 1980s.

This is not to argue that new spatial patterns were not emerging in the international automobile industry—indeed far from it. The point is that the growing influence of Japanese companies, and the market challenge which they posed, forced many corporate decisions on to a difficult knife edge, as companies tested the limits to and appropriate combinations of different strategies. Automobile producers sought to shorten their supply lines in tune with the stock reduction aspect of JIT—a very different animal from flexible specialization—and greater interdependence between plants emerged (either within the assembly company or via arm's length relationships). Yet whilst this was possible within the Japanese context precisely because of Japanese labour market and state regulatory conditions, it was not so straightforward in Western Europe or North America. The problems posed for such a strategy at times of industrial unrest were particularly apparent in the disputes at Ford UK in 1988 and 1990, which rippled out elsewhere to affect production in other parts of Ford's European operations. In this way then the limits to the geographical pattern of organization were being tested and integrated into corporate planning within a series of national contexts wholly different from Japan. At the same time, global geographic control of investment and production decisions meant that multinational corporations were able to encourage greater workplace flexibility by comparisons between plants, with the threat of production relocation as the ultimate sanction; though even in this they were partially constrained by the influence of national government policies to do with trade. In this way flexibility and relocation were not separate issues but interconnected via global corporate strategies. Different combinations were possible depending upon a wide range of circumstances.

Such issues were particularly apparent within and around the Nissan complex in north east England. Chosen for its lack of history of motor vehicle production, the area had been subjected to a traumatic state-backed programme of labour-market change before Nissan arrived. Decline in once staple industries such as coal and steel meshed with intensification of the labour process in what remained of those sectors and the emergence of a low-waged small-firm centred economic base which rested upon the collapse of the traditional economy to provide insecurity. It is in this very real sense, then, that the Japanese wave of manufacturing investment depended upon and took its shape from conditions created in regions like this by the UK state's chosen path of mediation of international market forces.

It is in this kind of contextual framework that the issue of the international and national integration of regional economies has to be addressed. In terms of north east England this analysis has focused on the intersection between two particular rounds of investment: that in coal and steel in the old industrial base, and that in motor vehicles as emblematic of the new economy. A number of points should be stressed here. Firstly, in all three sectors a key geographic scale was the international, regardless of the time-scale or period involved. Expansion of coal and steel production in the north east in the nineteenth century was integrally related to the imperial dominance of UK manufacturing in that era. Its subsequent decline was also part of the story of de-industrialization in the UK due to the rise of alternative centres of world power and global accumulation. This was typified in the rise of Japan and in particular its automobile producers, making Nissan's investment both a first in so many ways and a first class example of the new wave of international capital touching upon the north east. It was not so much a question, then, of greater pressures of international competition decimating the north east's old industrial base, although undoubtedly the international economic environment was becoming more and more competitive. Rather, it was a case of different phases or rounds of investment in the north east being associated with different kinds of global roles for the UK economy. International competition and its impact upon places and regions is not a new phenomenon. More importantly, as the global economy alters, the role of different regions changes—and this is happening at an increasing rate, given the faster turnover time of global fixed capital investment.

A second point to emphasize is the part played in all of this by the UK state. Behind a simple assertion that the north east is and has been a state-managed region lies a wealth of different, often conflicting, policies. In coal and steel, these range from the protected markets of the British Empire to the energy policies of post-1945 governments and the crucial part played by coal, coupled with the desire to keep alternative waged employment out of the north east coalfield for fear of disrupting production of this (then essential) fuel, to the collapse of over-ambitious investment programmes in the 1970s and the decimation of the region via British Steel and British Coal in the 1980s. In motor vehicles, the most obvious indicators were the UK government's massive financial subsidy to Nissan and the championing of its case against the UK's European Community partners over the issues of imports and local content. The influence of state policies extends far deeper than just production and trade, though, into issues to do with the reproduction of labour power through the provision of housing, and the creation of conditions conducive to profitable investment via labour market policies. In a whole variety of ways, the international market has been mediated by the impact of national state policies (the limits to which have in turn been set by that same international environment) in a fashion which has had particular consequences within the north east region.

This is not to argue that the region has been some kind of passive recipient of these processes. Opposition to decline of the old industrial base culminated locally in the campaign to save Consett steel works in 1980, and (more significantly) the national miners' strike in 1984/85. Generally though, the region's political institutions have come to play an active part in many of the changes described, accepting as inevitable the power of international market forces. In part, of course, this reflects an acute awareness of the limits to local government policies within the constraints of a national state, let alone an international capitalist economy, and the generalized acceptance of capitalist relations of production; but it also reflects a crisis of the dominant form of political representation, Labourism. For having taken part in its own downfall, so to speak, Labour within the region is faced with a crisis of imagination. The post-1945 style of public corporation has been tested and found wanting as a means of socialist transformation (indeed, it is arguable whether this was ever the intention of nationalization) and the rhetoric of the market has been imposed so forcibly that often it is difficult to see a way through to the alternatives which might exist.

In beginning to relate the pressures of international competition to regional change in this way, it is possible to see the active roles taken within the UK and the north east in the transition from one round of investment to another. In fact it is not so much a transition as an interaction—and here again the regional dimension is crucial to an understanding of global and national change. The geological analogy of rounds of investment begins to break down under this kind of conception, as the interplay between collapse in the old regional economy, the conditions which this created for new forms of investment (either in Japanese companies like Nissan, or in new small businesses created with the support of re-industrialization policies, or in the service sector), and the use which new companies make of this climate, all become evident. It is not so much a case of one round of investment overlapping another, as two different phases intersecting and cross-cutting in a fashion which depends upon a broad range of contingent circumstances with far from predetermined outcomes. It is in this lack of inevitability—indeed great uncertainty—that the potential exists for defining an alternative conception of the productive process. In every moment of crisis, there arises an opportunity for transformation, which need not be the capitalist solution.

What this suggests, then, is a framework within which capital washes globally over space, mediated by and partly subject to national states, each operating within the constraints set by capitalism as a system of production and the objectives of other states. This interlinking of investment flows becomes particularly evident in the regional context. It is in precisely this spatial grounding of capitalism as a system of production that both its greatest opportunities and problems arise. Just as command over space gives capital the opportunity for profit, so the limits to capital's power are set by its historic use of space. In the prevailing circumstances, though, it is difficult to see ways in which people living in regions such as north east England – or, for that matter, elsewhere –could play a more active role in deciding the grand trajectory of development without some radical changes to forms of political and economic organization. Coming to terms with the implications of this is indeed a far-reaching challenge for the 1990s, and probably beyond.

## Notes

1.  It would be wholly wrong not to at least mention a third potentially crucial set of issues for the 1990s: growing concern for the global environment. That they are included here in the form of a note is not intended as a reflection of some kind of marginal significance. Far from it; rather, they are considered in this form only because the precise impacts of environmental awareness are even more difficult to forecast than the two issues considered in detail in this section. There is no doubt though of the potential power of environmental issues. In terms of energy supply, for instance, questions to do with atmospheric emissions could play a decisive role for the UK coal industry. Control and reduction of noxious exhaust gases was also playing an increasing role in motor vehicle manufacture. While few proposals were as radical as the complete re-design of the combustion engine and passenger vehicle as a means of transport, the twin implications of energy shortage and pollution control were nonetheless proving of more rather than less significance. In a whole variety of often quite subtle ways, then, corporate horizons in the 1990s encompassed

respect for the power (and occasionally also profit potential) of global environmental concern.

2.   There were also some alternative views on the future of Europe. For instance, Lipietz (1989) argued that a united Europe could offer a means of resolving global crisis, replacing US hegemony through cooperation between the EC and NICs. Harmonization within Europe was necessary to restore global stability, entailing negotiated involvement with workforces, not low-wage policies. In this way Europe would be able:

> to offer a pole of co-development with Third World countries, to participate in laying the foundations for a new international monetary system, and to contribute to the gradual adjustment of the European balance of trade. (p.50).

# Bibliography

Adeney M, Lloyd J 1986 *The Miners' Strike 1984/85: Loss without Limit*. Routledge, London.

Aglietta M 1979 *A Theory of Capitalist Regulation*. New Left Books, London.

Altshuler A, Anderson M, Jones D, Roos D, Womack J 1985 *The Future of the Automobile: The Report of MIT's International Programme*. Unwin, London.

Amin A 1985 Restructuring in Fiat and the decentralisation of production into southern Italy. In Hudson R and Lewis J R (eds) *Uneven Development in Southern Europe*, pp. 155–91. Methuen, London.

Amin A 1989 Flexible specialisation and small firms in Italy: myths and realities. *Antipode* **21:** pp. 13–34.

Amin A, Robins K 1990 The re-emergence of regional economies? The mythical geography of flexible accumulation. *Society and Space* **8:** pp. 7–34.

Auer P 1985 *Industrial Relations, Work Organisation and New Technology: The Volvo Case*. Discussion paper IIM/LMP 85–10, WZB, Berlin.

Auty R M 1990 The impact of heavy industry growth poles on South Korean spatial structure. *Geoforum* **21:** pp. 23–33.

Bassett P 1986 *Strike Free: New Industrial Relations in Britain*. Macmillan, London.

Berggren C 1989 "New production concepts" in final assembly—the Swedish experience. In Wood S *The Transformation of Work?*, pp. 171–203. Unwin Hyman, London.

Beynon H 1984a *Working for Ford* (2nd edn). Penguin, Harmondsworth.

Beynon H 1984b The miners' strike in Easington. *New Left Review* **148:** pp. 104–15.

Beynon H (ed) 1985 *Digging Deeper: Issues in the Miners' Strike*. Verso, London.

Beynon H, Hudson R 1986 Memorandum to *Energy Committee*, pp. 279–81.

Beynon H, Cox A, Hudson R 1990 Opencast coalmining and the politics of coal production. *Capital and Class* **40:** pp. 89–114.

Beynon H, Hudson R, Sadler D 1986 Nationalised industry policies and the destruction of communities: some evidence from north-east England. *Capital and Class* **29:** pp. 27–57.

Beynon H, Hudson R, Sadler D 1991 *A Tale of Two Industries: The Contraction of Coal and Steel in the North East of England*. Open University Press, Milton Keynes.

Bloomfield G T 1981 The changing spatial organisation of multinational corporations in the world automotive industry. In Hamilton F E I, Linge G J R (eds) *Spatial Analysis, Industry and the Industrial Environment, vol II: International Industrial Systems*, pp. 375–94. Wiley, Chichester.

## The Global Region

Bluestone B, Harrison B 1982 *The Deindustrialization of America*. Basic Books, New York.

Boyfield K 1985 *Put Pits into Profit: Alternative Plans for Coal*. Centre for Policy Studies, London.

Bradbury J 1982 Some geographical implications of the restructuring of the iron ore industry. *Tijdschrift* **73:** pp. 295–306.

Brannen P, Batstone E, Fatchett D, White P 1976 *The Worker Directors*. Hutchinson, London.

Briggs P 1988 The Japanese at work: illusions of the ideal. *Industrial Relations Journal* **19:** pp. 24–30.

British Association of Colliery Managers 1986 Memorandum to *Energy Committee*, pp. 33–40.

Browett J 1986 Industrialisation in the global periphery: the significance of the newly industrialising countries of east and southeast Asia. *Society and Space* **4:** pp. 401–18.

Brusco S 1982 The Emilian model: productive decentralisation and social integration. *Cambridge Journal of Economics* **6:** pp. 167–84.

Bryer R A, Brignall T J, Maunders A R 1982 *Accounting for British Steel*. Gower, Aldershot.

Burns A, Newby M, Winterton J 1985 The restructuring of the British coal industry. *Cambridge Journal of Economics* **9:** pp. 93–110.

Bush R, Cliffe L, Sketchley P 1983 Steel: the South African connection. *Capital and Class* **20:** pp. 65–87.

Buss T F, Redburn F S 1983 *Shutdown at Youngstown: Public Policy for Mass Unemployment*. State University of New York Press, Albany.

Carney J, Hudson R, Lewis J (eds) 1980 *Regions in Crisis: New Perspectives in European Regional Theory*. Croom Helm, Beckenham.

Cecchini P 1988 *The European Challenge: 1992—The Benefits of a Single Market*. Wildwood, Aldershot.

Chadwick M J, Highton N H, Lindman N 1987 *Environmental Impacts of Coal Mining and Utilisation*. Pergamon, Oxford.

Christopherson S, Storper M 1986 The city as studio; the world as back lot: the impact of vertical disintegration on the location of the motion picture industry. *Society and Space* **4:** pp. 305–20.

Clark G L 1986 Restructuring the US economy: the NLRB, the Saturn project, and economic justice. *Economic Geography* **62:** pp. 289–306.

Clark G L 1987 Corporate restructuring in the steel industry: adjustment strategies and local labour relations. In Sternlieb G, Hughes J (eds) *America's New Economic Geography*. Rutgers University, New Jersey.

Clark G L 1989 *Unions and Communities under Siege: American Communities and the Crisis of Organised Labour*. Cambridge University Press, Cambridge.

Cleveland County Council 1983 *The Economic and Social Significance of the British Steel Corporation to Cleveland*. Cleveland County Council, Middlesbrough.

Cloke P, Philo C, Sadler D 1991 *Approaching Human Geography: An Introduction to Contemporary Theoretical Debates*. Paul Chapman, London.

Coal Information and Consultancy Services 1989 *Whose Coal in the Power Stations?* Coal Information and Consultancy Services, London

Commission of the European Communities 1989 *Energy and the Environment*, COM (89) 369. CEC, Brussels.

Commission of the European Communities 1990 *General Objectives Steel 1995*, COM (90) 201. CEC, Brussels.

Cox K, Mair A 1989 Levels of abstraction in locality studies. *Antipode* **21:** pp. 21–32.

Crowther S, Garrahan P 1988 Invitation to Sunderland: corporate power and the local economy. *Industrial Relations Journal* **19:** pp. 51–59.

Dicken P 1986 *Global Shift: Industrial Change in a Turbulent World.* Harper and Row, London.

Dicken P 1987 Japanese penetration of the European automobile industry: the arrival of Nissan in the United Kingdom. *Tijdschrift* **78:** pp. 94–107.

Dicken P 1988 The changing geography of Japanese foreign direct investment in manufacturing industry: a global perspective. *Environment and Planning A* **20:** pp. 633–53.

Dimbleby D, Reynolds R 1988 *An Ocean Apart: The Relationship between Britain and America in the Twentieth Century.* Hodder and Stoughton, London.

Dombois R 1987 The new international division of labour, labour markets and automobile production: the case of Mexico. Tolliday S, Zeitlin J (eds) *The Automobile Industry and Its Workers* pp. 244–57. Polity, Cambridge.

Douglass M 1988 The transnationalisation of urbanisation in Japan. *International Journal of Urban and Regional Research* **12:** pp. 425–54.

Dunning J 1986 *Japanese Participation in British Industry: Trojan Horse or Catalyst for Growth?* Croom Helm, Beckenham.

Energy Committee 1986 *The Coal Industry: Memoranda and Minutes of Evidence.* House of Commons paper 196 (two vols.), session 1985/86.

Energy Committee 1987 *The Coal Industry.* House of Commons paper 165, session 1986/87.

Energy Committee 1988 *The Structure, Regulation and Economic Consequences of Electricity Supply in the Private Sector.* House of Commons paper 307, session 1987/88.

Energy Committee 1989 *Energy Policy Implications of the Greenhouse Effect.* House of Commons paper 192 (3 vols.), session 1988/89.

Energy Committee 1990a *The Cost of Nuclear Power.* House of Commons paper 205 (two vols.), session 1989/90.

Energy Committee 1990b *The Flue Gas Desulphurisation Programme.* House of Commons paper 371, session 1989–90.

European Communities Committee 1983 *European Community Coal Policy.* House of Lords paper 80, session 1983/84.

Fevre R 1987 Subcontracting in steel. *Work, Employment and Society* **1:** pp. 509–27.

Fischer W H 1984 *Coal Trade Statistics 1979–83.* Robertson Research International, London.

Florida R L, Feldman M M A 1988 Housing in US Fordism. *International Journal of Urban and Regional Research* **12:** pp. 187–210.

Foley G 1987 *The Energy Question.* Penguin, Harmondsworth.

Foster J, Woolfson C 1989 Corporate reconstruction and business unionism: the lessons of Caterpillar and Ford. *New Left Review* **174:** pp. 51–66.

Frobel F, Heinrichs J, Kreye O 1980 *The New International Division of Labour.* Cambridge University Press, Cambridge.

Fujita K 1988 The technopolis: high technology and regional development in Japan. *International Journal of Urban and Regional Research* **12:** pp. 566–94.

Gamble A 1988 *The Free Economy and the Strong State: The Politics of Thatcherism.* Macmillan, London.

Garrahan P 1986 Nissan in the north east of England. *Capital and Class* **27:** pp. 5–13.

Gertler M S 1988 The limits to flexibility: comments on the post-Fordist vision of production and its geography. *Transactions of the Institute of British Geographers.* **13:** pp. 419–32.

Gibson K D 1990 Australian coal in the global context: a paradox of efficiency and crisis. *Environment and Planning* **22:** pp. 629–46.

Glasmeier A 1988 The Japanese Technopolis programme: high tech development strategy or industrial policy in disguise? *International Journal of Urban and Regional Research* **12:** pp. 268–84.

Glasmeier A K, McCluskey R E 1987 US auto parts production: an analysis of the organisation and location of a changing industry. *Economic Geography* **63:** pp. 142–59.

Gordon D 1988 The global economy: new edifice or crumbling foundations? *New Left Review* **168:** pp. 24–65.

Gordon R L 1987 *World Coal: Economics, Policies and Prospects.* Cambridge University Press, Cambridge.

Graham I 1988 Japanisation as mythology. *Industrial Relations Journal* **19:** pp. 69–75.

Gregory D 1989 Areal differentiation and post-modern human geography. In Gregory D, Walford R (eds) *Horizons in Human Geography* pp. 67–96. Macmillan, London.

Gwynne R N 1989 *New Horizons? The Third World Motor Vehicle Industry in an International Framework.* Paper presented to Institute of British Geographers' conference, Coventry.

Hall R W 1982 The Toyota kanban system. In Lee S M, Schwendiman G (eds) *Management by Japanese Systems*, pp. 144–51. Praeger, New York.

Harris L 1988 The UK economy at a crossroads. In Allen J, Massey D (eds) *The Economy in Question* pp. 7–44 Sage, London.

Harvey D 1982 *The Limits to Capital.* Blackwell, Oxford.

Harvey D, Scott A 1989 The practice of human geography: theory and empirical specificity in the transition from Fordism to flexible accumulation. In Macmillan B (ed) *Remodelling Geography* pp. 217–29. Blackwell, Oxford.

Helm D 1988 Regulating the electricity supply industry. *Fiscal Studies* **9**(3): pp. 86–105.

Hill R C 1986 Global factory and company town: the changing division of labour in the international automobile industry. In Henderson J, Castells M (eds) *Global Restructuring and Territorial Development.* Sage, London.

Hill R C 1989 Comparing transnational production systems: the automobile industry in the USA and Japan. *International Journal of Urban and Regional Research* **13:** pp. 462–80.

HMSO 1963 *The North East: A Programme for Regional Development and Growth,* Cmnd 2206. HMSO, London.

HMSO 1973 *British Steel Corporation: Ten Year Development Strategy* Cmnd 5226, London.

HMSO 1975 *British Leyland: The Next Decade,* House of Commons paper 342, session 1974/75.

HMSO 1978 *British Steel Corporation: The Road to Viability,* Cmnd 7149. HMSO, London.

HMSO 1988 *Privatising Electricity: The Government's Proposals for the Privatisation of the Electricity Supply Industry in England and Wales,* Cm 322. HMSO, London.

Hogan W T 1983 *World Steel in the 1980s: A Case of Survival.* D C Heath, Lexington.

# Bibliography

House of Lords 1985 *Causes and Implications of the Deficit in the UK Balance of Trade in Manufacturing.* Select Committee on Overseas Trade.

Hudson R 1986a Nationalised industry policies and regional policies: the role of the state in capitalist societies in the deindustrialisation and reindustrialisation of regions. *Society and Space* **4:** pp. 7–28.

Hudson R 1986b Producing an industrial wasteland: capital, labour and the state in north east England. In Martin R, Rowthorn B (eds) *The Geography of De-industrialisation*, pp. 169–213. Macmillan, London.

Hudson R 1988 Uneven development in capitalist societies: changing spatial divisions of labour, forms of spatial organisation of production and service provision, and their impacts on localities. *Transactions of the Institute of British Geographers* **13:** pp. 484–96.

Hudson R 1989a Labour market changes and new forms of work in "old" industrial regions: maybe flexibility for some but not flexible accumulation. *Society and Space* **7:** pp. 5–30.

Hudson R 1989b *Wrecking a Region: State Policies, Party Politics and Regional Change in North East England.* Pion, London.

Hudson R, Sadler D 1983 Region, class and the politics of steel closures in the European Community. Society and Space **1:** pp. 405–28.

Hudson R, Sadler D 1984 *British Steel Builds the New Teesside? The Implications of BSC Policy for Cleveland.* Cleveland County Council, Middlesbrough.

Hudson R, Sadler D 1986 Contesting works closures in western Europe's old industrial regions: defending place or betraying class? In Scott A J, Storper M (eds) *Production, Work, Territory: The Geographical Anatomy of Industrial Capitalism*, pp. 172–94 Allen and Unwin, London.

Hudson R, Sadler D 1987a *The Uncertain Future of Special Steels: Trends in the Sheffield, UK and European Special Steels Industries.* Sheffield City Council.

Hudson R, Sadler D 1987b Manufactured in the UK? Special steels, motor vehicles and the politics of industrial decline. *Capital and Class* **32:** pp. 55–82.

Hudson R, Sadler D 1987c *Easington Undermined? An Up-date of Undermining Easington: Who's Paying the Price of Pit Closures?* Easington District Council, Co. Durham.

Hudson R, Sadler D 1989 *The International Steel Industry: Restructuring, State Policies and Localities.* Routledge, London.

Hudson R, Sadler D 1990 State policies and the changing geography of the coal industry in the United Kingdom in the 1980s and 1990s. *Transactions of the Institute of British Geographers* **15:** pp. 435–54

Hudson R, Williams A 1986 *The United Kingdom.* Harper and Row, London.

Hudson R, Peck F, Sadler D 1985 *Undermining Easington: Who'll Pay the Price of Pit Closures?* Easington District Council, Co. Durham.

Industry and Trade Committee 1983 *The British Steel Corporation's Prospects.* House of Commons paper 212, session 1982/83.

Institute of Directors 1986 *Why Make Fuel Dear? An Energy Policy for Consumers.* Institute of Directors, London.

International Iron and Steel Institute 1983 *Steel and the Automotive Sector.* International Iron and Steel Institute, Brussels.

International Iron and Steel Institute 1985 *Indirect Trade in Steel.* International Iron and Steel Institute, Brussels.

Jones D, Womack J 1985 Developing countries and the future of the world automobile industry *World Development* **13:** pp. 393–407.

Jones K 1979 The process of change in the worker director scheme in the

British Steel Corporation. In Guest D, Knight A (eds) *Putting Participation into Practice*, pp. 206–228. Gower, Farnborough.

Jones K 1986 *Politics versus Economics in the World Steel Trade*. Allen and Unwin, London.

Kamata S 1983 *Japan in the Passing Lane*. Allen and Unwin, London.

Katz H 1987 Recent developments in US auto labour relations. In Tolliday S, Zeitlin J (eds) *The Automobile Industry and Its Workers*, pp. 282–304 Polity, Cambridge.

Keeling B 1988 *World Steel: A New Assessment of Trends and Prospects*. Economist Intelligence Unit Special Report No. 1124, London.

Krieger J 1986 *Reagan, Thatcher and the Politics of Decline*. Polity, Cambridge.

Krumme G 1981 Making it abroad: the evolution of Volkswagen's North American plans. In Hamilton F E I, Linge G J R (eds) *Spatial Analysis, Industry and the Industrial Environment, vol II: International Industrial Systems*, pp. 329–56. Wiley, Chichester.

Lash S, Urry J 1987 *The End of Organised Capitalism*. Polity, Cambridge.

Lewis J, Townsend A (eds) 1989 *The North-South Divide: Regional Change in Britain in the 1980s*. Paul Chapman, London.

Lipietz A 1986 New tendencies in the international division of labour: regimes of accumulation and modes of regulation. In Scott A J, Storper M (eds) *Production, Work Territory*, pp. 16–40. Allen and Unwin, London.

Lipietz A 1987 *Mirages and Miracles: The Crisis of Global Fordism*. Verso, London.

Lipietz A 1989 The debt problem, European integration and the new phase of world crisis. *New Left Review* **178**: pp. 37–50.

Lovering J 1990 Fordism's unknown successor: a comment on Scott's theory of flexible accumulation and the re-emergence of regional economies. *International Journal of Urban and Regional Research* **14**: pp. 159–74.

MacGregor I 1986 *The Enemies Within*. Collins, Glasgow.

Mair A, Florida R, Kenney M 1988 The new geography of automobile production: Japanese transplants in North America. *Economic Geography* **64**: pp. 352–73.

Malmberg A 1989 *Restructuring Swedish Manufacturing Industry: The Case of the Motor Vehicle Industry*. Paper presented to Institute of British Geographers' conference, Coventry.

Manwaring T 1982 The motor manufacturing industry in Britain: prospects for the 1980s. *Industrial Relations Journal* **14**: pp. 7–23.

Markusen A 1985a The military remapping of the United States. *Built Environment* **11**: pp. 171–80.

Markusen A 1985b *Profit Cycles, Oligopoly and Regional Development*. MIT, Cambridge, Mass.

Markusen A 1986 Neither ore, nor coal, nor markets: a policy oriented view of steel sites in the USA. *Regional Studies* **20**: pp. 449–62.

Martin R 1988 The political economy of Britain's north-south divide. *Transactions of the Institute of British Geographers* **13**: pp. 389–418.

Martin R, Rowthorn B (eds) 1986 *The Geography of De-industrialisation*. Macmillan, London.

Massey D 1984 *Spatial Divisions of Labour: Social Structures and the Geography of Production*. Macmillan, London.

Massey D 1986 The legacy lingers on: the impact of Britain's international role on its internal geography. In Martin R, Rowthorn B (eds) *The Geography of De-industrialisation*, pp. 31–52. Macmillan, London.

Massey D, Meegan R 1982 *The Anatomy of Job Loss*. Methuen, London.

Maunders A 1987 *A Process of Struggle: The Campaign for Corby Steelmaking in 1979*. Aldershot, Gower.

McCloskey G 1986 Memorandum to *Energy Committee*, pp. 379–83.

Meegan R 1988 A crisis of mass production? In Allen J, Massey D (eds) *The Economy in Question*, pp. 136–83. Sage, London.

Meyer P B 1986 General Motors' Saturn plant: a quantum leap in technology and its implications for labour and community organising. *Capital and Class* **30**: pp. 73–96.

Mohan J (ed) 1989 *The Political Geography of Contemporary Britain*. Macmillan, London.

Monopolies and Mergers Commission 1983 *National Coal Board*, Cmnd 8920. HMSO, London.

Monopolies and Mergers Commission 1989 *British Coal Corporation: A Report on the Investment Programme*, Cm 550. HMSO, London.

Morgan K 1983 Restructuring steel: the crises of labour and locality in Britain. *International Journal of Urban and Regional Research* **7**: pp. 175–201.

Morris J 1988 The who, why and where of Japanese manufacturing investment in the UK. *Industrial Relations Journal* **19**: pp. 31–40.

Motor Industry Research Project 1990 *Cowley Works: Why It Matters, Why It Must Be Saved*. Motor Industry Research Project, Oxford.

Motor Industry Research Unit 1988 *Rover: Profile, Progress and Prospects*. Motor Industry Research Project, Oxford.

Murray F 1987 Flexible specialisation in the "Third Italy". *Capital and Class* **33**: pp. 84–95.

National Audit Office 1989 *Department of Trade and Industry: Sale of Rover Group PLC to British Aerospace PLC*. House of Commons Paper 9, session 1989/90.

NEDO 1986a *Changing Working Patterns: How Companies Achieve Flexibility to Meet New Needs*. NEDO, London.

NEDO 1986b *Steel: The World Market and the UK Steel Industry*. NEDO, London.

NEI 1986 *The Power Plant Industry—The NEI View*. NEI, Newcastle upon Tyne.

North East Campaign for Coal 1987 *Energy and Employment: The Case for a New Coal-fired Power Station in the North-east*. North East Campaign for Coal, Newcastle upon Tyne.

NUM 1987 *New Proposed Working Practices in the British Deep Coal Mining Industry*. NUM, Sheffield.

NUM 1990 *The Case against Low Sulphur Coal Imports and for an Integrated Energy Policy for the North-east*. NUM, Sheffield.

Oberhauser A 1987 Labour, production and the state: decentralisation of the French automobile industry. *Regional Studies* **21**: pp. 445–58.

O'huallachain B 1987 Regional and technological implications of the recent build-up in American defence spending. *Annals of the Association of American Geographers* **77**: pp. 208–23.

Okayama R 1987 Industrial relations in the Japanese automobile industry 1945–70: the case of Toyota. In Tolliday S, Zeitlin J (eds) *The Automobile Industry and Its Workers*, pp. 168–89. Polity, Cambridge.

Oliver N, Wilkinson B 1988 *The Japanisation of British Industry*. Blackwell, Oxford.

Pemberton M 1988 *The World Car Industry to the Year 2000*. Economist Intelligence Unit, Automotive Special Report 12, London.

Pepler G, MacFarlane P W 1949 *North East Area Development Outline Plan*. Ministry of Town and Country Planning: interim confidential edition.

Philipson G 1988 *Aycliffe and Peterlee: New Towns 1946–1988*. Aycliffe and Peterlee Development Corporation.

Piore M, Sabel C 1984 *The Second Industrial Divide*. Basic Books, New York.

Pollert A 1988a The "flexible firm": fixation or fact? *Work, Employment and Society* **2**: pp. 281–316.

Pollert A 1988b Dismantling flexibility. *Capital and Class*. **34**: pp. 42–75.

Prior M, McCloskey G 1988 *Coal on the Market: Can British Coal Survive Privatisation?* FT International Coal Report, London.

Public Accounts Committee 1984 *Regional Industrial Incentives*. House of Commons paper 378, session 1983/84.

Public Accounts Committee 1985 *Control and Monitoring of Investment by British Steel Corporation in Private Sector Companies—the Phoenix Operations*. House of Commons paper 307, session 1984/85 London.

Rajan A 1987 *Services—The Second Industrial Revolution? Business and Jobs Outlook for UK Growth Industries*. Butterworth, London.

Revelli M 1982 Defeat at Fiat. *Capital and Class*. **16**: pp. 95–108.

Robertson I L 1989 *The UK Passenger Car Market*. Economist Intelligence Unit, Special Report 2001, London.

Robinson C 1988 A liberalised coal market? In Johnson C (ed) *Privatisation and Ownership: Lloyds Bank Annual Review*, pp. 93–109. Pinter, London.

Robinson C, Sykes A 1987 *Privatise Coal: Achieving International Competitiveness*. Centre for Policy Studies, London.

Robinson F, Gillespie A 1989 Let the good times roll? The North's economic revival. *Northern Economic Review* **17**: pp. 60–72.

Rutledge I, Wright P 1985 Coal worldwide: the international context of the British miners' strike. *Cambridge Journal of Economics* **9**: pp. 303–26.

Sadler D 1984 Works closure at British Steel and the nature of the state. *Political Geography Quarterly* **3**: pp. 297–311.

Sadler D 1990a Privatising British Steel: the politics of production and place. *Area* **22**: pp. 47–55.

Sadler D 1990b *Place-marketing, Competitive Places and the Construction of Hegemony in Britain in the 1980s*. Paper presented to Institute of British Geographers' conference, Glasgow.

Samuel R, Bloomfield B, Boanas G (eds) 1986 *The Enemy Within: Pit Villages and the Miners' Strike of 1984/85*. Routledge and Kegan Paul, London.

Sayer A 1986 New developments in manufacturing: the just-in-time system. *Capital and Class* **30**: pp. 43–72.

Sayer A 1989 Postfordism in question. *International Journal of Urban and Regional Research* **13**: pp. 666–95.

Schoenberger E 1987 Technological and organisational change in automobile production: spatial implications. *Regional Studies* **21**: pp. 199–214.

Schoenberger E 1989a Multinational corporations and the new division of labour: a critical appraisal. In Wood S (ed) *The Transformation of Work?*, pp. 91–101. Unwin Hyman, London.

Schoenberger E 1989b Thinking about flexibility: a response to Gertler. *Transactions of the Institute of British Geographers* **14**: pp. 98–108.

Scott A J 1987 The semiconductor industry in south east Asia: organisation, location and the international division of labour. *Regional Studies* **21**: pp. 143–60.

Scott A J 1988a *New Industrial Spaces*. Pion, London.

Scott A J 1988b Flexible production systems and regional development: the

rise of new industrial spaces in North America and Western Europe. *International Journal of Urban and Regional Research* **12:** pp. 171–86.
Scott A J, Cooke P 1988 The new geography and sociology of production. *Society and Space.* **6:** pp. 241–44.
Seddon V (ed) 1986 *The Cutting Edge: Women and the Pit Strike.* Laurence and Wishart, London.
Sheard P 1983 Auto-production systems in Japan: organisational and locational features. *Australian Geographical Studies* **21:** pp. 49–68.
Sinclair R, Walker D F 1982 Industrial development via the multinational corporation: General Motors in Vienna. *Regional Studies* **16:** pp. 433–42.
Sklair L 1989 *Assembling for Development: the Maquila Industry in Mexico and the United States.* Unwin Hyman, London.
Sleigh P A C 1988 *The UK Automotive Components Industry.* Economist Intelligence Unit, Automotive Special Report 10, London.
Sleigh P A C 1989 *The European Automotive Components Industry.* Economist Intelligence Unit Special Report 1186, London.
Sloman M 1986 Setting up the NCB Enterprise Initiative. *Regional Studies* **20:** pp. 184–87.
Smith I, Stone I 1989 Foreign investment in the North: distinguishing fact from hype. *Northern Economic Review* **18:** pp. 50–61.
Smith N 1989 Uneven development and location theory: towards a synthesis. In Peet R, Thrift N (eds) *New Models in Geography* (vol. I) pp. 142–163. Unwin Hyman, London.
Spooner D J, Calzonetti F J 1984 Geography and the coal revival: Anglo-American perspectives. *Progress in Human Geography* **8:** pp. 1–25.
Starkey K, McKinlay A 1989 Beyond Fordism? Strategic choice and labour relations in Ford UK. *Industrial Relations Journal* **20:** pp. 93–100.
Steenblik R 1987 *The British Coal Industry and the Wide World.* Paper presented to "Coal on the energy seesaw" conference, Nottingham.
Storper M, Christopherson S 1987 Flexible specialisation and regional industrial agglomeration: the case of the US motion picture industry. *Annals of the Association of American Geographers* **77:** pp. 104–17.
Storper M, Scott A J 1989 The geographical foundations and social regulation of flexible production complexes. In Wolch J, Dear M (eds) *The Power of Geography,* pp. 21–40. Unwin Hyman, London.
Taylor A J 1988 Consultation, conciliation and politics in the British coal industry. *Industrial Relations Journal* **19:** pp. 222–33.
Thrift N 1986 The geography of international economic disorder. In Johnston R J, Taylor P J (eds) *A World in Crisis?,* pp. 12–67. Blackwell, Oxford.
Thrift N, Leyshon A 1988 "The gambling propensity": banks, developing country debt exposures and the new international financial system. *Geoforum* **19:** pp. 55–70.
Townsend J 1988 Coal without miners: the Cerrejon North coal project. *Geography Review,* November 1988, pp. 14–16.
Townsend P, Phillimore P, Beattie A 1988 *Health and Deprivation: Inequality and the North.* Croom Helm, Beckenham.
Trade and Industry Committee 1984 *The British Steel Corporation's Prospects.* House of Commons paper 344, session 1983/84.
Trade and Industry Committee 1987 *The Motor Components Industry.* House of Commons paper 143, session 1986/87.
Turnbull P 1987 The limits to Japanisation—just in time, labour relations and the UK automotive industry. *New Technology, Work and Employment* **3:** pp. 7–20.

Tyne and Wear District Councils 1986 *The Future for NEI in Tyne and Wear*. Tyne and Wear District Councils, Newcastle upon Tyne.

UNCTC 1985 *Transnational Corporations in World Development: Third Survey*.

Upham M 1980 British Steel: retrospect and prospect. *Industrial Relations Journal* **11**: pp. 5–21.

Walker R, Huby M 1989 Social security spending in the United Kingdom: bridging the north-south economic divide. *Environment and Planning C: Government and Policy* **7**: pp. 321–40.

Walter I 1979 Protection of industries in trouble: the case of iron and steel. *World Economy* **2**: pp. 155–88.

Walter I 1983 Structural adjustment and trade policy in the international steel industry. In Cline W R (ed) *Trade Policy in the 1980s*, pp. 483–525.

West Midlands Industrial Development Association 1989 *Vehicle Component Sector Report*. West Midlands Industrial Development Association, Coleshill.

Wickens P 1988 *The Road to Nissan*. Macmillan, London.

Williams K, Williams J, Haslam C 1987 *The Breakdown of Austin Rover*. Berg, Leamington Spa.

Willman P 1984 The reform of collective bargaining and strike activity at BL Cars. *Industrial Relations Journal* **15**: pp. 1–12.

Willman P, Winch G 1985 *Innovation and Management Control: Labour Relations at BL Cars*. Cambridge University Press, Cambridge.

WOCOL 1980 *Coal: Bridge to the Future*. Ballinger, Cambridge, Mass.

Wood S (ed) 1989 *The Transformation of Work?* Unwin Hyman, London.

# Author Index

# Author Index

Gregory, D.  25
Gwynne, R.  171

Hall, R.  122
Harris, L.  30
Harrison, B.  2
Harvey, D.  2, 15
Haslam, C.  139
Heinrichs, J.  5
Helm, D.  51
Highton, N.  37
Hill, R.  122, 127, 168
HMSO  51, 97, 98, 138, 179
Hogan, W.  82
House of Lords  19
Huby, M.  20
Hudson, R.  2, 4, 11, 15, 19, 20, 24, 26, 64, 68, 72, 78, 98, 188, 190, 191, 213, 218, 220, 235

Industry and Trade Committee  241
Institute of Directors  71
International Iron and Steel Institute  79, 110, 114

Jones, D.  117, 126
Jones, K.  93, 100

Kamata, S.  123
Katz, H.  125
Keeling, B.  85, 86
Kenney, M.  168
Kreye, O.  5
Krieger, J.  17
Krumme, G.  131

Lash, S.  31
Lewis, J.  2, 20
Leyshon, A.  8
Lindman, N.  37
Lipietz, A.  9, 258
Lloyd, J.  216
Lovering, J.  15, 16

MacFarlane, P.  185
MacGregor, I.  222
Mair, A.  24, 168
Malmberg, A.  133
Manwaring, T.  134
Markusen, A.  18, 86
Martin, R.  2, 20
Massey, D.  2, 19, 25

Maunders, A.  97, 98
McCloskey, G.  42, 44, 51, 53, 59, 60, 61, 196
McCluskey, R.  168
McKinlay, A.  169
Meegan, R.  2, 11
Meyer, P.  125
Mohan, J.  20
Monopolies and Mergers Commission  46, 60, 62, 63, 66, 76
Morgan, K.  98
Morris, J.  8, 23
Motor Industry Research Project  173
Motor Industry Research Unit  139, 140, 141
Murray, F.  10

National Audit Office  173
NEDO  12, 198
NEI  69
Newby, M.  61
North East Campaign for Coal  69
NUM  58, 72

Oberhauser, A.  132
O'hUallachain, B.  18
Okayama, R.  119
Oliver, N.  8, 23

Peck, F.  218
Pemberton, B.  116, 121
Pepler, G.  185
Philipson, G.  186
Phillimore, P.  241
Philo, C.  15, 24
Piore, M.  10
Pollert, A.  12
Prior, M.  42, 44, 53, 59, 60, 61, 196
Public Accounts Committee  99, 210

Rajan, A.  21
Redburn, F.  87
Revelli, M.  131
Reynolds, R.  5
Robertson, I.  136
Robins, K.  14, 15
Robinson, C.  64, 171
Robinson, F.  240
Roos, D.  117
Rowthorn, B.  2
Rutledge, I.  37

# Subject Index

## Subject Index